THE LITURGY
OF THE
PRIMITIVE CHURCH

THE LITURGY

OF THE

PRIMITIVE CHURCH

by

REGINALD MAXWELL WOOLLEY, B.D.

Rector and Vicar of Minting, Lincs., formerly Scholar and
Naden Student of St John's College, Evans Prizeman
and Jeremie Prizeman in the University of Cambridge

Cambridge:
at the University Press
1910

CAMBRIDGE
UNIVERSITY PRESS

University Printing House, Cambridge CB2 8BS, United Kingdom

Published in the United States of America by Cambridge University Press, New York

Cambridge University Press is part of the University of Cambridge.

It furthers the University's mission by disseminating knowledge in the pursuit of education, learning and research at the highest international levels of excellence.

www.cambridge.org
Information on this title: www.cambridge.org/9781107416055

First published 1910
First paperback edition 2014

A catalogue record for this publication is available from the British Library

ISBN 978-1-107-41605-5 Paperback

PREFACE

THE history of the Liturgical uses of the Church must always be a matter of interest to all churchmen. It has, perhaps, a special interest to us in these days when we are hearing so much of proposals for the revision of the Liturgy of the Church of England.

In the consideration of our English Liturgy with a view to such revision we turn very naturally to the Latin use which was the immediate parent of our Prayer Book, and at the same time we are deeply interested in the Liturgies of the Eastern Churches.

It may, however, perhaps be questioned as to whether we are not inclined to neglect too much for these—comparatively speaking—late developments of the Liturgy in East and West, the more homely and less rigid Liturgical uses of the earliest centuries of the Church, those centuries in which the Church was more in touch than she has ever been since with the general life and the every day needs of her members.

But whether such be the case or not, I hope that this book may prove not unuseful to those who are beginning the study of Liturgiology, and that it may serve as an introduction, however unworthy, to such standard works as Brightman's "Liturgies Eastern and Western." I have to thank Professors Swete and Burkitt for kindly criticisms and suggestions during the preparation of this book, which has been accepted by the Divinity Professors of the University of Cambridge as sufficient for the degree of B.D.

R. M. W.

October 1910.

CONTENTS

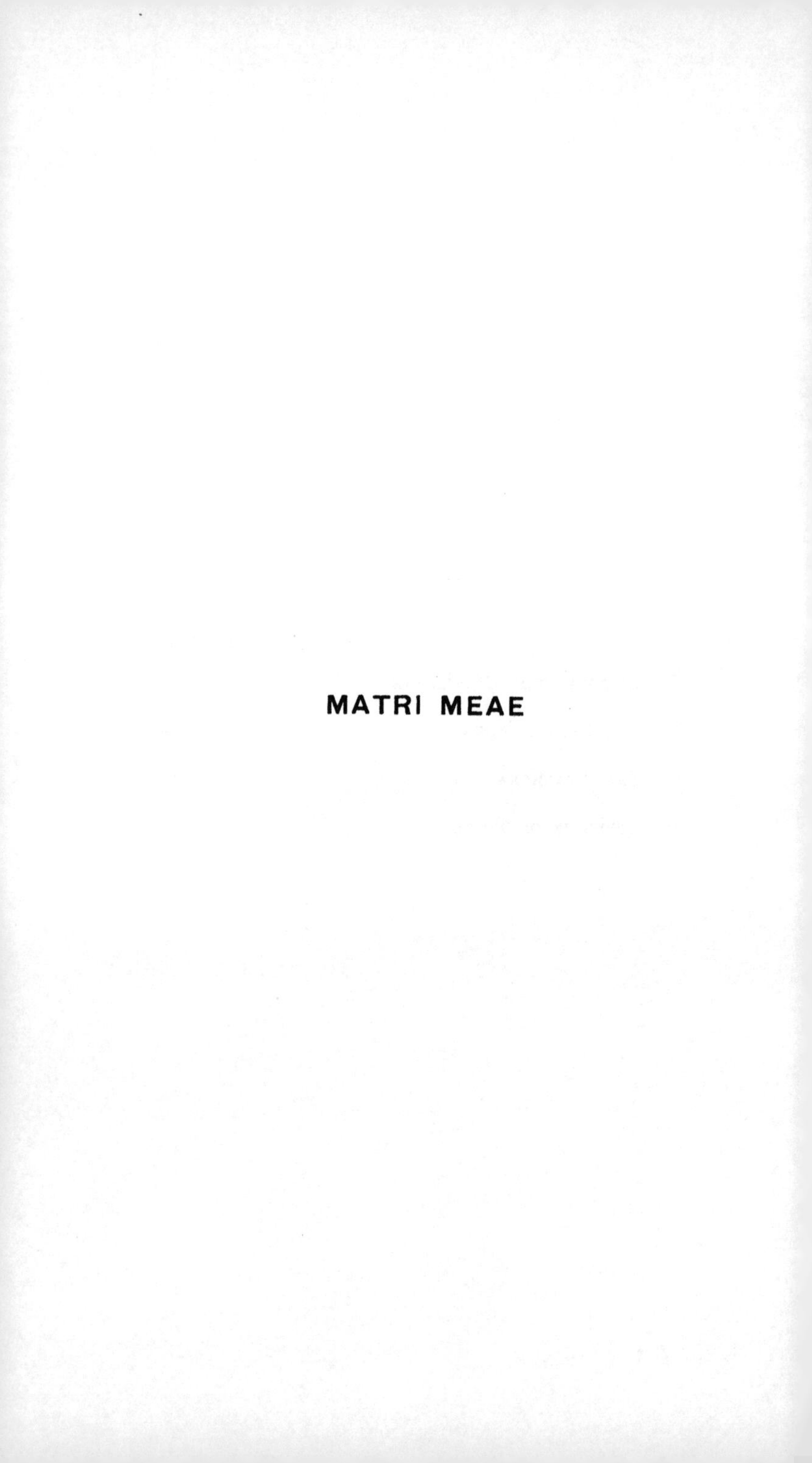

MATRI MEAE

I

INTRODUCTION. MATERIALS

THE authorities from which we derive our knowledge of the liturgy in the first three hundred years or so fall into two groups—

1. The Patristic writings,
2. The Church Order documents.

1. Of the Patristic writings it is not necessary to say much.

There is first the *Didache*, a work consisting of two different parts, the "Two Ways," cc. i.—vi., which is probably a Jewish work, and cc. vii.—end, containing certain disciplinary rules. It is the second part that is valuable for our purpose. The whole work in its present form is probably to be dated c. 110—130.

Of St Justin, of St Irenaeus, Tertullian and St Cyprian, it is not necessary to say anything.

Then there are two apocryphal works, the "Acts of John," and the "Acts of Thomas." These two works are apparently to be dated at c. 160 and c. 200 respectively. Certain descriptions and forms are given in connexion with the celebration of the Eucharist which are of great value, though from the point of view of later days these works were heretical.

But from all these works except the two last all the knowledge which we gain as to the Liturgy of the Eucharist is only incidental and therefore somewhat uncertain.

2. It is when we come to the Church Orders that we first come to definite forms. The dates of these documents are however at present unsettled and it is therefore necessary to deal with them somewhat fully in view of the date which we have assigned to them.

The Church Orders

By far the most important sources of our knowledge of the Liturgy of the first four hundred years are the "Church Orders."

The most complete form of the Church Order is to be found in the work which is known as the "Apostolic Constitutions."

The date of this work is very generally accepted as being somewhere about the last quarter of the fourth century, and need not be discussed here.

The important question is, What is the relation of this work to the other and smaller "Church Orders"? Are the "Apostolic Constitutions" the final form which the Church Orders took? or are the "Church Orders" simply extracts or epitomes of the eighth book of the Constitutions and so of later date?

The "Apostolic Constitutions" are made up from several sources.

Books I.—VI. are the Didaskalia, of which a somewhat earlier form in Syriac is still extant.

Book VII. is an amplification of the *Didache* and contains the whole of the latter work embedded in it.

Book VIII. is the most complete and finished form of Church Order, and it is with this portion of the Constitutions that we are chiefly concerned.

It contains the Liturgy in its completest form, Proanaphora and Anaphora. The Canons of the Apostles are given at the end.

The other works are as follows:

I. The *ἐπιτομή*, so called, of the eighth book of A. C.

This work is very closely related with A. C. VIII. It is either the immediate source from which A. C. VIII. is taken, or else is an immediate *ἐπιτομή*.

It is divided into five parts, each part having a special name.

(*a*) *Διδασκαλία τῶν ἁγίων ἀποστόλων περὶ χαρισμάτων.*

(*b*) *Διατάξεις τῶν ἁγίων ἀποστόλων περὶ χειροτονιῶν διὰ Ἱππολύτου.*

(*c*) *Παύλου τοῦ ἁγίου ἀποστόλου διατάξεις περὶ κανόνων ἐκκλησιαστικῶν.*

(*d*) *Πέτρου καὶ Παύλου τῶν ἁγίων ἀποστόλων διατάξεις.*

(*e*) *περὶ εὐταξίας διδασκαλία πάντων τῶν ἀποστόλων.*

The whole of the matter here contained occurs almost word for word in the text of A. C. VIII. and this work clearly stands between A. C. VIII. and the other Church Orders whether it be in the ascending or descending line[1].

[1] The text of the *ἐπιτομή* with critical apparatus is given in Funk's *Didaskalia et Constitutiones Apostolorum*, vol. II.

II. A group of documents closely related to each other and which constitute the "Church Orders" proper.

(1) The "Apostolic Church Order." This little work has been given the title of "Church Order," a name which really is not suitable. The work is, it would seem, a popular handbook rather for lay folk than others and cannot be regarded as dealing with church discipline. It is an enlarged form of the "Two Ways" (*Didache* i.—vi.) and dates apparently from the second century. The text is extant in Greek and in several versions.

(2) The Egyptian Hexateuch[1]. This work consists of six books and exists in Coptic both in the Sahidic and Bohairic dialects, in the latter of which the Canons of the Apostles occur as an appendix making a seventh book.

Book I. is the "Apostolic Church Order."

(3) The Ethiopic "Statutes of the Apostles[2]." This work is a translation of the Coptic Hexateuch, but is important as having among additional matter some that probably represents Coptic omissions.

(4) The "Canons of Hippolytus[3]." This work, existing only in Arabic, is a translation from the Coptic and represents a variant text, probably somewhat later, of the second book of the Coptic Hexateuch.

(5) The "Testamentum Domini nostri Jesu Christi[4]."

[1] The *Canones ecclesiastici* (Sahidic) published in de Lagarde's *Aegyptiaca*, and *The Apostolical Constitutions and Canons of the Apostles* (Bohairic) by H. Tattam, 1840, with an English translation which is inaccurate.

[2] Text and translation in G. Horner's *Statutes of the Apostles*.

[3] Text and Latin translation in von Haneberg's *Canones Hippolyti*, now out of print. A German translation is given by von Achelis in his *Canones Hippolyti*.

[4] The Syriac text with a Latin translation and notes was published by

This is an apocryphal work in Syriac which contains embedded in it a form of Book II. of the Coptic Hexateuch.

(6) "Canonum Reliquiae[1]." These are fragments of an ancient Latin version of the work represented by Book II. of the Coptic Hexateuch.

Thus all these documents are closely interrelated.

The two questions to be decided are:

I. What is their relationship exactly to each other?

II. What is the relationship between these "Church Orders" proper and A. C. VIII.?

I. The Egyptian Hexateuch or Egyptian Church Order seems to answer both these questions.

The first book is a version of the "Apostolic Church Order," and is of little moment.

The second book is the same work as the Canons of Hippolytus, the "Canonum Reliquiae," and the work embedded in the "Testamentum Domini."

The remaining Books III.—VI. (or §§ 64—77) are really a later edition of Book II. and cover exactly the same ground.

This is evident when the contents of Book II. are placed parallel to the contents of Books III.—VI.

Book II.	Books III.—VI.
§ 31 concerning Bishops. Their election, consecration, the Eucharist celebrated after the consecration, beginning with Sursum corda.	§§ 64, 65 concerning Bishops. Their election and consecration. Eucharist to follow, Gospel, sermon, washing of hands, deacon's proclamation, Invocation of Holy Spirit, etc.

Mgr Ignatius Rahmani, Uniat-Patriarch of Antioch. An English translation with notes has been made by Dr Cooper and Dr Maclean, *The Testament of our Lord.*

[1] M. E. Hauler's *Didascaliae apostolorum fragmenta veronensia latina.*

Book II.	Books III.—VI.
§§ 32, 33 Ordination of Priests according to the form we have given for the Bishop. Ordination of Deacons.	§ 66 Ordination of Priests and Deacons. Forms given.
§ 34 Confessors. The confessor not to be ordained to the diaconate or priesthood, but if appointed a Bishop is to have hands laid on him for that office.	§ 67 Confessors. Not to be ordained. If he has confessed he is worthy of great honour. If need to make him Bishop or Priest or Deacon he is to be duly ordained to such an office.
§ 35 Readers. To be appointed without laying on of hands.	§ 66 To the same effect.
§ 36 Subdeacons also to be appointed without the laying on of hands.	§ 66 The same, also of deaconesses.
§ 37 Widows. Not to be ordained. Their qualifications.	§ 67 To the same effect.
§ 38 Virgins not to be ordained. Virginity a matter of free choice.	§ 68 To same effect, not in contempt of marriage.
§ 39 Charismata of healing. No ordination for such; the power manifests itself.	§ 70 Exorcists and those possessing charismata not to be ordained. A gift of the Holy Ghost.
§ 40 concerning new men who come in to the Faith.	§ 74 To same effect but shorter.
§ 41 concerning works and crafts. Enquiries to be made into lives and occupations of all who seek admission to the church.	§ 75 The same but at greater length. Mention made of Easter, Ascension, Pentecost, Nativity of Christ, Baptism of Our Lord, Feast of the Apostles, and Feast of Stephen.
§ 42 Catechumenate to last three years.	§ 75 The same.

Book II.	Books III.—VI.
§ 43 The instruction of catechumens.	§ 75 Referred to.
§ 44 Blessing of catechumens after instruction even by lay instructors. Baptism of Blood.	§ 75 Mention of lay instructors. No mention of Baptism of Blood.
§§ 45, 46 Long and detailed account of rite of Baptism.	Nothing.
§ 47 Regulations for fasting.	Nothing.
§ 48 Grace to be said before meals.	Nothing.
§ 49 Agape not to be thrown open to unbelievers.	§ 75 To same effect.
§ 50 Eating and drinking to be with moderation.	§ 76 To same effect.
§ 51 Grace to be said after meals.	
§ 52 concerning the Agape. (Supper of widows.)	§ 76 Regulations dealing with suppers in commemoration of the departed.
§ 53 Firstfruits to be brought to the Bishop. Form of thanksgiving to be said over them.	§ 72 Tithes and firstfruits to be brought for the support of the clergy.
§ 54 List of produce which may be brought to be blessed.	
55 Strict fast to be kept on two days preceding Easter.	§ 75 Week before Easter to be kept free from work.
§ 56 Deacons to be diligent in their attendance on Bishops.	
§ 57 Believers to pray on waking. To go to any occasional services.	§ 75 Same but much more detailed.
§ 58 The Eucharist to be received fasting.	
§ 59 Care to be taken to guard the sacred elements.	
§ 61 No overcharge to be made for burying in the cemeteries.	

Book II.	Books III.—VI.
§ 62 Long details of hours of prayer.	§ 75 To same effect.
	§ 73 The εὐλογίαι which are not required for the Eucharist to be divided among the clergy.
	§ 77 concerning those who are persecuted for the faith.

Books III.—VI. begin with a long introduction (§ 63) that has no parallel in Book II. Also in Book II. there is nothing similar to § 77 which concludes VI.

This comparison shows us that in the Egyptian Church Order we have not two different works but a first and second edition of one and the same document.

It is most convenient perhaps to call these two recensions, the First Church Order and the Second Church Order.

The Second Church Order we shall deal with later on in connexion with the ἐπιτομή of A. C. VIII.

The First Church Order

As has been stated above, Book II. of the E.C.O., that is the "First Church Order," is also represented by the Ethiopic version in the Statutes of the Apostles, the Latin Verona fragments, the Canons of Hippolytus and the "Testamentum Domini." These different versions vary in certain points among themselves.

What was the origin of the First Order? The original text was beyond doubt in Greek and has long vanished.

The Coptic was made from the Greek as is evident from the fact that in the Sursum corda the Greek text is simply taken bodily into the translation.

The Latin is also from the Greek as is evident from such remarks as the following which occur in the text—"in exemplum, quod dicit graecus antitypum," and "calicem vino mixtum propter antitypum quod dicit graecus 'similitudinem sanguinis,'" where evidently the translator has before him ὁμοίωμα (cf. Sarapion).

The Ethiopic text is translated from the Coptic.

The "Testamentum Domini" is a translation from the Greek and this translation was made in the seventh century by James of Edessa.

The Canons of Hippolytus exist only in the Arabic, and this version clearly comes from the Coptic. In the translation, for example, of the description of the commencement of the liturgy at the consecration of a bishop where the Sursum Corda is preserved in Greek in the Coptic text, in the Arabic Canons of Hippolytus all is translated except these Greek words which are simply transliterated.

These different versions vary, some more, some less, among themselves. The oldest underlying text, we believe, is represented by the Coptic version and by the Latin.

The Ethiopic perhaps represents a slightly later recension of the Coptic, and the Canons of Hippolytus another and different recension of the Coptic.

The work has been incorporated into another in the Testament of Our Lord and has suffered some omissions and changes in the process. Probably all these documents have suffered somewhat from copyists.

Perhaps we should first indicate the more important variations.

One of the most important variations is in the liturgical texts given.

The Coptic only gives the commencement of the Eucharist, but there seems little room to doubt that the whole liturgy as given in the Latin version and in the Ethiopic (with additions and alternatives) was originally in the Coptic[1]. In the same way the Coptic omits the ordination prayers which are given by the Ethiopic and Latin[2]. Yet that the forms were once in the Coptic is clear from the direction given in the canon concerning the ordination to the priesthood (§ 32) in which it is directed "and let them pray over him according to the form which we said for the Bishop," though no such form occurs in the text as it has come down to us.

In the Canons of Hippolytus the liturgy is only partly given, thus following closely the text as we have it in the Coptic. In the ordination of priests, as in the Coptic, the same prayer of ordination is to be said as over a Bishop, and the prayer of ordination for a Bishop which is omitted by the Coptic occurs in the C. H. The C. H. also varies in order in the less important parts towards the end, into which also a long homily is inserted.

In the "Testament of Our Lord" there are several omissions.

The Latin version is unfortunately fragmentary but is very close to the text represented by the Coptic though it gives the liturgy, as does the Ethiopic, which is omitted from the Coptic. The Ethiopic gives some extra prayers which are not contained in the Latin.

[1] In the Canon on Confessors, when referring to their ordination, the Bishop is to celebrate the Eucharist: "Now the Bishop shall give thanks (ⲉⲩⲭⲁⲣⲓⲥⲧⲟⲩ) according to the things which we said before." Evidently this shows that the liturgy was once in the Coptic as in the Latin and Ethiopic.

[2] And some in the C. H.

Date.

What is the date of the First Church Order?

There are certain very striking regulations that are of the greatest value for the determining of the date of this work.

The most striking is perhaps the Canon on Confessors, which I give in full, so far as it concerns us:

> The confessor then if he has been in chains for the name of the Lord, they shall not lay hand upon him for a ministry[1] or presbyterate: for he has the honour of the presbyterate by his confession. But if he is to be ordained bishop, then hand shall be laid upon him. But if he is a confessor who was not brought before an authority, nor was punished with chains, nor shut up in prison nor condemned with any sentence, but in a casual way he was only insulted for our Lord, and he was punished with a punishment of house[2], though he confessed, hand is to be laid upon him for every office of which he is worthy.

The Canons of Hippolytus here follow the Coptic closely and have also an addition "and if he being a slave to anyone have endured punishment for Christ, such an one thereby is a priest to the flock[3]."

This canon is very striking and a proof that the document is early. It is inconceivable that if this document is an epitomised form of A. C. VIII. this canon could have appeared in such a form. At the same time it would suit excellently the period just before or the beginning of the Decian persecution and is an excellent example of the extravagant claims of the confessor made at that time.

The canon undoubtedly means that a confessor who has suffered torment is to be recognised as priest or deacon without ordination, his endurance under torment

[1] C. ⲟⲩⲇⲓⲁⲕⲟⲛⲓⲁ *i.e.* diaconate. The transl. is from Horner, p. 309.

[2] Probably meaning confinement by relations.

[3] C. H. can. v. The translation is Professor Burkitt's.

being sign of his possession of God's grace to an extent that renders ordination superfluous.

The Latin text is here wanting.

In the Ethiopic version the force of this canon has been weakened.

Concerning those who have confessed and were condemned for the name of our Lord Jesus Christ. If the confessor has been in a place of punishment, in chains for the name of Christ, they shall not lay hand on him for a ministering, for that is the honour of a deacon, but as for the honour of the presbyterate, though he hath the honour of the presbyterate by that which he confessed, yet the bishop shall ordain him having laid his hand upon him.

Here we find a little change that makes a great deal of difference. In the Coptic it is "he hath the honour of the presbyterate." Here the word for "honour," ⲧⲧⲙⲏ (G. τιμή), is certainly "the dignity of the office," including the power to exercise the functions of that office. By a slight change the Ethiopic translator has twisted the meaning into the confessor's right to rank in honour with the presbyterate.

The "Testament of Our Lord" also changes the force of this canon even more than the Ethiopic. "He who gives testimony and confesses that he has been in chains and prison and torments for the name of God [doubtless this should be 'so that he has been'], hands shall not be laid on him for this reason to the diaconate or priesthood. For he hath the honour of the clergy since by the hand of God he was protected through confession."

Now this Canon of Confession points to an approximate date. Saint Cyprian tells us what was the status and dignity of a confessor in his times. He not only ranked in honour with the presbyterate but at the time of the

Eucharist stood among the priests and even drew the salary of a priest.

"Caeterum presbyterii honorem designasse nos illis iam sciatis, ut et sportulis iisdem cum presbyteris honorentur et divisiones mensurnas aequatis quantitatibus partiantur, sessuri nobiscum provectis et corroboratis annis suis, etc.[1]"

He is speaking here of the confessors Celerinus and Aurelius. Cyprian, then, shows that the practice at Carthage in his day was to give confessors rank with the presbyterate and this practice is in accordance with the canon as given in the Ethiopic and Syriac. This may have been a compromise adopted with a view to the doing away with such claims as those recognised by the Coptic version and the Canons of Hippolytus. That the claims were made is clear from the corresponding canon of the Second Church Order and by A. C. VIII. xxiii. where it is added *εἰ δέ τις ὁμολογητὴς μὴ χειροτονηθεὶς ἁρπάσῃ ἑαυτῷ ἀξίωμά τι τοιοῦτον ὡς διὰ τὴν ὁμολογίαν οὗτος καθαιρείσθω καὶ ἀποβαλλέσθω.*

St Cyprian does not mention any such claim but it is probable that he would not mention it if possible, and we know that the claims of the confessors in his time were extravagant in the extreme.

At any rate it would seem that the canon in the Coptic version and in the C. H. cannot have been later than Cyprian's time and is probably earlier, while the forms of the canon in the Ethiopic and Syriac represent the usage and doubtless the period of St Cyprian.

Again in dealing with the professions and means of

[1] Cypr. *Ep.* xxxix. 5; cf. xliii. 3 "cumque semel placuerit tam nobis quam confessoribus et clericis urbicis."

livelihood of those who seek admission to the Church there is an objection shown to the military profession.

A soldier who is in authority, cause him not to kill men: if he should be commanded (to do it) cause him not to hasten to the work, nor cause him to swear; and being unwilling (to comply) let him be rejected (c. 41).

This attitude towards soldiers argues an early date, certainly a date before the Peace of the Church.

The corresponding passage in the Second Order (and A. C. VIII.) is changed into *στρατιώτης προσιὼν διδασκέσθω "μὴ ἀδικεῖν, μὴ συκοφαντεῖν, ἀρκεῖσθαι δὲ τοῖς διδομένοις ὀψωνίοις"* (Luc. iii. 14).

An objection is also shown to magistrates as having power of life and death. "One who has power over the sword, or a magistrate of a city who is clad in purple, either let him leave off or let him be rejected." This is omitted altogether in the Second Order.

Again in the Interrogatory Creed at Baptism we find evidence of an early date. The candidate is asked in the font:

"Dost thou believe[1] in Our Lord Jesus Christ the only Son of the Father?" So the Interrogatory Creed begins in the Coptic. The first article of the creed is subordinated to the second in a manner that recalls the regulae of St Irenaeus and Tertullian.

The Ethiopic version agrees with the Coptic.

The Canons of Hippolytus have however the three distinct articles: "Dost thou believe in God the Father Almighty?" "Dost thou believe in Jesus Christ the

[1] Horner in his translation, p. 318, does not give this in interrogatory form. But that it is interrogative is clearly shown by the reply of the candidate at the end, "again let him say 'I believe.'"

Son of God...?" "Dost thou believe in the Holy Spirit...?"

The Latin version follows the text represented by C.H. Though there is a lacuna in the Latin text where the first article occurs the form of the second article "postea dicat 'Credis in Christum Jesum Filium Dei?'...et cum ille dixerit 'Credo,' iterum baptizetur," shows clearly that the first article has a place in this version.

These examples are sufficient to show that the First Church Order cannot have been derived from A. C. VIII. or belong to the fourth century, but that the date of it must be placed not later than 250, and probably a little earlier than that time[1]. The versions differ, as has been seen, somewhat among themselves.

The relationship of the texts seems to be:

1. Oldest text—the Coptic. This forms Book II. of the Egyptian Hexateuch and is represented by the Ethiopic translation of that work. Some of the variations probably appeared in the text from which the Ethiopic version was made, and some changes were probably made at the time of the translation.

The Ethiopic is important as containing the liturgy and ordination forms which are omitted in the extant Coptic text.

2. The Canons of Hippolytus—an Arabic version of an early recension of the Coptic, and probably very little later than 250. This text has also suffered the omission of the liturgy, an omission probably due to much later times in both cases, in the process of copying.

3. The Latin text as represented by the Verona

[1] Of course there are later interpolations, *e.g.* the use of the word ὁμοούσιος of the Trinity.

fragments, made direct from the Greek and quite independent of the Coptic, very little later, if any, than the Coptic, about the year 250.

4. The Church Order as it is embodied in the Testamentum Domini. This work was translated into Syriac from the Greek by James of Edessa in the seventh century. The Greek original is lost. Dr Maclean and Dr Cooper date the compilation as being about the year 350.

The First Church Order which is embedded in it is perhaps the latest form in which the First Order exists. There are other liturgical forms besides the Eucharist, and the Eucharistic forms are fuller than those contained in any version of the order. The compiler evidently had the First Church Order before him, and took what he wanted out of it.

Note on the Canons of Hippolytus

The "Canons of Hippolytus" have perhaps obtained a greater importance than they deserve. They are not an independent work but an Arabic version of a Coptic text of the First Church Order which seems to have varied in places from the Coptic that is extant.

The chief differences between the text of the C. H. and the extant Coptic version of the First Order are as follows:

In Canon III. directions are given (as in the Latin and Ethiopic versions) for the blessing of oil if necessary, and for the blessing of the firstfruits immediately after the Eucharist.

The Consecration Prayer of a Bishop is given which is omitted from the Coptic, and the same prayer is ordered (as in Coptic) to be said for the ordination of a Priest.

The Ordination Prayer of a Deacon is given, and differs from that in the Latin version of the First Order, and also from the form of the Second Order, except in so far as it has a reference to St Stephen.

Canons XVII. and XVIII. on the conduct of women generally are an addition to the Coptic.

Canon XIX. agrees as we have seen with the Latin in the form of the interrogatory creed at Baptism against the Coptic.

Canon XXII. against the Jews is an addition.

Canon XXX. an homily to catechumens is an addition.

Canon XXX. end, and XXXI., directions on giving Communion, are an addition.

Canon XXXIII. on commemoration suppers is an addition.

Canon XXXIV. (first part) on much speaking, is an addition.

Canon XXXVI. gives a form for the blessing of the firstfruits which differs from that of the Coptic (and Latin and Ethiopic).

Canon XXXVIII. on the vestments of the clergy is not found in the Coptic, but compare A. C.

These are the chief differences—the Canon as to the vestments is probably a later interpolation, as is the reference to the use of the veil in churches. But we cannot be certain that either distinguishing vestments or the use of a veil were later than the third century.

There is a curious interpolation in the Creed teaching the double procession of the Holy Spirit, but this of course is very late.

Thus the C. H. it will be seen differs very little and only in unimportant details (and order in the latter end of the work) from the Coptic version of the First Order. The work was, as we have seen, translated from a Coptic text, and it seems to represent a different Coptic recension of the First Order, if anything rather a later one than the existing Coptic text.

It is unknown to what extent this work has any claim to its name. But it seems clear that the First Church Order used very largely the now lost work of Hippolytus περὶ χαρισμάτων. In the Epitome or "second Church Order" we find again two of its five sections associated with the name of Hippolytus.

The Second Church Order

We have seen that the Egyptian Hexateuch contains two recensions of a disciplinary work which we have called the First and Second Church Orders.

The Second Church Order consists of Books III.—VI. (§§ 63—78).

The Second Church Order in the Hexateuch is a version from the Greek, a recension of which is represented by the ἐπιτομή of A.C. VIII.

The Coptic (and Ethiopic) version is not however identical with the Greek text of the ἐπιτομή.

The liturgical matter in the Coptic text of the second Order is probably much later than the date of the recension itself and corresponds with a considerably developed form of liturgy. It has probably been brought into accordance with the later liturgical forms in the process of copying. Thus the words in which the ἐπίκλησις is described represent a considerably later date than that of the Apostolic Constitutions themselves.

The liturgical matter does not appear at all in the Greek ἐπιτομή.

The account of the Rites of Baptism which are given so fully in the First Church Order do not appear at all in either the Greek or Coptic of the Second Church Order.

The ordination prayers of the ἐπιτομή for Bishop and Priest are the same as in the Apostolic Constitutions except that they are very much longer in the latter work. The prayer for the ordaining of a deacon is quite different from that in the Constitutions.

In the Coptic, however, the ordination prayers are not given.

Of the two recensions the Greek ἐπιτομή is the nearer to A.C. VIII., and most of the text appears there word for word.

The corresponding portions of the Egyptian Hexateuch and the ἐπιτομή are as follows:

EGYPTIAN HEXATEUCH.

Book III. (§ 63)	=Διδασκαλία τῶν ἁγίων ἀποστόλων περὶ χαρισμάτων.
IV. and V. (§§ 64—73)	=Διατάξεις τῶν ἁγίων ἀποστόλων περὶ χειροτονιῶν διὰ Ἱππολύτου.
VI. (§§ 74—77)	=Παύλου τοῦ ἁγίου ἀποστόλου διατάξεις περὶ κανόνων ἐκκλησιαστικῶν.
	+Πέτρου καὶ Παύλου τῶν ἁγίων ἀποστόλων διατάξεις.
	+περὶ εὐταξίας διδασκαλία πάντων τῶν ἁγίων ἀποστόλων.

The relationship between the Second Church Order and A.C. VIII. is perhaps best seen by placing the contents of the parallel parts side by side.

SECOND CHURCH ORDER	A. C. VIII.
Διδασκαλία τῶν ἁγίων ἀποστόλων περὶ χαρισμάτων.	=cc. i., ii.
Διατάξεις τῶν ἁγ. ἀποστ. περὶ χειροτονιῶν διὰ Ἱππολύτου.	
1. On the character of one chosen for a bishop.	=iv.
2. Consecration of a Bishop and ordination prayer. (The ordination prayer is omitted from the Coptic.)	=c. v. in which the prayer is at much greater length.
In the Coptic text a partial description is given of the Eucharist. This is entirely lacking in the Greek.	=cc. v.—xv. which comprise the Clementine Liturgy.
3. The Bishop to lay hands on a priest at ordination 4. Prayer of ordination of a priest (omitted by the Coptic).	=c. xvi. where the prayer is much amplified.
5. Hands to be laid on a deacon. 6. Prayer of ordination of a deacon (omitted by the Coptic).	=cc. xvii., xviii. but the prayer of ordination is entirely different.

SECOND CHURCH ORDER.	A. C. VIII.
7. Ordination of a deaconess	=c. xix.
8. Prayer of ordination for a deaconess.	=c. xx.
9. Hands to be laid on subdeacon. 10. Prayer of ordination for subdeacon.	=c. xxi.
[In the Coptic § 66, which represents 7, 8, 9, 10, no forms are given, and it is expressly said of subdeacons, readers and deaconesses that "it is not right to ordain them."]	
11. Readers to have book given by the Bishop—no ordination.	=c. xxiii. But ordination by laying on of hands—also a prayer of ordination is given.
12. Confessors.	=c. xxiii.
13. Virgins.	=c. xxiv.
14. Widows.	=c. xxv.
15. Exorcists.	=c. xxvi.
16. Bishops to be ordained by three or two others.	=c. xxvii.
17. The power of the different orders of clergy.	=c. xxviii.
	c. xxix. Forms for blessing oil and water.
18. Firstfruits and tithes	=c. xxx.
19. Superfluous oblations for Eucharist to be given to clergy.	=c. xxxi.
Παύλου τοῦ ἁγ. ἀποστ. διατάξεις περὶ κανόνων ἐκκλησιαστικῶν.	
1. Inquiry into life of those who seek admission to the church.	=c. xxxii.
Πέτρου καὶ Παύλου τῶν ἁγ. ἀποστ. διατάξεις.	
1. About holy days.	=c. xxxiii.
2. Hours of prayer.	=c. xxxiv.
	c. xxxv. James ordains evening service daily.

Second Church Order.	A. C. viii.
	c. xxxvi. Deacon's bidding prayer.
	c. xxxvii. Bishop's prayer and dismissal.
	c. xxxviii. Morning service. Deacon's bidding prayer and Bishop's prayer.
	c. xxxix. Bishop's prayer of dismissal.
	c. xl. The thanksgiving over firstfruits.
	c. xli. Deacon's bidding prayer for the dead. Bishop's prayer.
3. Commemoration of the dead.	= cc. xlii., xliii.
4. Against drunkenness.	= c. xliv.
Περὶ εὐταξίας διδασκαλία πάντων τῶν ἁγίων ἀποστόλων. (Based on Clement cc. xl.—xliii.)	= c. xlvi.
	cc. xlvii.—xlviii. Canons of the Apostles.

In the first place the Greek text of the Second Church Order appears almost word for word in the corresponding parts of A. C. viii. It was practically unaltered except for additional matter.

The chief differences between the Greek of the Second Order and A.C. viii. are as follows:

In A.C. viii. c. iii. forms an introduction to the directions as to the ritual of the consecration of a bishop. This introduction does not appear in the "Epitome."

The prayer of consecration of a bishop in the Epitome is the same as that in the First Church Order (Latin and Ethiopic). The form in A.C. viii. is the same but much amplified.

In the A. C. viii. the Clementine Liturgy follows the consecration. The liturgy does not appear at all in the "Epitome" though it is described in the Coptic version.

In the prayer of ordination of a Priest the Epitome follows the First Order (Latin and Ethiopic) but at greater length. In the A.C. the form is still more amplified than that of the Epitome.

In the prayer of ordination of a Deacon the Epitome is word for word in agreement with A. C. Here the corresponding form in the First Order is quite different except for one petition.

The prayer of benediction of oil and water (A. C. VIII. xxix.) does not appear at all in the Epitome.

Chapters xxxv.—xli. of A.C. VIII. with details and rules as to the daily services do not occur at all in the Epitome.

Chapters xlvii., xlviii. of A. C. VIII. which consist of the Canons of the Apostles do not occur at all in the Epitome, though they form Book VII. of the Bohairic version of the Coptic, which book is wanting in the Sahidic version.

When we come to consider the Coptic version of the Epitome we find some important differences.

None of the ordination prayers are given, though as we have seen they occur in the Latin and Ethiopic versions of the First Order.

In the Coptic text a description of the liturgy is given where in A.C. the Clementine Liturgy is given at length. This description has evidently been tampered with by later hands, for the consecration by the ἐπίκλησις is spoken of in terms[1] which could only have been used at a period later than even that of the Clementine Liturgy.

The most important differences are in the regulations as to ordination. In the ordination of a deaconess, subdeacon and reader, the Epitome agrees with A.C. in enjoining ordination by the laying on of hands, and ordination prayers are given.

[1] See texts.

In the Coptic, however, it is expressly stated that these ministers are not to be ordained, for "it is not right to ordain them." They are simply to be appointed to the office and thus a great distinction is drawn between Holy Orders and Lesser Orders. The Coptic is here in agreement with the First Order. Also in the Second Order the objection of the First Order to the military profession is changed into something quite different; while the objection of the former document to magistrates as having power of life and death vanishes altogether.

What then is the relationship of the Second Church Order to A.C. VIII.? It seems as if the Egyptian Hexateuch has given us the key.

The Coptic is evidently a rather earlier form of the Epitome, in spite of some late interpolations. The Epitome on the other hand is word for word agreeing with the corresponding text of A.C. VIII.

But the underlying Greek text of the Coptic, as we have seen, must have varied considerably in places.

The conclusions then to which we are led are that the First Church Order is a document known to the greater part of the Church and having authority, so far as any document can be said to have had authority except by use and custom, before the days of the general councils.

It was known in Greek, in Latin[1], in Coptic and Ethiopic; that is to say to the whole Christian world.

[1] In a work on the "Ancient Church Orders" by the Bishop of Moray, Ross, and Caithness, now in the press, the proofs of which I have been permitted to see, Dr Maclean attributes the compilation of the earlier church orders in their present form to a later date than I have done.

He gives the first half of the fourth century, probably early, as the date of the Eg. C.O., the Eth. C. O., and the third part of the Verona fragments (*i.e.* the Latin version of the "First Church Order"). The

The incorporation of the work into the Syrian Testament of our Lord about 350 argues that the work was known before that time in Greek to the bilingual Syrian Church. The First Church Order is then one of the most important documents of the Primitive Church.

We cannot speak quite so certainly about the Second Order. Evidently its vogue was much more narrow. Egypt and Syria alone seem to have known it, and in Syria it developed into A.C. VIII. whereas it was probably soon forgotten in Egypt and does not appear to have been known in any more developed form.

If we only had extant the Greek text of the Epitome we should probably be forced to conclude from the close verbal agreement that it is merely an epitome of A.C. VIII. The existence of the Coptic version of this document however precludes such a view with its important differences. And we are forced to conclude that this document forms a Second Church Order intermediate between the First Order and A.C. VIII. The extant Greek text existing on side by side with A.C. VIII. soon got to be regarded as an Epitome of A.C. VIII. with the result that the text became very closely approximated to that of the last and finished recension.

Canons of Hippolytus he puts in the first half of the fourth century. The "Testamentum Domini" he assigns to c. 350.

Dr Maclean believes that all these documents are based ultimately on a lost Greek original but represent different lines of tradition.

II

THE PROANAPHORA

The Eucharistic liturgy has existed very much in its present form since the fifth century. In the sixth we come across the liturgy of St Basil by name, in the seventh the liturgy of St James. The general references to the liturgy in the fourth century and the liturgical remains of that time point to the fifth century as being the time in which the liturgy reached its final state on being reduced to a written form.

And though the two great types Roman and Eastern had already at that time acquired their special characteristics, it is evident from their general similarity in framework and component parts that both are derived from a common origin.

Eastern and Western liturgies alike can be divided into two distinct and clearly distinguishable parts: the Eastern into Proanaphora and Anaphora; the Western into the corresponding "Ordinary" and "Canon" of the Mass.

These two parts are already the two component parts of the liturgy by the fifth century. But there is evidence to show that before this time they were not so closely welded together and at the first were actually independent and separate services.

It is necessary then to enquire into the origin of these two parts, and into their gradual union into one finished whole.

The Christian Church was at the time of its foundation no new religion. It professed to be but the natural and looked for development and fulfilment of the Jewish Church. It was the more perfect dispensation which was to follow, and for which both the law and the prophets looked and prepared the way.

Indeed in the first few generations the Church of Christ was as much Jewish as Christian. To the outsider at first the Christians were but a more peculiar sect of Jews. To the Jew himself it was not quite clear for some time that the Christian was outside the pale of Judaism. The Church itself, in spite of its difficulties in reconciling the Gentile and Jewish elements within itself, was slow to break definitely with Judaism, and perhaps it was Judaism itself that brought about the final separation of Jew and Christian. If this is so we must expect to find within the Church of early days many relics of Judaism. Particularly should we expect to find in the Church's liturgy marks and characteristics of the older faith in whose public worship she was for so long content to take part. For the liturgy in its beginnings takes us back to a time when the Old Testament alone was the Canon of Scripture. For years before the New Testament came into being, before the Epistles of St Paul existed, before the Gospels were committed to writing, the liturgy was used in the Church's obedience to the command of her Lord, "Do this in remembrance of me."

In the pages of the Gospels we read time after time of Our Lord taking part in Jewish worship as a zealous observer of the ordinances of the Jewish faith. Time after time are we told of His presence among the worshippers on a Sabbath morning at the synagogue. Often He was the officiant. The frequency indeed of His ministration is incidentally shown by His reply before the High Priest, "I ever taught in the synagogue and in the temple, whither the Jews always resort, and in secret have I said nothing. Why askest thou me? Ask them which heard me what I have said unto them[1]."

And so the mode of worship with which the Disciples of Our Lord were most familiar was the Synagogue service, a service sanctified by their Lord's own participation in it. What more natural than that this form of service should be retained, gradually becoming, indeed, more and more distinctively Christian in its forms, and side by side with the distinctively Christian observance, the fulfilling of the Lord's command at the last supper, the proclaiming the deliverance of the new dispensation, the commemoration of the final act of the redemption the death and passion of the Saviour, with the participation of its benefits, the communion in His holy Body and Blood.

After the Ascension the apostles, as bidden by the Lord, remained for a time in Jerusalem, continuing "with one accord in prayer and supplication[2]." This "prayer and supplication" is further explained as the participating in the worship of the temple[3]. And we find them for many years frequenting the Temple for worship. At the same time they took part equally readily in the Synagogue service. It was at the synagogue of the Libertines and Cyrenians and Alexandrians and them of Cilicia and Asia that Stephen taught and ministered. In

[1] Joh. xviii. 20, 21. [2] Acts i. 14. [3] Acts ii. 46; iii. 1.

exactly the same way we find later on the Christian community attending the synagogues at Damascus. In the synagogues St Paul "preached Christ" immediately after his conversion, and so we find him present at the Synagogue service for years after during his missionary journeys.

It was only gradually and after many years that the synagogues began to be closed against Christians, and Christian places of assembly and worship came into existence. Perhaps it is some such temporary and makeshift Christian place of assembly that is alluded to in Acts xvi. 13, "And on the sabbath day we went forth without the gate, by a river side, where we supposed was a place of prayer (προσευχή)." And we find another mark of the separation that is beginning when we read of St Paul hiring a disused school for the Christian ministrations[1]. Finally in Troas we find the Christians with their own place of worship[2] where they gathered together for Agape and Eucharist and for the hearing of the word. During his captivity St Paul ministered in his own house.

The separation then was gradual. For a long time the Synagogue was the normal place of worship for the Christian assembly, except of course for the Eucharist. When the brethren began to be separated from the Jews it is difficult to believe that they immediately abandoned that form of service with which they had been so many years familiar in the synagogue.

Now if we compare the structure of the Christian morning service which in process of time became the

[1] "But when divers were hardened and believed not, but spake evil of that way before the multitude, he departed from them and separated the disciples, disputing daily in the school of one Tyrannus." Acts xix. 9.

[2] Acts xx. 6, 7.

Proanaphora of the liturgy, with the Synagogue Sabbath morning service, the similarity is so striking that we have every reason to conclude that the Christian service is derived from the Jewish.

We learn from the Mishnah[1] that the Synagogue service consisted of five parts:

1. The שמע (Hear, O Israel).
2. תפלה (The prayers).
3. התורה (The Lesson from the Law).
4. הנביא (The Lesson from the Prophets).
5. The תרגם (The paraphrase and exposition).

From the notices of the Synagogue services which occur in the Gospels we see that this was substantially if not identically the order of service followed in the synagogues in the time of Our Lord. We read of Our Lord taking part in a Synagogue service[2]:

καὶ ἐπεδόθη αὐτῷ βιβλίον τοῦ προφήτου Ἠσαΐου καὶ ἀνοίξας τὸ βιβλίον εὗρεν τὸν τόπον οὗ ἦν γεγραμμένον... καὶ πτύξας τὸ βιβλίον ἀποδοὺς τῷ ὑπηρέτῃ ἐκάθισεν... ἤρξατο δὲ λέγειν...

Here we have two of these parts of the Synagogue service mentioned as having been undertaken by Our Lord. It is noticeable that the lessons were chosen by the reader, for Our Lord manifestly chose the passage that He read Himself. Also the תרגם was no mere paraphrase of the Lessons but was of the nature of an exposition and homily. Elsewhere[3] it is called a *διδαχή*.

Of the prayers we know practically nothing: there cannot however be much room for doubt that they consisted

[1] Megill. iv. 3—6. [2] Lu. iv. 17—21.

[3] Lu. iv. 31 *ἦν διδάσκων, καὶ ἐξεπλήσσοντο ἐπὶ τῇ διδαχῇ αὐτοῦ.*

of a number of petitions and acts of praise, probably those which finally became the Shemoneh-esre.

Such then was the Synagogue service at the time of Our Lord.

Now let us turn to St Justin Martyr. He describes a form of service which was ordinarily a preliminary to the Eucharist. He tells us that when on the Lord's Day the Christian assembly is gathered together,

τὰ ἀπομνημονεύματα τῶν ἀποστόλων ἢ τὰ συγγράμματα τῶν προφητῶν ἀναγινώσκεται μέχρις ἐγχωρεῖ· εἶτα παυσαμένου τοῦ ἀναγινώσκοντος ὁ προεστὼς διὰ λόγου τὴν νουθεσίαν καὶ παράκλησιν τῆς τῶν καλῶν τούτων μιμήσεως ποιεῖται. ἔπειτα ἀνιστάμεθα κοινῇ πάντες καὶ εὐχὰς πέμπομεν. (Apol. I. 67.)

Then follows the Eucharist.

Again the last feature of this service was *αἱ εὐχαί*. "*ἀλλήλους φιλήματι ἀσπαζόμεθα παυσάμενοι τῶν εὐχῶν*[1]." The kiss was the introduction to the Eucharist.

Here then we find four out of the five constituent parts of the Synagogue Sabbath morning service:

1. Lesson from the Gospels.
2. Lesson from the Prophets.
3. Sermon by Bishop or celebrant.
4. The Prayers.

The שמע has of course gone[2].

Of the four parts that remain the order is changed. The lessons are not fixed in number. Apparently there might be only one[3]. In the short account given in the Didascalia (A. C. II. 57) apparently any lesson could be

[1] Ap. I. 65.

[2] It is interesting to note that even this was represented in later times by the introduction of the Creed. But this of course was unconscious.

[3] τὰ ἀπομνημονεύματα τῶν ἀποστόλων ἢ τὰ συγγράμματα τῶν προφητῶν.

read out of the Old or New Testament, and as many as desired[1].

At the same time Justin seems to imply that the length of the lessons and probably the choice of them was left to the *ἀναγνώστης*. He says: *ἀναγινώσκεται μέχρις ἐγχωρεῖ. εἶτα παυσαμένου τοῦ ἀναγινώσκοντος...*

At the same time the lessons might be taken from writings outside the later Canon of Scripture as there were probably almost as many varying Canons of Scripture in Justin's time as there were Bishops. We know that at the end of the second century the Epistle of Clement sometimes furnished one of the lessons in the Church of Corinth[2].

Tertullian too tells us incidentally of the composition of this Sunday morning service. He says (de anima ix.) "prout scripturae leguntur aut psalmi canuntur aut allocutiones proferuntur aut petitiones delegantur." Here we have lessons, sermon or sermons, and prayers. Psalms are mentioned for the first time. Elsewhere we are told that psalms were sung between the reading of the different lessons (A.C. II. 57). But in the third century the *ψάλτης* is mentioned several times and is evidently a recognised *τάξις* in the Church, his existence of course implying the use of psalms in public worship.

Of the subjects of the prayers we can gather a certain amount of information incidentally. They were a well recognised part of the service, occurring at the end and having already the recognised name *αἱ εὐχαί*.

It is probable that the long prayer which St Clement of Rome inserts into his letter[3] is reminiscent of *αἱ εὐχαί*.

[1] In A. C. VIII. 5. 11, five are contemplated, from the Law, Prophets, Epistles, Acts, and Gospels.

[2] Euseb. H. E. IV. xxxiii. 11.

[3] cc. lix.—lxi.

Possibly it may be a reminiscence of the Eucharistic Intercessions.

In the prayer of St Clement are petitions for the sick and weak, for the faint-hearted, for peace, for princes and governors, for the civil power generally. This seems to have been the scope of the prayers in the "Morning Service."

We find the same to be the case in the time of St Justin and Tertullian.

> *ὅθεν θεὸν μὲν μόνον προσκυνοῦμεν, ὑμῖν δὲ πρὸς τὰ ἄλλα χαίροντες ὑπηρετοῦμεν, βασιλεῖς καὶ ἄρχοντας ἀνθρώπων ὁμολογοῦντες καὶ εὐχόμενοι μετὰ τῆς βασιλικῆς δυνάμεως καὶ σώφρονα τὸν λογισμὸν ἔχοντας ὑμᾶς εὑρεθῆναι,*

says Justin (Ap. I. 17).

Tertullian (Apol. 30) goes more into detail. He says:

> precantes sumus omnes semper pro omnibus imperatoribus, vitam illis prolixam, imperium securum, domum tutam, exercitus fortes, senatum fidelem, populum probum, orbem quietum.

These prayers then occurred in the morning service to which catechumens were permitted to come. The catechumens were admitted to this service in Tertullian's[1] time. In later times when this preliminary service became united to the liturgy still the catechumens were permitted to attend, and one of the distinctive names of the Proanaphora was the Missa Catechumenorum.

The chief point to be noticed about the prayers would seem to be that while the intercessions in the Eucharistic Liturgy embraced the needs of the Church, special classes and all classes among believers, the "prayers" of this morning service seem to have rather been on behalf of the

[1] Speaking of the laxity of the heretical sects, he says (De praescr. haer. 41): "Inprimis quis catechumenus, quis fidelis incertum est: pariter adeunt, pariter orant."

unbelieving world, the emperors, the State, the catechumens etc. When in later times the two services were united into one there appeared two sets of intercessions. On the other hand, by this time the civil power had ceased to be unbelieving and the catechumens were becoming rapidly an inconsiderable body, with the result that these prayers in the Missa Catechumenorum tended to become shorter and shorter, while the Eucharistic Intercessions seem to have developed in proportion. This question will however be treated of more fully when we come to consider the Intercession of the Eucharist.

It would seem, then, that the portion of the later Eucharistic Liturgy which was called the Proanaphora, or "Missa Catechumenorum," was based on the Synagogue Sabbath morning service. It seems to have been ordinarily a preliminary service to the Eucharist on Sunday mornings, becoming in process of time the invariable preliminary adjunct to the liturgy and finally a definite part of the Eucharistic Liturgy.

We have said of this service that it was ordinarily a preliminary service to the Eucharist on Sunday mornings.

There remain two questions perhaps to be considered.

1. Was it from the first considered as necessarily preliminary or introductory to the Eucharist?

2. Was it a separate service and ever used as such?

1. It is clear that the gatherings together of the brethren for worship recorded in the Acts are not all for Eucharists. Such expressions as "they continued with one accord in prayer" would include their worship in the Temple, and their worship in the Synagogue services, as well as the purely Christian gatherings of the Church.

The expression "the breaking of bread" which is found accompanying the phrase does not, strictly speaking, refer to the Eucharist, though probably sometimes it includes it. Properly speaking it seems to denote the Agape only, and includes the Eucharist at times, only in so far as the gathering together of the brethren at this social meal seems to have been regarded as offering a suitable occasion for the celebration of the Eucharist.

The Eucharist in apostolic or early apostolic days was probably always celebrated at night. In the first place there was the example of the Institution; in the second place it seems generally to have followed the Agape, and we can understand how the evening would be the most suitable time for such an assembly, as being the freest time for the humble class that formed the greater part of the Church, and also as securing as much freedom from publicity as possible.

At Corinth we know that the Eucharist was celebrated in the evening after the Agape.

The only other celebration of the Eucharist that seems to be more or less certain is that recorded at Troas[1], and here again it takes place in the evening.

If this is so it must have been of necessity quite independent of the Sunday morning service taken into Christian usage from the Jews. By the time of Pliny however the celebration seems to have been very generally transferred from the evening to the early morning[2].

[1] Acts xx. 7—11. The Peshitta version has in v. 7 ܟܕ ܟܢܝܫܝܢ ܕܢܩܨܐ ܐܘܟܪܣܛܝܐ

[2] Probably the idea in these very early celebrations was to escape observation as much as possible.

From this time forward, then, there is no reason to doubt that ordinarily the "morning service" preceded the Liturgy, and we can see how very naturally the two were welded into one.

But for some time the union of these two portions was very loose. Thus we find in St Justin's account of the ordinary Sunday worship (Ap. I. 67) that the Eucharist follows at once on the "morning service[1]." But if there was any other event taking place before the Eucharist, the "morning service" seems to have been dispensed with altogether.

Thus St Justin elsewhere (I. 65) describes the celebration of the Eucharist following on a baptism. He makes no mention whatsoever of the "morning service" and it is evident that it did not occur on this occasion.

The same thing is seen in the First Church Order. The Eucharist follows at once on the Consecration of a Bishop[2]. But there is no sign of the "morning service" as a preliminary to the Eucharist. Evidently it did not appear. The Eucharist begins at once with the kiss and the "sursum corda."

Again in the description of Holy Baptism[3] which the Eucharist follows, as in Justin the proanaphora is not yet a part of the Liturgy, and does not occur at all.

And we find, in short, that in all the descriptions of the Eucharist and in all the texts up to the time of St Cyril the Liturgy is regarded as beginning at the kiss, and there is no sign that the "morning service" was considered to

[1] Cf. Tertull. de an. ix., and Orig. in Rom. x. xxxiii. "mos ecclesiis traditus est ut post orationes osculo se invicem suscipiant fratres."

[2] § 31 Copt. text. It is noticeable that the proanaphora already is part of the liturgy in the corresponding place in the Second Order.

[3] § 41.

be in any way a part of the Liturgy itself, however closely connected it may have been with it. And even St Cyril in describing the Liturgy to his catechumens (C. M. v.) begins at the kiss.

So, on the whole, we may conclude that up to nearly the end of the fourth century "the morning service" was no part of the Liturgy, and though on Sundays it ordinarily preceded the Eucharist, yet the connection of the two services was only loose. The connection of the two was only a chance connection, and any other service such as the celebration of Baptism or the ordination of clergy displaced the morning service altogether.

Towards the end of the fourth century the two drew closer together, and in the fifth century had become one whole, forming together the Proanaphora and Anaphora of the Eucharistic Liturgy.

2. The "morning service" then was no part properly speaking of the Liturgy, but ordinarily preceded it on Sunday mornings. The question remains, Was this service ever used apart from the Eucharist? Was it in any sense a complete service in itself? It was certainly a complete service in itself and was regularly used as such.

Tertullian[1] describes for us the service which was used on Station Days. He tells us that the Kiss of peace was not used, and distinguishes it from the Sunday services by saying that the "orationes sacrificiorum" were omitted. The "orationes sacrificiorum" are the Eucharistic forms or liturgy. Thus then the regular Station Day service was the Christian "morning service," which had originally been derived from the Synagogue service.

But Tertullian also gives a name to this service[2]. In

[1] de orat. 14. [2] de cult. fem. II. 11.

speaking of the duties of a Christian as opposed to the idle pleasures of the Gentile, he insists upon attendance at public worship on every occasion that is offered. There are two ordinary occasions: "aut sacrificium offertur, aut Dei verbum administratur." There were evidently, then, other services than the Eucharist of regular occurrence. Their name, "administratio Dei verbi," clearly indicates their nature. The chief feature is evidently a sermon or instruction. The sermon we know from Justin occurred in the "morning service," and we cannot doubt that this service was the same as that in use on the Station Days, even if Tertullian is not here actually referring to the Station Day services, and that this service is the "morning service."

Origen as we have noticed uses the general term "orationes" of this service recalling Justin's general name for it (*αἱ εὐχαί*).

The First Church Order bears out Tertullian's evidence very closely even in the matter of the name.

"And if there should be the word of instruction (Veron. si qua autem per verbum catechizatio fit) let them choose rather for themselves to go and hear the word of God for the confirming of their soul, and let them hasten to go to the church where the Spirit breaks forth (Ver. floret)[1]."

"The word of instruction," "per verbum catechizatio," "ut audiat verbum Dei" are manifestly equivalent to Tertullian's "administratio Dei verbi." The service referred to in the First Order is either an occasional service, or a service in some places regular, perhaps daily. It would seem that all services additional to the Eucharist (except

[1] § 57 Coptic. Veron. vers. lxxvii. Hauler, p. 117.

of course Baptisms and ordinations) were of this one type, the old "morning service" and sermon.

The "Peregrinatio ad loca sancta[1]" of the end of the fourth century throws further light on the use and one of the developments of this service.

Dom F. Cabrot in his "Les origines liturgiques[2]" remarks:

> A Jérusalem au IVe siècle l'avant-messe se célèbre dans une église comme un rite séparé. Puis cette cérémonie terminée on va dans une autre église où les fidèles baptisés sont seuls admis et l'on célèbre la messe des fidèles.

Perhaps it is more exact to say that in the "Peregrinatio" we find this service occurring as a preliminary to the Eucharist, and also with suitable variations serving as the office for the different hours observed.

Thus the authoress describing the services says[3]:

> et sunt omnia secundum consuetudinem quae ubique fit die dominica. Sane quia hic consuetudo sic est ut de omnibus presbiteris qui sedent quanti volunt praedicent: et post illos omnes episcopus praedicat: quae praedicationes propterea semper dominicis diebus sunt ut semper erudiatur populus in scripturis et in Dei dilectione: quae praedicationes dum dicuntur grandis mora fit ut fiat missa[4] ecclesiae: et ideo ante quartam horam aut horam quintam missa (non) fit. At ubi autem missa facta fuerit ecclesiae iuxta consuetudinem qua et ubique fit; tunc de ecclesia monazontes cum ymnis ducunt episcopum usque ad Anastasim. Cum autem ceperit venire aperiuntur omnia ostia de basilica Anastasis. Intrat omnis populus, fidelis tamen nam catechumini non.

Then follows the Eucharist.

This service is then the same at Jerusalem as elsewhere, the preliminary to the Liturgy. Its essential separateness

[1] Ed. by Joh. Franciscus Gamurrini. [2] p. 138.

[3] pp. 80, 81.

[4] The word "missa" is used here, as frequently, not of the Eucharist but of "dismissal."

as a service is clearly shown by the practice at Jerusalem of holding it in one church and then proceeding to another for the Eucharist.

The most important thing is the sermon or sermons. The purpose of this, "ut semper erudiatur populus in scripturis," shows that it was an exposition of, or an homily on some passage of Scripture, which seems to point to at least one such lection being made. The fact that there were or might be several such homilies[1] points to there having been several lections.

But not only is this service the preliminary to the Eucharist. It supplies with suitable variations the services for the different hours observed through the day.

Mattins is thus described (pp. 76, 77):

singulis diebus ante pullorum cantum... ex ea hora usque in lucem dicuntur ymni et psalmi respondentur similiter et antiphonae: et cata singulos ymnos fit oratio.... iam autem ubi ceperit lucescere tunc incipiunt matutinos ymnos dicere. Ecce et supervenit episcopus cum clero et statim ingreditur intro spelunca et de intro cancellos primum dicet orationem pro omnibus: commemorat etiam ipse nomina quorum vult: sic benedicet catechuminos. Item dicet orationem et benedicet fideles.

Sext (p. 77).

dicuntur psalmi et antiphonae donec commonetur episcopus. Similiter descendet et non sedet sed statim intrat in cancellos intra Anastasim, id est intra speluncam... et inde similiter primum facit orationem sic benedicet fideles...

Nones.

Ita ergo et hora nona fit sicuti et ad sexta.

Vespers (p. 78).

dicuntur ymni vel antiphonae. Et ad (finem) ubi perducti fuerint iuxta consuetudinem levat se episcopus et stat ante cancel-

[1] There are also sermons by several priests in the account of the turgy in A. C. II. 57.

lam id est ante speluncam : et unus ex diaconibus facit commemorationem singulorum sicut solet esse consuetudo. Et diacono dicente singulorum nomina semper pisinni plurimi stant respondentes semper 'Kyrie eleyson,' quod dicimus nos 'miserere, Domine,' quorum voces infinitae sunt. Et ubi diaconus perdixerit omnia quae dicere habet, dicet orationem primum episcopus et orat pro omnibus : et sic orant omnes tam fideles quam et catechumini simul.

Then follows the blessing of catechumens and faithful.

The descriptions are not perhaps very clear—but the services at the different hours are evidently the same, with variations doubtless of the hymns and psalms.

The service closes with prayers for all, catechumens and other classes. It is true that the lections are not mentioned actually in these accounts, but they are implied elsewhere. In the description of the services on the Monday in Holy Week we are told "lectiones etiam aptae diei et loco leguntur, interpositae semper orationes." The mention here of lections suitable to the day implies the occurrence of lections in the services on other days.

Thus then the Peregrinatio shows us the twofold development of the old Sunday morning service. It is on the one hand the preliminary to the Liturgy and almost already the Proanaphora. On the other hand it provides the offices for the hours. So the occurrence of the Proanaphora in the Liturgy a little later and of the "offices" on the same day is simply a reduplication of one and the same service.

But the old morning service lingered on into the fifth century as a distinct and separate service. Socrates in the well-known passage[1] describing the varying uses and customs of the Church, speaks of the use of Alexandria on Wednesdays and Fridays. He says,

[1] Hist. Eccl. v. 22.

αὖθις δὲ ἐν Ἀλεξανδρείᾳ τῇ τετράδι καὶ τῇ λεγομένῃ παρασκευῇ, γραφαί τε ἀναγινώσκονται καὶ οἱ διδάσκαλοι ταύτας ἑρμηνεύουσι, πάντα τε τὰ συνάξεως γίνεται δίχα τῆς τῶν μυστηρίων τελετῆς.

He adds *τοῦτο ἐστίν ἐν Ἀλεξανδρείᾳ ἔθος ἀρχαῖον.* The use is exactly the same as it was in Tertullian's days for the Station Day services.

And Tertullian tells us that the same services were used during the Pascha, the fasting days preparatory to the celebration of Easter. This use seems to have been the origin of the Liturgy of the Presanctified. Already in the ninth century we find the Liturgy of the Presanctified in use[1]. The Blessed Sacrament was reserved for the purpose of communicating the people on the week-days in Lent, on which days it was not permitted to celebrate the Eucharist.

But this seems to have been an intermediary step. There was the practical difficulty of preserving incorrupt the Consecrated Cup.

The Consecrated Bread was early given to the faithful that they might receive it at home and communicate themselves every day[2]. Such a method of communion seems also to have been practised by solitaries[3]. The reservation in one kind only was practised because of the practical impossibility of reserving the Cup under these circumstances.

And so we find an earlier Liturgy of the Presanctified intermediate between the service of Tertullian and the Alexandrian Church of the fifth century, and the later Liturgy of the Presanctified.

This, "the signing of the chalice," was used among the

[1] Brightman p. 345.

[2] Tertull. ad uxor. II. 5.

[3] Bas. ep. xciii.

Jacobites until comparatively recent times, but is evidently an earlier form of the Liturgy of the Presanctified, though existing on side by side with it.

This rite consisted of reserving the Host from the Sunday and on week-days placing a portion of It into an unhallowed chalice, thus consecrating the wine. Even a deacon could perform this consecration.

The use seems to have been very early in the East at any rate, and dates from the time of John of Tella (538) and Severus of Antioch (511—538)[1].

It would seem then that the third development of the Sunday "morning service" was into the Liturgy of the Presanctified through the rite called "the signing of the chalice."

Thus we have originally the Synagogue morning service taken into the use of the Church and becoming

1. The ordinary Sunday morning service before the Eucharist.

2. The ordinary service at all times[2] when the Eucharist was not celebrated, *e.g.* during Pascha, and on Station Days, and forming the service for the different hours.

3. The Proanaphora of the Liturgy.

4. The signing of the chalice and finally the "Liturgy of the Presanctified."

[1] Texts of this rite are printed in J. T. S. iv. 69, v. 369 (Jacobite) and v. 535 (Nestorian).

[2] Yet another occasion on which this service was used is given by A. C. VIII. xlii. *ἐπιτελείσθω δὲ τὰ τρίτα τῶν κεκοιμημένων ἐν ψαλμοῖς καὶ ἀναγνώμασιν καὶ προσευχαῖς.* In the corresponding canon *περὶ μνημοσυνῶν* of the Second Church Order the same words occur except for the omission of *καὶ ἀναγνώμασιν.*

III

THE ANAPHORA OR LITURGY PROPER

We come now to the consideration of the Eucharistic Liturgy proper, the Anaphora of later days.

The sub-apostolic age is almost a blank so far as our knowledge of the liturgy is concerned. It is not till we come to the time of Justin Martyr that we get definite information, and when we reach the Church Orders of the beginning of the third century we find a form of liturgy that is the parent of all later families.

But how far is this liturgy of the third century representative of the liturgical use of the Church in the foregoing period? Can we say that there was one liturgical use from Apostolic days? The evidence goes rather to show that this liturgical use was the use that prevailed of several that at one time existed side by side.

When we turn to the records of the Institution we find that we are told three things of Our Lord's words and acts.

1. That He took bread and brake it and blessed (*εὐχαριστήσας, εὐλογήσας*) the broken bread and the cup.

2. That He said of the blessed Bread and Cup, "This is my Body," "This is my Blood," and gave Them to His disciples.

3. That He laid on them the commandment "Do this in remembrance of me."

Of the institution nothing more seems to have been known than this. St Paul's tradition is more or less the same as the description in the Synoptists, and by the time the Liturgy comes into full view there can be little doubt that the account of the Synoptists represents the sum total of the Church's knowledge of what took place at the Institution itself. We have no certain knowledge as to the nature of the blessing or consecration of the Bread and the Cup—εὐχαριστήσας and εὐλογήσας, which seem to be synonymous terms, are but of vague meaning to us, and were probably no less vague to men generally by the time the Gospels became popularly known and read.

On the other hand every time the Church celebrated the Eucharist she was fulfilling the Divine command "Do this in remembrance of me." We find no sign of any claim on the part of the Church to any secret tradition as to the form used in the Consecration of the Eucharist. In fact St Basil expressly denies any such thing.

τὰ τῆς ἐπικλήσεως ῥήματα ἐπὶ τῇ ἀναδείξει τοῦ ἄρτου τῆς εὐχαριστίας καὶ τοῦ ποτηρίου τῆς εὐλογίας τίς τῶν ἁγίων ἐγγράφως ἡμῖν καταλέλοιπεν; οὐ γὰρ δὴ τούτοις ἀρκούμεθα ὧν ὁ ἀπόστολος ἢ τὸ εὐαγγέλιον ἐπεμνήσθη, ἀλλὰ καὶ προλέγομεν καὶ ἐπιλέγομεν ἕτερα ὡς μεγάλην ἔχοντα πρὸς τὸ μυστήριον τὴν ἰσχὺν ἐκ τῆς ἀγράφου διδασκαλίας παραλαβόντες (De Spir. S. c. 66).

The extent then to which the accounts of the Institution could be regarded as a guide to the Church in her liturgical use seems to be confined to the injunction "Do this in remembrance of me." If this is so there was no reason why the Church should confine herself to any one particular form. So long as she expressed the fact that her celebration of the Eucharist was in fulfilment of the

Divine command, there would seem to be no other essential. And this expression of fulfilment of the command might be made in different ways.

Now this is borne out by what evidence we have before the year 200 A.D. There are signs of three or perhaps four different uses, based on different ideas, and yet all expressing the fact that in the Eucharist the Church is doing as her Lord bids her.

The three or four different uses, which we shall consider one by one, would seem to be as follows:

1. The use of the grace before meals adapted to the blessing of the spiritual food of the Eucharistic Feast. This is probably the nearest to Our Lord's own words of Consecration which are described by *εὐχαριστήσας* or *εὐλογήσας*.

2. The adaptation of the only sacramental form actually given to His disciples by our Lord, the Baptismal formula, and the blessing of the bread and wine in the name of the Father and of the Son and of the Holy Ghost.

3. Possibly the use of the Lord's Prayer as a consecration form. In such case *ἐπιούσιον* has the sense of "supersubstantialem." But this use of the Lord's Prayer as a consecration form is very doubtful, for, except for the statement of St Gregory the Great that this was the "mos apostolorum," we have little or no other evidence.

4. A use existing from the first with other uses had by the latter half of the third century so far become general, that all other uses were not only obsolete but already forgotten. It is the Scriptural use, embodying more or less the account of the Institution. The *εὐχαριστία* or form of blessing may for convenience be divided into two parts.

1. A recitation of God's manifold dispensations of

love toward mankind leading up to the story of the Passion and of the Institution of the Blessed Sacrament.

2. The ἀνάμνησις or expression that the Church is hereby fulfilling the Divine command, followed by prayer that the Holy Spirit may come upon the offering of the Church that all who communicate may receive the Sacrament to salvation, and concluding with petitions for all classes and conditions of the Church.

This is the mother of all families of liturgies from the third century onwards.

How far were all these uses recognised by the Church? Apparently in the earliest times each local church used the greatest freedom in the management of its own affairs. This freedom would extend even to its liturgical use.

The prevalence of each of these varying uses is hard to gauge. But it is evident that the last, obtaining from the first, was so far the most familiar use and the most general that other uses were altogether unknown even by persons of wide experience and knowledge of other churches. St Justin for example seems only to know the one use which he describes. Those liturgical uses, too, which appear in the Acts of John and Thomas occur, it must be remembered, in works which from a later point of view were distinctly heretical, whatever may have been the official view of them at the time when they were written, and probably represent only a very limited part of the Church. Be that as it may, however, they are of value as showing a contemporary view of what would be sufficient for a "valid" Eucharist, and there is little room to doubt that they do represent actual historical uses, however limited may have been the sphere in which they were in vogue.

On the other hand the use of St Justin, which is the

undeveloped form of the later universal form of liturgy, was undoubtedly the chief and most widely spread use from earliest days. That there were definite official uses in earliest days would seem to be proved by the assertions of both Justin and Tertullian that the Christian Eucharistic liturgy was distinctly and deliberately imitated in the Mithraic celebration of the Mysteries.

Whichever was actually the borrower, one thing seems to be clear, that there was one or more distinctly official and definite outline or outlines in use in the Church, and however much the mere wording and phraseology were left to the powers of the individual celebrant (as was the case in the time of Justin Martyr, and in the time of the First Church Order, and probably well on into the fourth century), yet there was some sort of restriction to a customary and authoritative scheme and arrangement of contents.

Both Justin and Tertullian seem explicit on the subject.

> *ὅπερ καὶ ἐν τοῖς τοῦ Μίθρα μυστηρίοις παρέδωκαν γίνεσθαι μιμησάμενοι οἱ πονηροὶ δαίμονες· ὅτι γὰρ ἄρτος καὶ ποτήριον ὕδατος τίθεται ἐν ταῖς τοῦ μυομένου τελεταῖς μετ' ἐπιλόγων τινῶν, ἢ ἐπίστασθε ἢ μαθεῖν δύνασθε*[1].

And Tertullian[2]:

> qui (sc. diabolus) ergo ipsas res de quibus sacramenta Christi administrantur, tam aemulanter affectavit exprimere in negotiis idolatriae. Utique et idem et eodem ingenio gestiit et potuit instrumenta quoque divinarum rerum et sanctorum Christianorum, sensum de sensibus, verba de verbis, parabolas de parabolis profanae et aemulae fidei attemperare.

It is evident that Justin and Tertullian are thinking of something more than a mere imitation of the Christian Sacraments. *μετ' ἐπιλόγων τινῶν* and still more decidedly

[1] Just. Apol. I. 66.

[2] de praescript. c. 40.

the expression "verba de verbis" of Tertullian point to a borrowing by the Mithraic rite of the recognised forms of a recognised and general Christian Liturgy.

We shall proceed now to consider the varying uses which seem to have existed at the first side by side.

I. The adaptation of the grace before meals to the blessing of the elements of the Eucharistic Feast.

The words used in the synoptists and by St Paul that our Lord blessed the bread and the cup at the Institution (εὐχαριστήσας, εὐλογήσας) are interpreted most simply of the grace or of some adaptation of the grace.

There was apparently in our Lord's time a general outline of the grace to be used at meals, and this He probably followed. What the actual words were does not appear, but something of their general form may be gathered from Berachoth.

In B. VI. 1 we read

How do they give thanks for the fruits of trees? by saying "Who createst the fruit of the tree"—except for wine. On wine they say "who createst the fruit of the vine." And on fruits of the earth, saying, "who createst the fruits of the earth." Excepting on bread. On bread they say "who broughtest forth bread from the earth." And on olives they say "who createst the fruits of the earth" etc.

In B. VII. 3 there are further particulars. He who says grace begins 'Let us bless' (נברך), or 'Bless ye' (ברכו), with slight variations according to the numbers present. The whole company answered then it would appear, or rather perhaps joined in

ברוך ה׳ אלהינו אלהי ישראל אלהי הצבאות יושב הכרובים על המזון שאכלנו

Blessed (art Thou), O Lord our God, the God of Israel, the God of Hosts, who dwellest between the Cherubim, for the food which we eat.

From these directions we can get some idea of the general form of the grace, and there seems to be a considerable similarity of idea in the forms in the Didache.

That the forms there given in cc. ix. x. are a form or part of a form of the Eucharistic Liturgy can hardly be seriously doubted. The expression *πνευματικὴ τροφή* in c. x. cannot be used of anything but the Eucharist, and the compiler of the A.C. certainly regarded these forms as liturgical.

Now this form consists of two parts:

I. A thanksgiving over the elements, before partaking.

II. A thanksgiving for the participation of the spiritual Food and Cup received, concluding with a prayer for the Church.

There appears but little reason to doubt that these two forms make up what in later times was called the *προσφορά* or Canon.

They are on the same principle, both graces or thanksgivings, the one before the Eucharistic Feast, and thus a consecration; the other a grace or thanksgiving after communion.

It is interesting to compare these forms with our information from the Mishnah.

c. ix. *εὐχαριστοῦμέν σοι, πάτερ ἡμῶν, ὑπὲρ τῆς ἁγίας ἀμπέλου Δαβὶδ τοῦ παιδός σου, ἧς ἐγνώρισας κ.τ.λ.*	נברך (or ברוך) לאלהינו אלהי ישראל אלהי (B. vii. 3) בורא פרי הגפן (B. vi. 1)

In c. x. the grace is equally well marked and is adapted

by the slightest additions to a thanksgiving after receiving the Communion.

εὐχαριστοῦμέν σοι... σὺ, Δέσποτα, παντοκράτορ, ἔκτισας τὰ πάντα ἕνεκεν τοῦ ὀνόματός σου τροφήν τε καὶ πότον ἔδωκας τοῖς ἀνθρώποις εἰς ἀπόλαυσιν, ἵνα σοι εὐχαριστήσωσιν, ἡμῖν δὲ ἐχαρίσω πνευματικὴν τροφὴν καὶ πότον καὶ ζωὴν αἰώνιον διὰ τοῦ παιδός σου. πρὸ πάντων εὐχαριστοῦμέν σοι κ.τ.λ.

The close parallel which these forms offer to the directions of the Mishnah would appear to show that the liturgy of the Didache is based on the grace before and after meals used by the Jews and doubtless taken from them into Christian ordinary use.

At any rate that the Didache forms are an adaptation of the Christian grace before and after meals, is put more or less beyond doubt by the fact that Pseudo-Athanasius[1] in his tractate περὶ παρθενίας has preserved for us forms of grace used before and after meals which are more or less identical with the forms underlying the Didache liturgy.

The grace before meals in St Athanasius represents the underlying matter of the thanksgivings in the Didache over the cup and bread; the grace after meals the substance of the thanksgiving μετὰ τὸ ἐμπλησθῆναι.

The graces before and after meals preserved by St Athanasius are as follows:

περὶ παρθενίας XIII. καὶ ὅταν καθεσθῇς ἐπὶ τῆς τραπέζης καὶ ἔρχῃ κλᾶσαι τὸν ἄρτον, σφραγίσασα αὐτὸν τρίτον, οὕτως εὐχαριστοῦσα λέγε· "εὐχαριστοῦμέν σοι, πάτερ ἡμῶν, ὑπὲρ τῆς ἁγίας ἀναστάσεως σοῦ. διὰ γὰρ Ἰησοῦ τοῦ παιδός σου ἐγνώρισας ἡμῖν αὐτήν. καὶ καθὼς ὁ ἄρτος οὗτος ἐσκορπισμένος ὑπάρχει ὁ ἐπάνω ταύτης τῆς τραπέζης καὶ συναχθεὶς ἐγένετο ἕν, οὕτως ἐπισυναχθήτω σου ἡ ἐκκλησία ἀπὸ τῶν περάτων τῆς γῆς εἰς τὴν βασιλείαν σου, ὅτι σοῦ ἐστιν ἡ δύναμις καὶ ἡ δόξα εἰς τοὺς αἰῶνας τῶν αἰώνων, ἀμήν."

[1] There is very little reason why this work should not be regarded as a genuine work by Athanasius himself.

The grace after meals c. xiv.

ὁ Θεὸς ὁ παντοκράτωρ καὶ κύριος ἡμῶν Ἰησοῦς Χριστὸς τὸ ὄνομα τὸ ὑπὲρ πᾶν ὄνομα, εὐχαριστοῦμέν σοι καὶ αἰνοῦμέν σοι ὅτι κατηξίωσας ἡμᾶς μεταλαβεῖν τῶν ἀγαθῶν τῶν σῶν, τῶν σαρκικῶν τροφῶν. δεόμεθα καὶ παρακαλοῦμέν σε, κύριε, ἵνα καὶ τὰς ἐπουρανίους τροφὰς ἡμῖν δωρήσῃ κ.τ.λ.[1]

The forms are evidently, with slight variations, the same as those underlying the Didache prayers. It is possible, of course, that they may have been taken from the Didache, which is referred to in the work. But the more probable explanation is that they are a typical form of the Christian grace which was derived ultimately from the Jewish usages which we have seen were laid down in the Mishnah.

So then it would appear that one of the earliest usages for the consecration of the Eucharist was the adaptation of the grace before meals, and was probably the closest parallel to the *εὐχαριστία* of Our Lord Himself.

εὐχαριστοῦμέν σοι, πάτερ ἡμῶν, ὑπὲρ τῆς ἁγίας ἀμπέλου Δαβὶδ τοῦ παιδός σου, ἧς ἐγνώρισας ἡμῖν διὰ Ἰησοῦ τοῦ παιδός σου. σοὶ ἡ δόξα εἰς τοὺς αἰῶνας.

εὐχαριστοῦμέν σοι, πάτερ ἡμῶν, ὑπὲρ τῆς ζωῆς καὶ γνώσεως ἧς ἐγνώρισας ἡμῖν διὰ Ἰησοῦ τοῦ παιδός σου. σοὶ ἡ δόξα εἰς τοὺς αἰῶνας. ὥσπερ ἦν τοῦτο κλάσμα διεσκορπισμένον ἐπάνω τῶν ὀρέων καὶ συναχθὲν ἐγένετο ἕν, οὕτω συναχθήτω σου ἡ ἐκκλησία ἀπὸ τῶν περάτων τῆς γῆς εἰς τὴν σὴν βασιλείαν· ὅτι σοῦ ἐστιν ἡ δόξα καὶ ἡ δύναμις διὰ Ἰησοῦ Χριστοῦ εἰς τοὺς αἰῶνας.

The grace after the Eucharistic meal, the Liturgical thanksgiving, is as we have seen adapted to its Eucharistic purpose. But there is also another thing noticeable about it. The grace is amplified it would seem by the Lord's Prayer, of which reminiscences are frequent.

[1] Ed. von der Goltz. Leipzig, 1905.

εὐχαριστοῦμέν σοι **πάτερ ἅγιε ὑπὲρ τοῦ ἁγίου ὀνόματός σου** οὗ κατεσκήνωσας ἐν ταῖς καρδίαις ἡμῶν, καὶ **ὑπὲρ τῆς γνώσεως καὶ πίστεως καὶ ἀθανασίας ἧν ἐγνώρισας** ἡμῖν διὰ Ἰησοῦ τοῦ παιδός σου· σοὶ ἡ δόξα εἰς τοὺς αἰῶνας.	πάτερ ἡμῶν...ἁγιασθήτω τὸ ὄνομά σου... γενηθήτω τὸ θέλημά σου ὡς ἐν οὐρανῷ καὶ ἐπὶ γῆς.
σὺ Δέσποτα παντοκράτορ **ἔκτισας τὰ πάντα ἕνεκεν τοῦ ὀνόματός σου τροφήν τε καὶ πότον ἔδωκας τοῖς ἀνθρώποις εἰς ἀπόλαυσιν** ἵνα σοι εὐχαριστήσωσιν, ἡμῖν δὲ ἐχαρίσω πνευματικὴν τροφὴν καὶ πότον καὶ ζωὴν αἰώνιον διὰ τοῦ παιδὸς σοῦ. πρὸ πάντων εὐχαριστοῦμέν σοι ὅτι δύνατος εἶ. σοὶ ἡ δόξα εἰς τοὺς αἰῶνας.	τὸν ἄρτον ἡμῶν τὸν ἐπιούσιον δὸς ἡμῖν σήμερον.
μνήσθητι, κύριε, τῆς ἐκκλησίας σου τοῦ ῥύσασθαι αὐτὴν ἀπὸ παντὸς πονηροῦ καὶ τελειῶσαι αὐτὴν ἐν τῇ ἀγάπῃ σου, καὶ σύναξον αὐτὴν ἀπὸ τῶν τεσσάρων ἀνέμων τὴν ἁγιασθεῖσαν εἰς τὴν σὴν βασιλείαν ἣν ἡτοίμασας αὐτῇ. ὅτι σοῦ ἐστὶν ἡ δύναμις καὶ ἡ δόξα εἰς τοὺς αἰῶνας.	ῥῦσαι ἡμᾶς ἀπὸ τοῦ πονηροῦ.

Perhaps the parallel is not very close in places, but it is noticeable, and the fact is all the more interesting and important when we see the Lord's Prayer worked in, as it were, into the end of the thanksgiving in the Liturgy contained in the Testamentum Domini, and the position of the Lord's Prayer generally in the type of Liturgy that prevailed.

The Intercession so marked and comprehensive in later days is represented by *μνήσθητι, κύριε, τῆς ἐκκλησίας σου τοῦ ῥύσασθαι αὐτήν κ.τ.λ.*

The matter that follows these forms would seem to be

no part of the forms but simply the pious ejaculations of the writer.

ἐλθέτω χάρις καὶ παρελθέτω ὁ κόσμος οὗτος. ὡσαννὰ τῷ υἱῷ Δαβίδ. εἴ τις ἅγιός ἐστιν ἐρχέσθω. εἴ τις οὐκ ἔστι, μετανοείτω. μαραναθά. ἀμήν.

If they have anything to do with the preceding forms, they must refer to the Communion and be out of place.

These forms are a general model. If the officiants be endowed with special gifts of speech (προφῆται) they are allowed to use those gifts as they will and apparently need not feel bound down closely to these forms.

One of the forms given in the Acts of John is probably a form of adapted grace. It is considerably developed in comparison with the Didache forms and the text is almost certainly corrupt in places; but the underlying idea seems to be that of a thanksgiving for the spiritual food given in the Eucharist.

Acts of John c. 85.

καὶ ταῦτα εἰπὼν ὁ Ἰωάννης ἐπευξάμενος καὶ λαβὼν ἄρτον...εἶπε·

Δοξάζομέν σου τὸ ὄνομα τὸ ἐπιστρέφον ἡμᾶς ἐκ τῆς πλάνης καὶ ἀνηλεοῦς ἀπάτης· δοξάζομέν σε τὸν παρ' ὀφθαλμοῖς δείξαντα ἡμῖν ἃ εἴδομεν· μαρτυροῦμέν σου τῇ χρηστότητι ποικίλαις φανίσιν· αἰνοῦμέν σου τὸ ἀγαθὸν ὄνομα, κύριε, ἐλέγξαντι τοὺς ὑπὸ σοῦ ἐλεγχομένους· εὐχαριστοῦμέν σε, κύριε Ἰησοῦ Χριστέ, ὅτι πεπείσμεθα ἀμετάβολον οὖσαν· εὐχαριστοῦμέν σοι τῷ χρήσαντι φύσιν φύσεως σωζομένης· εὐχαριστοῦμέν σοι τῷ τὴν ἀπαραίτητον ἡμῖν δεδωκότι ταύτην, ὅτι σὺ μόνος καὶ νῦν καὶ ἀεί· οἱ σοὶ δοῦλοι εὐχαριστοῦμέν σοι μετὰ προφάσεως συλλεγόμενοι καὶ ἀναλεγόμενοι ἅγιε.

The text is unfortunately corrupt in places. But the form is a thanksgiving over the elements, a grace considerably more developed and adapted than that of the Didache.

II. Another use for the consecration of the Eucharist

seems to have been by an adaptation of the Baptismal formula. As being the only definite formula given by our Lord, and that for the other great Sacrament of Holy Baptism, such an adaptation would be not only reasonable but likely in the absence of any definite command or tradition as to the consecration of the Eucharist.

There is also the analogy of the use of the name of our Lord in the healing of the sick and the casting out of evil spirits. Both in the Sacrament of Baptism and in the performing of miracles the forms used indicate the presence of the divine power to consecrate and to make strong.

This use occurs only in the two apocryphal works, the Acts of John and the Acts of Thomas. It would appear therefore to have been used in a very limited region only and perhaps we may regard it as one of the uses of a distinctively Gentile origin.

At the same time the forms there given present certain parallels to the great scriptural use that existed side by side with all other uses from the first and ultimately prevailed over them all. The text which we give of the Acts of Thomas is Wright's version of the Syriac which was probably the original language of the work. The Greek version varies often and considerably from the Syriac in many places.

Acts of Thomas C. (see appendix).

He brought bread and wine, and placed it on the table and began to bless it, and said:

"Living bread, the eaters of which die not! Bread that fillest hungry souls with thy blessing! Thou that art worthy to receive the gift and to be for the remission of sins, that those who eat thee may not die! we name the name of the Father over thee; we name the name of the Son over thee; we name the name of the Spirit over thee, the exalted name that is hidden from all."

And he said :

"In thy name, Jesus[1], may the power of the blessing and the thanksgiving come and abide upon this bread, that all the souls which take of it may be renewed and their sins may be forgiven them[2]."

Here we have a form of the "Canon," and it consists of two parts, (1) The Blessing of the Elements, (2) A prayer for a good communion, the early form, as we shall see later, which developed into the ἐπίκλησις of the Holy Spirit.

The form of blessing or consecration is beyond doubt based on the Baptismal formula in the name of the Holy Trinity.

Acts of Thomas A.

Jesus, who hast deemed us worthy[3] to draw nigh unto Thy holy Body, and to partake of Thy life-giving Blood ; and because of our reliance upon Thee we are bold and draw nigh, *and invoke Thy holy Name*, which has been proclaimed by the prophets as Thy Godhead willed; and Thou art preached by Thy apostles through the whole world according to Thy grace, and art revealed by Thy mercy to the just ; we beg of Thee that Thou wouldest come and communicate with us for help and for life and for the conversion of Thy servants unto Thee, that they may go under Thy pleasant yoke and under Thy victorious power, and that it may be unto them for the health[4] of their souls and for the life of their bodies in Thy living world.

[1] This reference to the name of Jesus alone when the foregoing text shows the use of the Trinitarian formula may perhaps throw some light on the Baptism into the name of Jesus in the Acts of the Apostles.

[2] Acts of Thomas in Wright's Apoc. Acts. See appendix for text and the variations of the Greek version.

[3] Cf. in Anamnesis of First Church Order "gratias tibi agentes quia nos dignos habuisti adstare coram te et tibi ministrare."

[4] Cf. the language of St Ignatius ad Eph. 20, *ἕνα ἄρτον κλῶντες ὅς ἐστι φάρμακον ἀθανασίας ἀντίδοτος τοῦ ἀποθανεῖν ἀλλὰ ζῆν ἐν Ἰησοῦ Χριστῷ διὰ παντός*. It is significant that both Ignatius and the Acts of Thomas belong to Syria. Cf. also the words of administration of Acts of Thomas p. 58 *infra*.

The expression *φάρμακον ζωῆς* occurs in the *ἐπίκλησις* of Sarapion.

Then follows an ἐπίκλησις:

And he began to say:

Come, gift of the Exalted: come, perfect mercy; come, holy Spirit; come, revealer of the mysteries of the chosen among the prophets; come, Proclaimer by His Apostles of the combats of our victorious Athlete; come, treasure of majesty; come, beloved of the mercy of the Most High; come, (thou) silent (one), revealer of the mysteries of the Exalted; come, utterer of hidden things and shewer of the works of Our God; come, giver of life in secret and manifold in Thy deeds; come, giver of joy and rest to all who cleave unto Thee; come, power of the Father, and wisdom of the Son, for Ye are one in all; come and communicate with us in this Eucharist which we celebrate, and in this offering which we offer, and in this commemoration which we make.

In these forms the blessing of the elements seems to be by the calling over them of the name of Our Lord, a parallel use to Baptism ἐπὶ τῷ ὀνόματι Ἰησοῦ Χριστοῦ.

The Invocation that follows is theologically confused, and it is not until the end that we get clear indications as to Whom it is addressed. The words at the end "come, power of the Father, and wisdom of the Son, for Ye are one in all" in conjunction with the words at the beginning "come, holy Spirit," make it clear that the Invocation is addressed to the Holy Trinity. Such an invocation addressed to the Trinity appears in the Liturgy of the Testamentum Domini, as we shall see later.

It is to be noticed also that the Invocation of the Holy Trinity is not that the Divine power may descend upon the elements but rather that it may be present in the communion of the faithful.

There remains one more form which seems to belong to this type of liturgy, and it is from the Acts of John. Although rather earlier than the Acts of Thomas, I give it last because it is not so clear an example of this type as the first at least of the forms from the Acts of Thomas.

Acts of John c. 109.

καὶ αἰτήσας ἄρτον εὐχαρίστησεν οὕτως·

τίνα αἶνον ἢ ποίαν προσφορὰν ἢ τίνα εὐχαριστίαν κλῶντες τὸν ἄρτον τοῦτον ἐπονομάσωμεν ἀλλ' ἢ σὲ μόνον Ἰησοῦ; δοξάζομέν σου τὸ λεχθὲν ὑπὸ τοῦ πατρὸς ὄνομα. δοξάζομέν σου τὸ λεχθὲν διὰ υἱοῦ ὄνομα. δοξάζομέν σου τὴν εἴσοδον τῆς θύρας. δοξάζομέν σου τὴν δειχθεῖσαν ἡμῖν διά σου ἀνάστασιν. δοξάζομέν σου τὴν ὁδόν. δοξάζομέν σου τὸν σπόρον, τὸν λόγον, τὴν χάριν, τὴν πίστιν, τὸ ἅλας, τὸν ἄλεκτον μαργαρίτην, τὴν θησαυρὸν, τὸ ἄροτρον, τὴν σαγήνην, τὸ μέγεθος, τὸ διάδημα, τὸν δι' ἡμᾶς λεχθέντα υἱὸν ἀνθρώπου, τὸν χαρισάμενον ἡμῖν τὴν ἀλήθειαν, τὴν ἀνάπαυσιν, τὴν γνῶσιν, τὴν δύναμιν, τὴν ἐντολὴν, τὴν παρρησίαν, τὴν ἐλπίδα, τὴν ἀγάπην, τὴν ἐλευθερίαν, τὴν εἰς σὲ καταφυγήν. σὺ γὰρ εἶ μόνος, κύριε, ἡ ῥίζα τῆς ἀθανασίας καὶ ἡ πηγὴ τῆς ἀφθαρσίας καὶ ἡ ἕδρα τῶν αἰώνων, λεχθεὶς ταῦτα πάντα δι' ἡμᾶς νῦν ὅπως καλοῦντές σε διὰ τούτων γνωρίζωμέν σου τὸ μέγεθος ἀθεώρητον ἡμῖν ἐπὶ τοῦ παρόντος ὑπάρχον, καθαροῖς δὲ θεωρητὸν μόνον ἐν τῷ μόνῳ σου ἀνθρώπῳ εἰκονιζόμενον.

Then follows the ἐπίκλησις on the Communion of the faithful:

καὶ κλάσας τὸν ἄρτον ἐπέδωκεν πᾶσιν ἡμῖν, ἑκάστῳ τῶν ἀδελφῶν ἐπευχόμενος ἄξιον ἔσεσθαι αὐτὸν τῆς τοῦ κυρίου χάριτος καὶ τῆς ἁγιωτάτης εὐχαριστίας.

Here is a form of blessing the elements. It begins by calling upon the name of Jesus and the last words ὅπως καλοῦντές σε διὰ τούτων γνωρίζωμέν σου τὸ μέγεθος ἀθεώρητον ἡμῖν ἐπὶ τοῦ πάροντος show that the elements were consecrated by the invocation of the name or names of the Father and of Our Lord upon them. The ἐπίκλησις which follows, and its purpose, is clearly marked. It is combined with the words of administration to each of the communicants.

The confusion of the Persons of the Father and the Son recalls the confusion of the Persons in Hermas. Probably one of the many epithets that follow denote the Holy Spirit and so we have a consecration by the Invocation of the name of the Father and of the Son and of the Holy Spirit.

In these texts there are also given forms of administration of the consecrated elements. In the Acts of John c. 110 as we have seen the *ἐπίκλησις* is united with the words of administration and said over each communicant. In the communicating of himself John says *κἀμοὶ μέρος ἔστω μεθ' ὑμῶν.*

The congregation is then dismissed immediately after communion with the words *εἰρήνη μεθ' ὑμῶν ἀγαπητοί.*

In the Acts of Thomas in A there are two distinct forms of administration.

And he made the sign of the Cross upon the bread and began to give (it) and he gave first to the woman, and said to her:

"Let it be unto thee for remission of transgressions and sins, and for everlasting resurrection."

And after her he gave to the persons who were baptized with her.

Then he gave to everyone and said to them:

"Let this Eucharist be unto you for life and rest, and not for judgement and vengeance."

And they said "Amen."

In extract B the administration words are almost identical with the second of the foregoing forms:

He...broke the Eucharist and gave unto all of them and said unto them:

"Let this Eucharist be unto you for grace and mercy and not for judgement and vengeance."

And they said "Amen."

In extract D.

And he brake the Eucharist and gave... and said:

"Let this Eucharist be to you for life and rest and joy and health and for the healing of your souls and of your bodies."

And they said, "Amen."

III. The use of the Lord's Prayer as a form of Consecration.

St Gregory the Great in his letter to John of Syracuse (ix. 12) states that it was the custom of the Apostles to consecrate by means of the Lord's Prayer simply. This seems to be the meaning of his words, which are not however very clear. He says:

> "orationem vero dominicam idcirco mox post precem dicimus quia mos apostolorum fuit ad ipsam solummodo orationem oblationis hostiam consecrarent. Et valde mihi inconveniens visum est ut precem quam scholasticus composuerat super oblationem diceremus et ipsam traditionem quam Redemptor noster composuit super eius corpus et sanguinem non diceremus. Sed et Dominica Oratio apud Graecos ab omni populo dicitur, apud nos vero a solo sacerdote. In quo ergo Graecorum consuetudines secuti sumus qui aut veteres nostras reparavimus aut novas et utiles constituimus, in quibus tamen alios non probamur imitari."

This letter was written at a time when St Gregory had given considerable offence to the Church in Rome by his alteration of certain parts of the Liturgy. This was the chief change, the saying of the Lord's Prayer, which immediately followed the Canon, by the people and no longer as hitherto by the celebrant alone.

It is noticeable that he is not able to say that he has simply reverted to the ancient use of the Roman Church. It is evident that he had devoted himself to some research in the hope of finding that he was simply going back to an older use. He can find no evidence of this, but apparently finds something somewhere which satisfies him as to the "mos apostolorum" in the consecration of the Eucharist.

As a matter of fact his statement is without the support of any other author, and there is hardly a shred of evidence to support it.

Some light is thrown on the position of the Lord's Prayer in the Roman Church before the days of St Gregory by the portions of the Canon preserved in Pseudo-Ambrose de Sacramentis, a work perhaps really to be attributed to St Ambrose. Here it is evident that the Lord's Prayer is used twice. Once by the celebrant at the end of the Canon and said by him alone.

ubi Christi verba deprompta fuerint iam non panis dicitur sed corpus appellatur. quare ergo in oratione dominica quae postea sequitur....

(V. iv. 24.) And that the priest says the Lord's Prayer here is equally evident from the writer's words (VI. v. 24):

sed libera nos a malo. quid sequitur? audi quid dicat sacerdos: per dominum nostrum Jesum Christum, in quo tibi est, cum quo tibi est honor, laus, gloria, magnificentia, potestas, cum Spiritu sancto, a saeculis et nunc et semper, et in omnia saecula saeculorum. Amen.

The liturgical doxology to the Lord's Prayer is of great interest and evidently very ancient.

The second place in which the Lord's Prayer occurs in the time of the author of the de Sacramentis is after Communion. It is here said apparently by the communicant alone as an act of thanksgiving.

"Ergo venisti ad altare, accepisti Corpus Christi" he says (v. iii. 12), and goes on (v. iv. 18) Nunc quid superest nisi oratio? et nolite putare mediocris esse virtutis scire quemadmodum oretis. Apostoli sancti dicebant ad Dominum Jesum: Domine, doce nos orare.... Tunc ait Dominus orationem "Pater Noster." And so he concludes (19) ergo attolle oculos ad Patrem... qui te per Filium redemit et dic "Pater Noster[1]."

[1] See an apparently similar use of the Lord's Prayer in the thanksgiving of the communicant after his communion in the Liturgy of the Testamentum Domini.

Here we find lingering on a sign of the older use in which after communion the people said the Lord's Prayer as an act or as part of an act of thanksgiving. In the process of development and in the gradual hedging of the mystery the Lord's Prayer became confined to the priestly act of consecration[1]. But already in the Canon of the de Sacramentis the Lord's Prayer has the same position in the Canon as in St Gregory's days. How far can we believe that St Gregory had any ground for his statement as to the use of the Apostles? St Basil expressly denies that there is any tradition.

The Lord's Prayer was regarded, at any rate in private devotion, as filling up any deficiency in private prayers and as giving them virtue as by a sort of consecration. This idea is expressed by Tertullian (de orat. 9) thus:

> ab ipso igitur ordinata religio orationis et de spiritu ipsius iam tunc cum ex ore divino ferretur, animata, suo privilegio ascendit in caelum, commendans Patri quae Filius docuit. quoniam tamen Dominus, prospector humanarum necessitatum, seorsum post traditam orandi disciplinam, petite inquit et accipietis, et sunt, quae petantur pro circumstantia cuiusque, praemissa legitima et ordinaria oratione quasi fundamento.

Doubtless it is with some such idea that the Lord's Prayer is to be found at all times in every office of the Church. But as being in itself a form of consecration in the Eucharist there is no sign in Tertullian, who would hardly have passed by such a fact without mention. Nor does Cyprian in his *de oratione dominica* make any reference to such a use.

There remains the expression used by Justin Martyr

[1] It is interesting to note that in spite of St Gregory's restoration the Lord's Prayer has again in the Latin rite been taken from the people except for the response "sed libera nos a malo."

in speaking of the form of consecration *τὴν δι' εὐχῆς λόγου τοῦ παρ' αὐτοῦ εὐχαριστηθεῖσαν τροφήν* (Apol. I. 66).

By these words St Justin may mean that the Eucharist was consecrated by a prayer to the Word. He may mean again that it was consecrated by a prayer which contained or had some reference to Our Lord's words at the institution. He may mean that the Eucharist was consecrated by a prayer in fulfilment of His command to "do this," and it is possible that the expression means the Lord's Prayer.

It may be so, but it is difficult to believe that Justin would have used such an obscure (in that case) expression to denote the Lord's Prayer. And the words which follow and describe what happened at the institution are much in favour of the second of the above interpretations.

And so as to St Gregory's statement:

In the first place it is not quite certain that his words mean that the Lord's Prayer was, according to the "mos apostolorum," the actual consecrating form. "Ad ipsam solummodo orationem" may mean that the Lord's Prayer was the culminating point of the consecration. Secondly, with our evidence, there is no ground for believing that the Lord's Prayer was ever in itself a consecration form. But of course St Gregory may have had evidence which we have not. In the variety of uses that obtained in the early days of the Church, such a use may well have obtained among the others.

But St Gregory seems to have put himself to considerable pains to try and find early evidence in support of his unpopular action, and it seems to me quite possible, even though it may seem presumptuous to lay such a charge against so able and learned a Saint, that in his historical investigations it is not unlikely that in some early document he may have confused the Prex Domini, or Oratio Domini, the general name for the Consecration Form, with the Oratio Dominica or Lord's Prayer.

IV. We come now to the chief liturgical use of early days which at the beginning of the third century has so far ousted all other uses as to be generally prevalent.

It may be possible to draw some distinction between this use and those which we have been considering. It seems very probable that the foregoing were Gentile uses which had their origin in the more distinctively Gentile Churches, while the use we are about to consider may be regarded as the distinctive use of the Jewish Churches. As we have suggested before, the final general acceptance of this use may be attributed to the fact that it is by far the most scriptural, and also at the same time from a practical point of view it would be much easier to lay down a general outline of this use and obtain adherence to it than would have been the case in the other and much more free uses.

Thus to the Gentile such uses as a grace adapted to the Eucharistic Feast, or a form closely akin to the divinely appointed Baptismal form, or perhaps the Lord's Prayer as a consecrating formula, would all seem suitable, while the Jew looking on Christianity as the fulfilment of the old Covenant and no new thing would be more likely to connect the memorial of salvation from the captivity of sin with the older memorial of salvation from the captivity of Egypt, more especially as the Eucharist was instituted either at the Paschal Supper itself, or at least as a new Paschal Commemoration.

And this last and perhaps distinctively Jewish use

seems to be based on the older ritual of the Paschal Supper.

The Passover ritual of Our Lord's time is probably represented by the directions in Pesachim. Here (Pes. x. 4) the ritual begins with the questions and answers of son and father as to why unleavened bread is used this night and bitter herbs etc.

And according to the capacity of his son shall the father teach him: first he shall begin with the disgrace and finish with praise, and shall expound "a Syrian ready to perish...' (Deut. xxvi. 5) till he have finished the whole section.

Pes. x. 5 is more explicit.

Rabbi Gamaliel said "whosoever does not mention these three things at passover time does not fulfil his duty," פסח מצה ומרור. פסח (Passover) because God passed over the houses of our fathers in Egypt; מצה (unleaven) because our fathers were redeemed from Egypt; מרור (bitter herbs) because of the bitter treatment of our fathers in Egypt. In every generation one is bound to show himself as if he were going forth from Egypt, as it is said (in Exod. xiii. 8).

Immediately there follows

לפיכך אנחנו חייבין להודות להלל לשבח לפאר לרומם להדר לברך לעלה ולקלס למי שעשה לאבותינו ולנו את כל הניסים האלו הוציאנו מעבדות לחרות מיגון לשמחה ומאבל ליום טוב ומאפילה לאור גדול ומשעבור לגאלה ונאמר לפניו הללויה :

Wherefore we are bound to confess, praise, glorify, honour, exalt, celebrate and bless, extol and magnify, Him who wrought for our fathers and for us all these wonders. He brought us forth from slavery to liberty, from sadness to joy, from grief to festival, from darkness into great light, from subjection to redemption, and we say before Him, "Alleluia."

This form of praise, so strikingly similar to the Eucharistic preface, taken word for word from Pesachim is in the Passover ritual to this day.

Thus in Our Lord's time the Passover liturgy begins with ritual question and answer, and then the celebrant begins the "Haggadah" or recital of God's mercies to Israel, speaking of the bitter treatment of the fathers in Egypt, of the first passover in Egypt, and of their redemption from Egypt by the power of God, and closing with the burst of worship and praise given above.

The celebrant was left to choose his own words, only he was tied to the subjects of his recital, and perhaps the final form of worship and praise was already fixed in our Lord's time.

It is still a vexed question whether the Institution took place at a Passover supper or not. The chronology of the synoptists and of St John is irreconcilable. But the matter is not of much importance. It is clear that either this meal was the Passover meal, or if not the authorized meal it was a new Passover meal instituted by Our Lord. Such expressions as "the New Testament in my blood," "do this in remembrance of me" place it beyond doubt that the Passover ritual was in Our Lord's mind. We may be sure then that, whether this was the Passover meal proper or a new Christian Passover, Our Lord followed the passover ritual at the meal.

If so the order at the Institution of the blessed sacrament would probably be

1. The Haggadah.
2. The blessing of the bread and the cup and the giving them to the disciples.
3. The command "Do this in remembrance of me."

In the account of the Institution there is no reference to the reciting of an Haggadah by Our Lord. The words *εὐχαριστήσας* and *εὐλογήσας* seem to be synonymous. Both St Matthew and St Mark use *εὐλογήσας* of the bread and *εὐχαριστήσας* of the cup. St Luke followed by St Paul uses *εὐχαριστήσας* of the bread and the cup.

In St Matthew and St Mark the words must signify something of the nature of a grace. In St Luke and St Paul possibly the word is used more generally as of an *εὐχαριστία*, a consecrating thanksgiving, and if so may cover the Haggadah.

But the most probable explanation is that the *εὐχαριστία* of the Liturgy, containing as it does the Christian Haggadah, has derived its name from the word *εὐχαριστήσας* of the Institution as a general name without any special technical meaning. By the time of Justin the whole consecrating form was already known as the *εὐχαριστία*, so that the Consecrated Bread could be spoken of as *ἄρτος εὐχαριστηθείς*.

When we pass on to St Paul we find the first signs of the beginnings of an official liturgy, and at the same time we begin to find such ceremonial uses as the Kiss of Peace coming or already come into use. In the liturgical forms used by St Paul we probably find the origin of that type of liturgy which finally prevailed by the beginning of the third century. If this is so we find some explanation for the much greater prevalence of this liturgical use than of other uses when we remember how great a proportion of the primitive church owed its origin to the great Apostle of the Gentiles.

The Eucharist seems to have begun from earliest times with the "Kiss of Peace." This was an introduction into worship of what had hitherto been only a social custom. Although St Justin first mentions the Kiss as occurring at the beginning of the Eucharist there can be little doubt from the reference to this observance in the books of the New Testament[1] that it was customary for the believers when they assembled together so to greet one another. It is the Jewish greeting שָׁלוֹם; the Syriac translation of ἀσπάσασθε is ܫܐܠܘ ܒܫܠܡܐ; it is the unchanging salaam of the East. There is no sign of it in Jewish worship, and though it occurs in the Samaritan rites there can be little doubt that there it has been borrowed from Christian ritual.

Other contemporary evidence as to the use of the Apostolic Church we have only in St Paul's stern rebuke of the abuses connected with the celebration of the Eucharist at Corinth. Perhaps it was not only with the unseemly and uncharitable results of the close connection of Eucharist with agape that St Paul was dealing, but with the method of celebrating or consecrating the Eucharist. He is insistent on the example or form which he committed to them (ὃ παρέδωκα ὑμῖν) and which he states he received (παρέλαβον) from the Lord[2]. This the Corinthians seem not to have kept to. St Paul therefore reminds them of what he had received, of what he had handed to them, a recital of the circumstances of the Institution and of Our Lord's words.

1 ἀσπάσασθε ἀλλήλους ἐν φιλήματι ἁγίῳ. Ro. xvi. 16, 1 Cor. xvi. 20, 2 Cor. xiii. 2.

ἀσπάσασθε τοὺς ἀδελφοὺς πάντας ἐν φιλήματι ἁγίῳ. 1 Thes. v. 26.

ἀσπάσασθε ἀλλήλους ἐν φιλήματι ἀγάπης. 1 Pet. v. 14.

2 Both these words παραλαμβάνω and παραδίδωμι are used elsewhere of the receiving and tradition of a σύμβολον. 1 Cor. xv. 3, cf. 1 Cor. xi. 2.

ἐγὼ γὰρ παρέλαβον ἀπὸ τοῦ Κυρίου ὃ καὶ παρέδωκα ὑμῖν ὅτι ὁ Κύριος Ἰησοῦς ἐν τῇ νυκτὶ ᾗ παρεδίδετο ἔλαβεν ἄρτον καὶ εὐχαριστήσας ἔκλασεν καὶ εἶπεν· Τοῦτό μου ἐστὶν τὸ σῶμα τὸ ὑπὲρ ὑμῶν. τοῦτο ποιεῖτε εἰς τὴν ἐμὴν ἀνάμνησιν. ὡσαύτως καὶ τὸ ποτήριον μετὰ τὸ δειπνῆσαι, λέγων· Τοῦτο τὸ ποτήριον ἡ καινὴ διαθήκη ἐστὶν ἐν τῷ ἐμῷ αἵματι· τοῦτο ποιεῖτε, ὁσάκις ἐὰν πίνητε εἰς τὴν ἐμὴν ἀνάμνησιν. 1 Cor. xi. 23—25.

The words with which St Paul introduces this account of the institution, the connexion in which he repeats them, and their closeness to the account of the Institution as recorded in St Luke's Gospel[1], all make it most probable that he is reciting words which he himself used in the celebration of the Eucharist. Also, as we shall see later, his language following this passage seems reminiscent of an ἐπίκλησις[2]. If this is so it is all the more probable that the words of Institution were used, or at least some reference to the Institution was made, by St Paul when he celebrated the Holy Sacrament.

From St Paul[3] we must go on past the Didache, which seems to know another liturgical use, as we have seen, to the information which St Justin Martyr gives us of what would seem to be the only liturgical use known to him.

St Justin Martyr.

Justin gives us in his first Apology an account of the

[1] Unless indeed we hold the "Western" to represent the original text.

[2] It is of course a great anachronism to use the word ἐπίκλησις (which we first find mentioned technically by St Basil) of the liturgy in these times. But in dealing with the historical development of the liturgy it is impossible not to use the later technical terms which distinguish the different component parts of the whole service.

[3] Perhaps such words as ἄρτον τοῦ θεοῦ θέλω ὅ ἐστι σὰρξ Ἰησοῦ Χριστοῦ... καὶ πόμα θέλω τὸ αἷμα αὐτοῦ, Ign. Rom. 7, are reminiscent of the occurrence of the words of Institution in Ignatius' liturgy; cf. ad Smyrn. 7.

Liturgy of his day. He then goes on to explain what Christians believed of the Eucharist.

Apol. I. 65.

ἀλλήλους φιλήματι ἀσπαζόμεθα παυσάμενοι τῶν εὐχῶν. εἶτα προσφέρεται τῷ προεστῶτι τῶν ἀδελφῶν ἄρτος καὶ ποτήριον ὕδατος καὶ κράματος, καὶ οὗτος λαβὼν αἶνον καὶ δόξαν τῷ πατρὶ τῶν ὅλων διὰ τοῦ ὀνόματος τοῦ υἱοῦ καὶ τοῦ πνεύματος τοῦ ἁγίου ἀναπέμπει καὶ εὐχαριστίαν ὑπὲρ τοῦ κατηξιῶσθαι τούτων παρ' αὐτοῦ ἐπὶ πολὺ ποιεῖται. οὗ συντελέσαντος τὰς εὐχὰς καὶ τὴν εὐχαριστίαν, πᾶς ὁ παρὼν λαὸς ἐπευφημεῖ λέγων, Ἀμήν... εὐχαριστήσαντος δὲ τοῦ προεστῶτος καὶ ἐπευφημήσαντος παντὸς τοῦ λαοῦ, οἱ καλούμενοι παρ' ἡμῖν διάκονοι διδόασιν ἑκάστῳ τῶν παρόντων μεταλαβεῖν ἀπὸ τοῦ εὐχαριστηθέντος ἄρτου καὶ οἴνου καὶ ὕδατος, καὶ τοῖς οὐ παροῦσιν ἀποφέρουσιν.

After "Prayers," *αἱ εὐχαί*, *i.e.* the morning service, the Eucharist begins.

Here is the description of the Liturgy of Justin's time.

1. The Kiss of Peace.
2. The offertory.
3. The *εὐχαριστία*

containing (*a*) *αἶνος καὶ δόξα*,

(*b*) prayer *ὑπὲρ τοῦ κατηξιῶσθαι τούτων*.

The *εὐχαριστία* was the form, or contained the form, which was regarded as effecting the Sacrament—and therefore it is used as more or less equivalent to "consecration" (*τοῦ εὐχαριστηθέντος ἄρτου*).

The expression *τὰς εὐχὰς καὶ τὴν εὐχαριστίαν* would appear to denote the nature of the *εὐχαριστία* as a whole, which contained not only thanksgiving and praise, *εὐχαριστία* in the narrower sense, but, in addition, prayer over the elements for their consecration (see next extract) and also for a worthy participation by the communicants.

St Justin goes on to explain further in c. 66.

οὐ γὰρ ὡς κοινὸν ἄρτον οὐδὲ κοινὸν πόμα ταῦτα λαμβάνομεν· ἀλλ' ὃν τρόπον διὰ λόγου Θεοῦ σαρκοποιηθεὶς Ἰησοῦς Χριστὸς ὁ σωτὴρ ἡμῶν καὶ σάρκα καὶ αἷμα ὑπὲρ σωτηρίας ἡμῶν ἔσχεν, οὕτως καὶ τὴν δι' εὐχῆς λόγου τοῦ παρ' αὐτοῦ εὐχαριστηθεῖσαν τροφὴν, ἐξ ἧς αἷμα καὶ σάρκες κατὰ μεταβολὴν τρέφονται ἡμῶν, ἐκείνου τοῦ σαρκοποιηθέντος Ἰησοῦ καὶ σάρκα καὶ αἷμα ἐδιδάχθημεν εἶναι.

οἱ γὰρ ἀπόστολοι ἐν τοῖς γενομένοις ὑπ' αὐτῶν ἀπομνημονεύμασιν, ἃ καλεῖται εὐαγγέλια, οὕτως παρέδωκαν ἐντέταλθαι αὐτοῖς. τὸν Ἰησοῦν λαβόντα ἄρτον εὐχαριστήσαντα εἰπεῖν· Τοῦτο ποιεῖτε εἰς τὴν ἀνάμνησίν μου· τοῦτό ἐστι τὸ σῶμά μου· καὶ τὸ ποτήριον ὁμοίως λαβόντα καὶ εὐχαριστήσαντα εἰπεῖν, Τοῦτό ἐστι τὸ αἷμά μου· καὶ μόνοις αὐτοῖς μεταδοῦναι.

The actual formula of consecration is here further indicated. It was δι' εὐχῆς λόγου τοῦ παρ' αὐτοῦ, whatever that may mean[1].

Further, Justin seemed to know no other source of information as to the way in which the Eucharist should be celebrated, than the accounts of the Institution in the Gospels. It is possible that he means also that the use of the words of Institution is enjoined upon the Church in the *εὐχαριστία*.

Dial. cum Tryph., c. 41.

καὶ ἡ τῆς σεμιδάλεως δὲ προσφορὰ, ὦ ἄνδρες, ἔλεγον, ἡ ὑπὲρ τῶν καθαριζομένων ἀπὸ τῆς λέπρας προσφέρεσθαι παραδοθεῖσα, τύπος ἦν τοῦ ἄρτου τῆς εὐχαριστίας ὃν εἰς ἀνάμνησιν τοῦ πάθους οὗ ἔπαθεν ὑπὲρ τῶν καθαιρομένων τὰς ψυχὰς ἀπὸ πάσης πονηρίας ἀνθρώπων, Ἰησοῦς Χριστὸς ὁ Κύριος ἡμῶν παρέδωκε ποιεῖν, ἵνα ἅμα τε εὐχαριστῶμεν τῷ Θεῷ ὑπέρ τε τοῦ τὸν κόσμον ἐκτικέναι σὺν πᾶσι τοῖς ἐν αὐτῷ διὰ τὸν ἄνθρωπον, καὶ ὑπὲρ τοῦ ἀπὸ τῆς κακίας ἐν ᾗ γεγόναμεν ἠλευθερωκέναι ἡμᾶς, καὶ τὰς ἀρχὰς καὶ ἐξουσίας καταλελυκέναι τελείαν κατάλυσιν διὰ τοῦ παθητοῦ γενομένου κατὰ τὴν βουλὴν αὐτοῦ.

St Justin in this passage, besides referring again to the making of an *ἀνάμνησις* in the liturgy, tells us some of the subject-matter of the *εὐχαριστία*. Thanks and praise were offered in it,

[1] See above, p. 62.

(*a*) for the creation of the world for man's sake;

(*b*) for our redemption from sin;

(*c*) for the trampling on the powers of evil through the Passion of Christ.

He further alludes to the *ἀνάμνησις*:

Dial. c. 70. ὅτι μὲν οὖν καὶ ἐν ταύτῃ τῇ προφητείᾳ περὶ τοῦ ἄρτου ὃν παρέδωκεν ἡμῖν ὁ ἡμέτερος Χριστὸς ποιεῖν εἰς ἀνάμνησιν τοῦ τε σωματοποιήσασθαι αὐτὸν διὰ τοὺς πιστεύοντας εἰς αὐτόν, δι' οὓς καὶ παθητὸς γέγονε, καὶ περὶ τοῦ ποτηρίου, ὃ εἰς ἀνάμνησιν τοῦ αἵματος αὐτοῦ παρέδωκεν εὐχαριστοῦντας ποιεῖν, φαίνεται.

c. 117. ὅτι μὲν οὖν καὶ εὐχαὶ καὶ εὐχαριστίαι ὑπὸ τῶν ἀξίων γενόμεναι τέλειαι μόναι καὶ εὐάρεστοί εἰσι τῷ θεῷ θυσίαι καὶ αὐτὸς φημί. ταῦτα γὰρ μόνα καὶ Χριστιανοὶ παρέλαβον ποιεῖν καὶ ἐπ' ἀναμνήσει τῆς τροφῆς αὐτῶν ξηρᾶς τε καὶ ὑγρᾶς ἐν ᾗ καὶ τοῦ πάθους ὃ πέπονθε δι' αὐτοὺς ὁ υἱὸς τοῦ θεοῦ μέμνηται.

The liturgy of Justin then would appear to be as follows:

1. The Kiss.
2. The offertory.
3. The *εὐχαριστία* consisting of

(*a*) *αἶνος καὶ δόξα* for the creation of the world; for our redemption from sin; for the loosing of the powers of evil.

(*b*) the *ἀνάμνησις*. The expression of obedience to Our Lord's command "Do this in remembrance of me." Very probably the words of Institution, or some reference to the Institution preceded this *ἀνάμνησις* or was part of it.

(*c*) The *ἐπίκλησις* in its early and undeveloped form, a prayer *ὑπὲρ τοῦ κατηξιῶσθαι αὐτούς*.

The order of these three component parts is not clearly indicated in Justin, but as they correspond to the actual matter of the Canon when it emerges into view, it is probable that the order was the same in Justin's time.

The whole Canon, 3 *a*, *b*, and *c*, was probably regarded as the consecrating form, not one part of it alone. The whole is the *εὐχαριστία*, and the bread when consecrated is called *ἄρτος εὐχαριστηθείς*. Another name for this whole *εὐχαριστία* would seem to be *αἱ εὐχαί*[1], which would correspond to Tertullian's "orationes (sacrificiorum)" Justin's description of the Eucharistic service is remarkably full, occurring as it does in a work intended for non-Christian readers. Technical names for the component parts of the liturgy had doubtless not come into existence, at any rate in any narrow or exact senses. So it is not safe to read the meanings of a later day into the names which he applies to his general description of the liturgy.

St Irenaeus.

Irenaeus gives us no express information as to the actual forms of the liturgy of his day. He uses certain expressions to denote the actual consecration form, but what that form was he does not say. The names by which he refers to the consecration form are:

1. *ὁ λόγος τῆς ἐπικλήσεως*[2], and goes on to show what he means by *ἐπίκλησις* by referring again to it in the words *ἡ ἐπίκλησις αὐτοῦ* *i.e.* the celebrant's, thus showing that he is using *ἐπίκλησις* as more or less equivalent to *εὐχή*.

2. *ἡ ἐπίκλησις τοῦ θεοῦ*[3]. The bread after this is no longer *κοινὸς ἄρτος* but *εὐχαριστία.*

3. *ὁ λόγος τοῦ θεοῦ*[4]. *ὁ γεγονὼς ἄρτος ἐπιδέχεται τὸν λόγον τοῦ θεοῦ καὶ γίνεται ἡ εὐχαριστία.* This expression at once recalls Justin's name for the consecration

[1] This would only be a general term when speaking of the Eucharist itself. As we have seen the term is also used of the "Morning service."

[2] I. vii. 2. [3] IV. xxxi. 4. [4] V. ii. 2.

form εὐχὴ λόγου τοῦ παρ' αὐτοῦ and is a description as well as a name, though unfortunately it is not clear what it means.

There is only one passage in which Irenaeus perhaps gives us a hint of the composition of the εὐχαριστία, and this suggests that the words of Institution had a place in it.

sed et suis discipulis dans consilium primitias Deo offerre ex suis creaturis, non quasi indigenti, sed ut ipsi nec infructuosi nec ingrati sunt, eum qui ex creatura est panis accepit et gratias egit, dicens; "Hoc est corpus meum"; et calicem similiter qui est ex ea creatura quae est secundum nos, suum sanguinem confessus est, et novi testamenti novam docuit oblationem, quam ecclesia ab Apostolis accipiens in universo mundo offert Deo...[1]

Here referring to the Eucharistic sacrifice he seems to turn naturally to the account of the Institution in the Gospels which contains the command to the Church for its perpetual offering. He would seem to know of no other authority to the Church in this matter than the gospel account[2], and he seems to mean this when he speaks of the Church receiving the "novi testamenti novam oblationem" ab apostolis.

We may then have here a hint that the words of Institution, or some reference to the Institution, had a place in the εὐχαριστία of Irenaeus' liturgy.

Tertullian.

There is not very much in Tertullian's writings that bears on the question of the liturgy. He tells us that in the service with the Canon omitted which took the place of the Eucharist on the Saturday before Easter and on Station days, the kiss was omitted[3]. Also that the Sanctus was used[4]. He called the Canon proper "orationes

[1] IV. xxix. 5. [2] Cf. St Justin Martyr. [3] de orat. 14.
[4] de spectac. c. 25. The first occurrence of the name.

sacrificiorum[1]." It is only incidentally that we can draw deductions. It would seem that the words of Institution had a place in his Canon and were used moreover in the consecration even if not as a consecration form.

He evidently regards Our Lord's words as being the actual consecration form at the Last Supper.

Tum quod et corpus eius in pane censetur: "Hoc est corpus meum[2]."

Still more clearly he says:

acceptum panem et distributum discipulis corpus suum illum fecit "Hoc est corpus meum" dicendo, id est figura corporis mei[3].

Thus at the Last Supper Our Lord's words "This is my Body," "This is my Blood," were regarded by Tertullian as consecrating the bread and cup. If this is so, it is not improbable that these words have at least a place in the Canon of Tertullian's liturgy even if they were not the consecrating form itself.

But that is not all. "'Hoc est corpus meum': id est figura corporis mei" recall at once the liturgical forms of Sarapion *προσηνέγκαμεν τὸν ἄρτον τοῦτον τὸ ὁμοίωμα τοῦ σώματος τοῦ μονογενοῦς*. Also the Canon preserved in Ps.-Ambrose de Sacramentis. In this latter work, which Mgr. Duchesne dates at c. 400[4], we find in the Canon itself this expression of Tertullian;

Fac nobis, inquit (sacerdos), hanc oblationem adscriptam, ratam, rationabilem, acceptabilem; quod figura est corporis et sanguinis Domini nostri Jesu Christi[5].

The author goes on expressly to state that the words

[1] de orat. 14.
[2] de orat. 6.
[3] adv. Marc. IV. 40.
[4] Christian worship (E. T. ed. 1904) p. 177.
[5] de Sacramentis IV. v. 21.

of Institution not only at the Last Supper, but in the liturgy are the actual consecrating form.

Antequam consecretur panis est: ubi autem verba Christi accesserint, corpus est Christi. Denique audi dicentem "Accipite et edite ex eo omnes; hoc est corpus meum." Et ante verba Christi, calix est vini et aquae plenus: ubi verba Christi operata fuerint, ibi sanguis efficitur qui plebem redemit[1].

The similarity is striking. We may perhaps say that it is probable that the words of Institution occurred in Tertullian's liturgy.

Acts of Thomas.

We have seen that there are in the liturgical matter in this work an example of a form of consecrating the Eucharist by means of a formula based on the Baptismal Form. There seem to be some grounds for thinking that the author was also familiar with the use which we are now considering.

... he brought bread and the mingled cup, and spake a blessing over it and said:

Thy holy Body, which was crucified for our sake, we eat, and Thy life-giving Blood, which was shed for our sake, we drink. Let Thy Body be to us for life, and Thy Blood for the remission of sins. For the gall which Thou drankest for us, let the bitterness of our enemy be taken away from us. And for Thy drinking vinegar for our sake, let our weakness be strengthened. And for the spit which Thou didst receive for us, let us receive Thy perfect life. And because Thou didst receive the crown of thorns for us, let us receive from Thee the crown that withereth not. And because Thou wast wrapped in a linen cloth for us, let us be girt with Thy mighty strength which cannot be overcome. And because Thou wast buried in a new sepulchre for our mortality, let us too receive intercourse with Thee in heaven. And as Thou didst arise, let us be raised, and let us stand before Thee at the judgment of truth.

And he brake the Eucharist and gave...[2].

[1] IV. v. 23.

[2] Wright II. p. 290. The combination of the reference to the Passion

Here there is distinct reference to the Passion of Our Lord. This form is a strange combination of the ἐπίκλησις with the "mentio passionis eius." Still it would seem to be an example of the liturgy which we are now considering, of which the Passion of Our Lord is the central point.

We may quote two passages from Origen which have a bearing on the liturgy.

(*a*) *contra Cels.* viii. 53.

ἡμεῖς δὲ τῷ τοῦ παντὸς δημιουργῷ εὐχαριστοῦντες καὶ τοὺς μετ' εὐχαριστίας καὶ εὐχῆς ἐπὶ τοῖς δοθεῖσι προσαγομένους ἄρτους ἐσθίομεν, σῶμα γενόμενον διὰ τῆς εὐχῆς, ἅγιόν τι καὶ ἁγίαζον τοὺς μετὰ ὑγιοῦς προθέσεως αὐτῷ χρωμένους.

(*b*) *in Matt.* xi. 14.

τὸ ἁγιαζόμενον βρῶμα διὰ λόγου θεοῦ καὶ ἐντεύξεως (1 Tim. iv. 5)[1] κατ' αὐτὸ μὲν τὸ ὑλικὸν εἰς τὴν κοιλίαν χωρεῖ καὶ εἰς ἀφεδρῶνα ἐκβάλλεται. κατὰ δὲ ἐπιγενομένην αὐτὸ εὐχὴν, κατὰ τὴν ἀναλογίαν τῆς πίστεως ὠφέλιμον γίνεται καὶ τῆς τοῦ νοῦ αἴτιον διαβλέψεως ὁρῶντος ἐπὶ τὸ ὠφελοῦν, καὶ οὐχ ἡ ὕλη τοῦ ἄρτου ἀλλ' ὁ ἐπ' αὐτῷ εἰρημένος λόγος ὁ ὠφελῶν τὸν μὴ ἀναξίως τοῦ Κυρίου ἐσθίοντα αὐτόν.

From these two extracts (the latter of which is shown by its concluding words to refer to the Eucharist) we can gather two and perhaps three features of Origen's liturgy:

1. A thanksgiving (εὐχαριστία) to the Father.

2. The Consecration of the elements. This is called the εὐχή[1], and its matter is referred to in the expression ὁ ἐπ' αὐτῷ εἰρημένος λόγος (cf. St Justin and St Irenaeus).

3. We may perhaps conclude from the words ἁγίαζον τοὺς μετὰ ὑγιοῦς προθέσεως αὐτῷ χρωμένους, a prayer for worthy communion.

with the ἐπίκλησις is very curious and practically inverts the usual order of the two.

[1] Thus even in Origen the consecration of the Eucharist is as it were the grace which hallows the Eucharistic meal.

St Cyprian and St Firmilian.

We must pass on from Origen to St Cyprian and St Firmilian. In Cyprian we find definite references and technical names to parts at least of the liturgy.

"Sursum Corda," Preface, and Prayer (of Consecration) all appear by name.

de Orat. Dom. c. xxxi.

Ideo et sacerdos ante orationem praefatione praemissa parat fratrum mentes dicendo "Sursum Corda," ut dum respondet plebs "Habemus ad Dominum," admoneatur nihil aliud se quam Dominum debere cogitare.

This short extract is full of information. The Sursum Corda is already a fixed introduction to the liturgy[1]. It is followed (unless here the Sursum Corda is the praefatio) by the "praefatio" which we may identify with the εὐχαριστία of St Justin and Origen and that part of the liturgy to which Tertullian refers when he speaks of the Sanctus.

Then follows "Oratio," the Prayer, that is the prayer of consecration whatever it may have been.

He gives us in Ep. lxiii. a good deal of information incidentally.

§ 14. Nam si Jesus Christus Dominus et Deus noster Ipse est summus sacerdos Dei Patris, et sacrificium Patris se ipsum primus

[1] The "Sursum Corda" is referred to by another writer, Commodian, perhaps contemporary with St Cyprian. But his date is probably the fifth century.

Sacerdos Domini cum "Sursum corda" praecepit
In prece fienda ut fiant silentia vestra
Limpide respondis, nec temperas quae promittas.
Instruct. II. xxxvi.

The reference to the "Sursum Corda" is the first that we have of this introduction to the liturgy.

obtulit, et hoc fieri in sui commemorationem praecepit: utique ille sacerdos vice Christi vere fungitur qui id quod Christus fecit imitatur, et sacrificium verum et plenum tunc offert in ecclesia Deo Patri, si sic incipiat offerre secundum quod ipsum Christum videat obtulisse.

The officiating priest then is in the place of Christ. "Id quod Christus fecit imitatur" means more than the assertion of the oneness of the offering and sacrifice but implies it would seem the copying of Our Lord's actions and words at the time of the Institution so far as they are known.

§ 17. Et quia passionis eius mentionem in sacrificiis omnibus facimus—Passio est enim Domini sacrificium quod offerimus—Nihil aliud quam quod ille fecit facere debemus. Scriptura enim dicit (1 Cor. xi. 26) "quotiescunque enim ederitis panem istum et calicem istum biberitis, mortem Domini annuntiabitis quoadusque veniat." quotiescunque ergo calicem in commemorationem Domini et passionis eius offerimus, id quod constat Dominum fecisse faciamus.

Here we are told that in the Cyprianic liturgy there was a mention of the Passion of the Lord. The concluding words "quotiescunque ergo calicem in commemorationem Domini et passionis eius offerimus" seem to imply an ἀνάμνησις.

It is the "traditio Domini" which is in all cases to be followed. He quotes the account of the Institution several times in this Epistle, evidently as being the source from which we derive our knowledge of "quod fecit Dominus," in §10 quoting St Paul's account as a confirmatory "traditio" of the Apostle (ab apostolo eius hoc idem confirmatur et traditur). His words "nisi eadem quae Dominus fecit nos quoque faciamus," and others similar, would equally well apply to Our Lord's actions and what He spoke, as well as to the use of wine in the chalice.

In Ep. LXV. he apparently mentions the consecration form by its name.

LXV. § 2. quomodo putat manum suam transferri posse ad Dei sacrificium et precem Domini quae captiva fuerit sacrilegio et crimini?

§ 4. quando nec oblatio sanctificari illic possit, ubi Spiritus sanctus non sit, nec cuiquam Dominus per eius orationes et preces prosit qui Dominum ipse violavit.

In these two passages we probably get the name of the Consecration form "Prex Domini" or "preces." The expression "manum suam transferri" seems to be a reminiscence of manual acts. It is interesting to compare with the second passage the words of the *ἀνάμνησις* of the First Church Order "gratias tibi agentes quia nos dignos habuisti adstare coram te et tibi ministrare[1]."

So then in Cyprian we find the following component parts of the liturgy of his day.

1. Sursum Corda.
2. Praefatio.
3. "Prex Domini" or "Oratio" or "Preces" containing a mention of the Passion (and probably the words and actions of the institution) and the *ἀνάμνησις*.

The Forms of the Church Orders, and others

We now come to the definite liturgical forms. The earliest of these are those of the First Church Order. The variations in the forms which are given in the different versions of the First Order are due to the fact, it would seem, that the different versions also represent different recensions of this document and yet without being very distant from each other in date.

[1] Didasc. Apost. et fragmenta Veron. Ed. Hauler, p. 107.

The Second Church Order, which apparently had much less vogue than the first and had authority only in Egypt (and in its latest form in the Apostolic Constitutions in parts of Syria), is of little value to us, because in those parts of it which deal with the liturgy it has suffered many late alterations to bring it into line with later views and usages.

But as we have seen the First Order seems to have been known nearly all over the world, and if it was not generally accepted as an authoritative body of Canons yet its very general acceptance is a proof and a witness that the form of liturgy there given was the type of liturgy generally accepted and in general use throughout the Church.

Yet the liturgical forms given in the First Order are a model liturgy or an example only. No celebrant is to be bound to use it word for word. We have seen how in the Didache those celebrants who are endowed with gifts of ready speech are to be allowed full liberty to exercise those gifts in the celebration of the Eucharist[1].

In the same way St Justin tells us that full liberty was given to the celebrant in his day to use what gifts he had (*ὅση δύναμις αὐτῷ*) in his actual wording of the liturgy.

So too in the First Order this same liberty is definitely recognised and permitted to the celebrant:

It is not altogether necessary for him to recite the same words which we said before, as if learning to say them by heart in his thanksgiving to God; but according to the ability of each one he is

[1] This is probably the meaning of "the prophet" in this connection. There is no reason why prophecy should be taken as a "charismatic order" rather than a spiritual gift. St Barnabas was endowed with this gift and was a prophet (Acts xiii. 1) as well as an apostle (Acts xiv. 14). So was St Paul. The "order" of prophets in the N. T. seem to have

to pray. If indeed he is able to pray sufficiently well with a grand prayer, then it is good: but if also he should pray and recite a prayer in due measure, no one may forbid him, only let him pray being sound in orthodoxy[1].

This liberty as to actual phraseology used seems to have been permitted up to the end of the fourth century[2].

In addition to the forms of the Church Orders there are also the liturgical prayers of Sarapion Bishop of Thmuis, the contemporary of St Athanasius. The very name "The prayer of Sarapion" given to these forms proves how unfixed in wording the liturgy was about the year 350, though we find the general outline of this liturgy well marked and defined in structure.

Lastly there is the description of the liturgy which is contained in the Catecheseis of St Cyril of Jerusalem. Unfortunately the forms are not given, but the description of the different parts of the Canon is so full that we can gather from it a very fair idea as to what the liturgy of the Church of Jerusalem was like in his day.

For convenience sake it is proposed to consider the Canon in two divisions, although any such dividing up of the Canon is foreign to the time with which we are dealing.

The constituent parts of the Canon from the later point of view are as under.

been a class of men endowed with unusual gifts of speech in teaching and preaching and were accordingly of much value to the early Church.

[1] First Ch. Order Sahid. version, § 34.

[2] Canon 26 of the Council of Hippo (393) forbids any "oratio" to be addressed to the Son, but all to the Father. No one is to use his own prayers except after consultation with instructed brethren. Probably this canon is dealing with liturgical practice. Anyhow it would cover the liturgy.

The Canon or εὐχαριστία consists of

1. A great thanksgiving for God's mercies toward mankind, leading up to the "mentio passionis" and an account of the Institution of the Blessed Sacrament.

2. The Anamnesis or expression that the Church is therefore carrying out the Divine command "Do this in remembrance of Me"; followed by a prayer (the later ἐπίκλησις, but as yet undeveloped) that the Holy Spirit may be present at the offering, in order that the communicant may receive in the Sacrament the virtue of the Sacrament; concluding with the "Intercession" or prayers for all estates in the Church.

3. The Communion and Dismissal.

(1) and (2) are really a whole, indivisible. Both together form the εὐχαριστία, the consecrating formula. In later days when doctrine had become more fixed, the Eucharistic liturgy was naturally subjected to theological inquiry and was divided up into different portions, each of which acquired a technical name. Even then it was not till long after that such inquiry went so far as to determine what was the actual moment of consecration[1].

But in considering the early liturgy it is necessary for convenience to treat it in parts, and it is sometimes necessary to give to each part that name by which it was afterwards known. It is difficult to know how best to divide the early liturgy for this purpose, but it is perhaps most convenient to divide it into two parts. I propose

[1] The first occurrence, so far as I am aware, of any such idea as the "moment of consecration" occurs in the "Homilies of Narsai" († 502). Mr Edmund Bishop in his appendix to Dom Conolly's edition of this work says (p. 128) that the common people who filled the Syrian churches at the end of the fifth century were already in actual possession of "that certitude as to the 'moment of consecration' which was only to be acquired by the common Christian people in the west in the twelfth century or at the earliest in the eleventh."

therefore to consider separately, first (1) and then (2) and then (3).

(1) *The Thanksgiving*

The Church Orders.

The two descriptions in the First Church Order.

(*a*) In connexion with the consecration of a Bishop. The text is from the Coptic (Coptic § 31, Horner transl. Stat. of the Apostles p. 307, Canons of Hipp. c. iii., Ethiopic § 22, Horner's transl. p. 139. Latin version, Hauler p. 106).

Let everyone give peace to him (*i.e.* the newly ordained Bishop) with his mouth, saluting him.

Let the deacons then offer to him the Oblation. And having put his hand on the oblation with the presbyters, let him say in giving thanks:

The Lord with you all.

And all the people say:

With thy spirit.

And he says:

Lift up your hearts.

And the people say:

We have them with the Lord.

And he says again:

Let us give thanks to the Lord.

And all the people say:

Meet and right.

And let him pray also thus, and say the things which come after these according to the custom of the holy Oblation.

The variations in C.H., the Latin and the Ethiopic are slight and unimportant.

(*b*) Second description, in connexion with the administration of Baptism. From the Coptic text (Copt. § 46, Horner's transl. p. 319, Ethiop. § 35, Horner pp. 155, 156. C.H. c. xix., Latin version, Hauler p. 112).

Let the deacons bring the Oblation to the Bishop and he shall give thanks over bread because that (it is) the form of the Flesh of the Christ; and a cup of wine because it is the Blood of the Christ which will be shed (Latin "effusum est") for all who believe him; and milk and honey mingled, in fulfilment of the promises of the fathers, because he said: I will give to you a land flowing with milk and honey.

This is the Flesh of the Christ, which he gave to us to nourish us with it like children, namely we who believe him; It will cause the bitterness of the heart to be dissolved by the sweetness of the word. All these things shall the bishop recount to him who shall be baptized. And when the bishop therefore has now broken the bread let him give a piece to each one of them saying:

This is the bread of heaven, the Body of the Christ Jesus.

Let him who receives answer "Hamen."

Further, if there is no [more] priest, let the deacons take hold of the cup and stand in right order and give to them the Blood of the Christ Jesus our Lord: and he who has the milk and honey.

Let him who gives the cup say:

This is the Blood of Jesus the Christ, our Lord.

And he who receives also shall answer: "Hamen[1]."

The expression "because that it is the form of the Flesh of the Christ: and a cup of wine because it is the Blood of the Christ which will be shed for all who believe him" is evidently reminiscent of a form of the words of institution.

We come now to the actual liturgical text which survives in the Latin and Ethiopic versions and in a developed form in the Syriac.

That it was once in the Coptic is evident from the concluding words of the first of the foregoing descriptions. "Let him pray also then and say the things which come after these according to the custom of the holy oblation."

The Latin version of the liturgy of the First Order (with the Ethiopic variations) (Hauler, Didascal. Apost. fragmenta Veron. Lat. pp. 106, 107).

[1] For the various readings of the different versions see Appendix.

Illi (episcopo) vero offerant diacones oblationem, qui imponens manus in eam cum omni presbyterio dicat gratias agens :

Dominus vobiscum.

Et omnes dicant :

Et (E. "perfectly," see App.) cum spiritu tuo.

Sursum corda.

Habemus ad Dominum (E. "The Lord our God").

Gratias agamus Domino.

Dignum (E. "it is right and meet") et iustum est.

Et sic iam prosequatur:

Gratias tibi referimus, Deus, per dilectum puerum tuum Jesum Christum, quem in ultimis temporibus misisti nobis, salvatorem et redemptorem, et angelum voluntatis tuae ; qui est verbum tuum inseparabile, per quem omnia fecisti et beneplacitum tibi fuit ; misisti de caelo (E. adds "Thy Son") in matricem virginis ; qui in utero habitus incarnatus est et filius tibi ostensus est ex spiritu sancto et virgine natus ; qui voluntatem tuam complens et populum sanctum tibi acquirens extendit manus cum pateretur (E. "for suffering"), ut a passione (E. "the sufferers") liberaret eos qui in te crediderunt : qui cum traderetur voluntariae passioni ut mortem solvat, et vincula diaboli dirumpat, et infernum calcet, et iustos illuminet (E. "lead forth"), et terminum figat et resurrectionem manifestet, accipiens (E. "on that night on which He was betrayed He took") panem gratias tibi agens dixit : Accipite, manducate ; hoc est corpus meum quod pro vobis confringitur (E. future). Similiter et calicem dicens (E. "having given thanks He said") : Hic est sanguis meus qui pro vobis effunditur (E. future) ; quando hoc facitis meam commemorationem facitis.

The Syriac version gives an amplified form of the same prayer. (Testament of Our Lord, Cooper and Maclean, p. 71.)

Then let the bishop say, giving and rendering thanks with an awed voice :

Our Lord [be] with you.

And let the people say :

And with thy spirit.

Let the bishop say : [Lift] up your hearts.

Let the people say : They are [lifted] up unto the Lord.

Let the bishop say : Let us give thanks unto the Lord.

And let all the people say: It is meet and right.

And let the bishop cry: Holy things in holy [persons].

And let the people call out: In heaven and on earth without ceasing.

Eucharist, or Thanksgiving over the offering.

Let the bishop immediately say:

We render thanks to Thee, O God, the Holy One, Confirmer of our souls, and Giver of our life, the Treasure of incorruptibility, and Father of the Only-begotten, our Saviour, whom in the latter times Thou didst send to us as a Saviour and Proclaimer of Thy purpose. For it is Thy purpose that we should be saved in Thee. Our heart giveth thanks unto Thee, [our] mind, [our] soul, with all its thinking, that Thy grace may come upon us, O Lord, so that we may continually praise Thee, and Thy Only-begotten Son and Thy Holy Ghost, now and alway and for ever and ever. Amen.

O Thou Power of the Father, the Grace of the nations, Knowledge, true Wisdom, the Exaltation of the meek, the Medicine of Souls, the Confidence of us who believe, for Thou art the Strength of the righteous, the Hope of the persecuted, the Haven of those who are buffeted, the illuminator of the perfect, the Son of the living God, make to arise in us out of Thy gift which cannot be searched into, courage, might, reliance, wisdom, strength, unlapsing faith, unshaken hope, the knowledge of Thy Spirit, meekness [and] uprightness, so that alway, O Lord, we Thy servants and all the people, may praise Thee purely, may bless Thee, may give thanks to Thee Lord at all times, and may beseech Thee.

And also let the Bishop say:

Thou, Lord, the Founder of the heights, and King of the treasuries of light, Visitor of the heavenly Sion, King of the orders of Archangels, of Dominions, Praises, Thrones, Raiments, Lights, Joys, Delights, the Father of kings, who holdest all in Thy hands, and suppliest all by Thy reason, through Thine Only-begotten Son who was crucified for our sins: Thou, Lord, didst send Thy Word, who is of Thy counsel and covenant, by whom Thou madest all things, being well pleased with Him, into a virgin womb; Who when He was conceived [and] made flesh, was shown to be Thy Son, being born of the Holy Ghost and the Virgin; Who fulfilling Thy will and preparing a holy people, stretched forth His hands to suffering that He might loose from sufferings and corruption and death those who have hoped in Thee: Who when He was betrayed to voluntary suffering that He might raise up those who had slipped and find those who were lost, and give life to the dead, and loose [the pains of] death, and rend the bonds of the devil, and fulfil the counsel of the Father, and tread down Sheol, and open the way of life, and guide the righteous to light, and fix the boundary, and lighten the darkness and nurture the babes, and reveal the resurrection; taking bread, gave it to His disciples, saying, Take, eat, this is My Body which is broken for you for the forgiveness of sins. When ye do this, ye make My resurrection. Also the cup of wine which He mixed He gave for a type of the Blood which He shed for us.

It will be seen that this is an expanded form of the liturgy of the Latin and Ethiopic versions. Its phraseology reminds one very much of the forms contained in the Acts of John and the Acts of Thomas.

The second prayer, "O Thou Power of the Father" etc., calls for notice. It has all the force of an ἐπίκλησις and is perhaps best explained as an alternative form of ἐπίκλησις in an alternative position, *i.e.* before the words of institution.

The most interesting point in these prayers lies in the omission of the words of institution relating to the cup. Mgr. Rahmani attributes the omission to accident. But as Dr Cooper and Bishop Maclean point out (Test. of Our Lord, p. 170) the same omission is noticeable in the Abyssinian Anaphora of Our Lord which is derived from the liturgy of the Testament[1].

It is more likely that the words of institution being given relating to the bread, the words relating to the cup and so similar, were left to the memory of the celebrant. In the derived Abyssinian liturgy however it is clear from the wording that this was the actual form in that liturgy.

[1] "Likewise also the cup of wine after they had supped, mixing, giving thanks, blessing and sanctifying, Thou didst give to them, Thy true blood which was shed for our sins." Cooper and Maclean, "Testament of our Lord," App. I. p. 247. The Abyssinian anaphora there translated is from the Latin version of Ludolf, Commentar. ad suam histor. Aeth.

And although the omission may have been copied by the Abyssinian translator without his being conscious of an omission, on the other hand it is quite likely that the form as it stands in the Syriac is actually the complete form.

Sarapion's liturgy.

When we leave the Church Orders and come to Sarapion's liturgy and to the description of that used by St Cyril of Jerusalem we notice a considerable development. They represent the transitional stage between the more primitive liturgy of the Church Orders and the final developed liturgy of the fifth century.

However it is chiefly the ἐπίκλησις in which, when we come to consider that part of the εὐχαριστία, we shall notice the most marked development.

Sarapion Bishop of Thmuis was the contemporary of St Athanasius and four letters addressed to him by Athanasius are still extant. Bishop Wordsworth dates these liturgical forms about 350—356.

Εὐχὴ προσφόρου Σαραπίωνος ἐπισκόπου.

ἄξιον καὶ δίκαιόν ἐστιν σὲ τὸν ἀγένητον πατέρα τοῦ μονογενοῦς Ἰησοῦ Χριστοῦ αἰνεῖν ὑμνεῖν δοξολογεῖν· αἰνοῦμεν σὲ, ἀγένητε Θεὲ, ἀνεξιχνίαστε, ἀνέκφραστε, ἀκατανόητε πάσῃ γενητῇ ὑποστάσει· αἰνοῦμεν σὲ τὸν γιγνωσκόμενον ὑπὸ τοῦ υἱοῦ τοῦ μονογενοῦς, τὸν δι' αὐτοῦ λαληθέντα καὶ ἑρμηνευθέντα καὶ γνωσθέντα τῇ γενητῇ φύσει· αἰνοῦμεν σὲ τὸν γιγνώσκοντα τὸν υἱὸν καὶ ἀποκαλύπτοντα τοῖς ἁγίοις τὰς περὶ αὐτοῦ δόξας· τὸν γιγνωσκόμενον ὑπὸ τοῦ γεγεννημένου σου λόγου καὶ ὁρώμενον καὶ διερμηνευόμενον τοῖς ἁγίοις· αἰνοῦμεν σὲ, πάτερ ἀόρατε, χορηγὲ τῆς ἀθανασίας· σὺ εἶ ἡ πηγὴ τῆς ζωῆς, ἡ πηγὴ τοῦ φωτὸς, ἡ πηγὴ πάσης χάριτος καὶ πάσης ἀληθείας, φιλάνθρωπε καὶ φιλόπτωχε, ὁ πᾶσιν καταλλασσόμενος καὶ πάντας πρὸς ἑαυτὸν διὰ τῆς ἐπιδημίας τοῦ ἀγαπητοῦ σου υἱοῦ ἕλκων. δεόμεθα ποίησον ἡμᾶς ζῶντας ἀνθρώπους· δὸς ἡμῖν πνεῦμα φωτὸς, ἵνα γνῶμεν σὲ τὸν ἀληθινὸν καὶ ὃν ἀπέστειλας Ἰησοῦν Χριστόν· δὸς ἡμῖν Πνεῦμα ἅγιον, ἵνα δυνηθῶμεν ἐξειπεῖν καὶ διηγήσασθαι τὰ ἄρρητά σου μυστήρια. λαλησάτω ἐν ἡμῖν ὁ Κύριος Ἰησοῦς καὶ ἅγιον Πνεῦμα καὶ ὑμνησάτω σὲ δι' ἡμῶν· σὺ γὰρ ὁ ὑπεράνω πάσης ἀρχῆς καὶ ἐξουσίας καὶ δυνάμεως καὶ κυριότητος καὶ παντὸς ὀνόματος ὀνομαζομένου οὐ μόνον ἐν αἰῶνι τούτῳ ἀλλὰ καὶ ἐν τῷ μέλλοντι· σοὶ παραστήκουσι χίλιαι χιλιάδες καὶ μύριαι μυριάδες ἀγγέλων ἀρχαγγέλων θρόνων κυριοτήτων ἀρχῶν ἐξουσιῶν· σοὶ παραστήκουσι τὰ δύο τιμιώτατα σεραφεὶμ ἑξαπτέρυγα, δυσὶν μὲν πτέρυξιν καλύπτοντα τὸ πρόσωπον, δυσὶ δὲ τοὺς πόδας, δυσὶ δὲ πετόμενα καὶ ἁγιάζοντα, μεθ' ὧν δέξαι καὶ τὸν ἡμέτερον ἁγιασμὸν λεγόντων· Ἅγιος ἅγιος ἅγιος Κύριος σαβαώθ, πλήρης ὁ οὐρανὸς καὶ ἡ γῆ τῆς δόξης σου· πλήρης ἐστὶν ὁ οὐρανὸς, πλήρης ἐστὶν καὶ ἡ γῆ τῆς μεγαλοπρεποῦς σου δόξης· Κύριε τῶν δυνάμεων, πλήρωσον καὶ τὴν θυσίαν ταύτην τῆς σῆς δυνάμεως καὶ τῆς σῆς μεταλήψεως· σοὶ γὰρ προσηνέγκαμεν ταύτην τὴν ζῶσαν θυσίαν τὴν προσφορὰν τὴν ἀναίμακτον· σοὶ προσηνέγκαμεν τὸν ἄρτον τοῦτον, τὸ ὁμοίωμα τοῦ σώματος τοῦ μονογενοῦς. ὁ ἄρτος οὗτος τοῦ ἁγίου σώματός ἐστιν ὁμοίωμα, ὅτι ὁ Κύριος Ἰησοῦς Χριστὸς ἐν ᾗ νυκτὶ παρεδίδοτο ἔλαβεν ἄρτον καὶ ἔκλασεν καὶ ἐδίδου τοῖς μαθηταῖς αὐτοῦ λέγων· Λάβετε καὶ φάγετε, τοῦτό ἐστιν τὸ σῶμά μου τὸ ὑπὲρ ὑμῶν κλώμενον εἰς ἄφεσιν ἁμαρτιῶν· διὰ τοῦτο καὶ ἡμεῖς τὸ ὁμοίωμα τοῦ θανάτου ποιοῦντες τὸν ἄρτον προσηνέγκαμεν καὶ παρακαλοῦμεν διὰ τῆς θυσίας ταύτης· καταλλάγηθι πᾶσιν ἡμῖν καὶ ἱλάσθητι, Θεὲ τῆς ἀληθείας· καὶ ὥσπερ ὁ ἄρτος οὗτος ἐσκορπισμένος ἦν ἐπάνω τῶν ὀρέων καὶ συναχθεὶς ἐγένετο εἰς ἕν, οὕτω καὶ τὴν ἁγίαν σου ἐκκλησίαν σύναξον ἐκ παντὸς ἔθνους καὶ πάσης χώρας καὶ πάσης πόλεως καὶ κώμης καὶ οἴκου, καὶ ποίησον μίαν ζῶσαν καθολικὴν ἐκκλησίαν· προσηνέγκαμεν δὲ καὶ τὸ ποτήριον τὸ ὁμοίωμα τοῦ αἵματος, ὅτι ὁ Κύριος Ἰησοῦς Χριστὸς λαβὼν ποτήριον μετὰ τὸ δειπνῆσαι ἔλεγε τοῖς ἑαυτοῦ μαθηταῖς· Λάβετε, πίετε, τοῦτό ἐστιν ἡ καινὴ διαθήκη, ὅ ἐστιν τὸ αἷμά μου τὸ ὑπὲρ ὑμῶν ἐκχυνόμενον εἰς ἄφεσιν ἁμαρτημάτων. διὰ τοῦτο προσηνέγκαμεν καὶ ἡμεῖς τὸ ποτήριον ὁμοίωμα αἵματος προσάγοντες.

The chief points of interest here are that there is something very like an *ἐπίκλησις* before the words of institution *δὸς ἡμῖν πνεῦμα φωτὸς, ἵνα γνῶμεν σέ κτλ.*, though the purpose of the prayer seems to be that the celebrant may be granted utterance fitting for the celebration of the Holy mysteries. Perhaps the *ἐπίκλησις* in Sarapion's liturgy originally occurred in this position, though a full *ἐπίκλησις* of the Word occurs later on. It is interesting to compare the form from the Acts of Thomas in which an inverted order (from the later point of view) occurs, the *ἐπίκλησις* coming first.

As we have seen, too, there are signs of an ἐπίκλησις in this place in the liturgy of the Testament of Our Lord[1].

The other point of interest is the somewhat strange position of the ἀνάμνησις. It is introduced twice in connexion with the words of institution, in connexion with the bread, and in connexion with the cup. And it does not occur again as is usual as an introduction to the ἐπίκλησις.

St Cyril of Jerusalem.

St Cyril, though he does not give us the actual wording of his liturgy except here and there, gives us a very full description of it. It is noticeable in the first place that there is no proanaphora, and that Baptism immediately precedes, probably occupying the place that on ordinary occasions would be filled by the proanaphora. His outline of the part of the εὐχαριστία which we are considering is as follows:—Catechesis Myst. v. cc. 3—6.

ὁ διάκονος·

ἀλλήλους ἀπολάβετε, καὶ ἀλλήλους ἀσπαζώμεθα.

ὁ ἱερεύς·

ἄνω τὰς καρδίας.
ἔχομεν πρὸς τὸν Κύριον.
εὐχαριστήσωμεν τῷ Κυρίῳ.
ἄξιον καὶ δίκαιον.

μετὰ ταῦτα μνημονεύομεν οὐρανοῦ καὶ γῆς καὶ θαλάσσης, ἡλίου καὶ σελήνης, ἄστρων καὶ πάσης τῆς κτίσεως λογικῆς τε καὶ ἀλόγου, ὁρατῆς τε καὶ ἀοράτου, ἀγγέλων ἀρχαγγέλων δυνάμεων κυριοτήτων ἀρχῶν ἐξουσιῶν θρόνων, τῶν χερουβὶμ τῶν πολυπροσώπων, δυνάμει λέγοντες τὸ τοῦ Δαβὶδ, μεγαλύνατε τὸν Κύριον σὺν ἐμοί. μνημονεύομεν καὶ τὰ σεραφὶμ ἃ ἐν τῷ Πνεύματι ἁγίῳ ἐθεάσατο Ἡσαίας παρεστηκότα κύκλῳ τοῦ θρόνου τοῦ Θεοῦ, καὶ ταῖς μὲν δυσὶ πτέρυξι κατακαλύπτοντα τὸ πρόσωπον, ταῖς δὲ δυσὶ τοὺς πόδας, καὶ ταῖς δυσὶ πετόμενα, καὶ λέγοντα Ἅγιος, ἅγιος, ἅγιος, Κύριος σαβαώθ.

διὰ τοῦτο γὰρ τὴν παραδοθεῖσαν ἡμῖν ἐκ τῶν σεραφὶμ θεολογίαν

[1] See p. 87.

ταύτην λέγομεν, ὅπως κοινωνοὶ τῆς ὑμνῳδίας ταῖς ὑπερκοσμίοις γενώμεθα στρατιαῖς.

So far St Cyril. He then passes on to the *ἐπίκλησις*.

There are two points noticeable here. From the last words above it seems likely that considerable progress has been made even to the verbal fixing of the liturgy. But perhaps this must not be pressed.

The most interesting and important point is the omission of any reference to the Institution and to any occurrence in St Cyril's liturgy of the words of institution.

The fact that Cyril does not mention this is no proof as to its non-occurrence in his liturgy, for after all he is only giving an outline.

But whatever may have been the case earlier, it would seem that at this date, this, the prevailing type of liturgy, did contain a reference at least to the Institution if not a use of the words of institution in some form or other.

The only evidence against this view is the extant liturgy of Adai and Mari used by the East Syrian Nestorians and which Drs Cooper and Maclean[1] date as probably before 431. In its present form and perhaps for centuries there is no use of the words of institution. But the probable explanation is that they have been omitted from the Service books as being familiar to the clergy, and gradually and inadvertently have long ago passed out of use.

But the actual wording of the liturgy of Adai and Mari seems to require at least a reference to the Institution: "We ...who are assembled in Thy name and stand before Thee at this moment have received by tradition the example which came from Thee..." Surely here after "the example that came from Thee" there originally occurred an account

[1] *Op. cit.* p. 35.

of the Institution. It is especially noticeable that in the liturgy of the Apostolic Constitutions immediately before the account of the Institution occur the words *τὴν διάταξιν αὐτοῦ πληροῦμεν.*

It would appear probable, then, that by St Cyril's time an account of the Institution was general throughout the Church, and that, though not referred to, it did occur in the liturgy of Jerusalem in his time.

The Second Church Order.

We come finally to the account of the consecration of a Bishop and the Eucharist that follows in the Second Church Order.

I believe that this account has been largely edited and brought up to date by later hands.

The account is as follows (Copt. text § 64. Horner's Statutes pp. 342—4):

And when they have saluted him with the salutation which is in the Lord, let them read in the holy Gospels. And when they have finished reading the Gospel, let the Bishop who has been ordained salute all the Church, saying: The grace of Our Lord Jesus Christ and the love of God the Father, and the fellowship of the Holy Spirit, (be) with you all. And let them all answer "With thy spirit also." And when he has finished saying this, let him also speak to the people with words of exhortation[1]; then having finished his instruction, let the deacon mount upon a high place and proclaim:

Let no unbeliever remain in this place.

[1] It is not clear that this part of the description is of part of the Proanaphora. It looks more like a description of the service belonging to the consecration of a Bishop. The Gospel mentioned is perhaps not the proanaphoral lection from the Gospels as there are no other lections mentioned. But probably by this time a part at least of the Proanaphora was used even when there was such an event as a Baptism or Ordination service preceding the Eucharist.

And then when the bishop has finished all the prayers which it is right for him to make, whether for the sick and also for the rest, let the deacon say to them all:

Salute one another with a holy kiss.

And let the clergy salute the bishop, and let the laymen salute one another, and let the women also salute the women.........Then let the subdeacon bring water, and let the priests wash their hands, for a sign of purity of their souls, lifted up to God the Almighty. And let another deacon cry out:

Let not any of those who only hear the word but do not communicate of the Holy Mysteries, stand in this place.

Let not any of the unbelievers remain.

Let not any of the heretics stand in this place with us to-day.

Mothers, hold your children.

Let no one have a quarrel in his heart with another.

Let none stand in this place playing the hypocrite or with hypocrisy.

Be all of you sincere toward the Lord God.

Let us stand in fear of God and trembling.

....

... and thus let the chief priest supplicate over the oblation....

(2) *The ἀνάμνησις and the ἐπίκλησις*

We come now to the consideration of that part of the Canon which has become to the whole Eastern Church the essential part of it, the actual consecration form. As has been said before it was quite foreign to the mind of the third and fourth century to divide up the liturgy into parts and to regard either one part or another as the actual consecration formula. The whole liturgy was the consecrating form.

It has been rather difficult to know where to make the division for convenience of treatment, but on the whole it seems best to take the *ἀνάμνησις* and *ἐπίκλησις* together. The climax of the *εὐχαριστία* has been reached when the account of the Institution concludes with the injunction "Do this in remembrance of me." It remains for the Church to proclaim her obedience as she does in the Anamnesis and pray for the presence of the Holy Spirit that those who partake in the sacred mysteries may be the recipients of heavenly benediction.

There remain the words of administration in the communion of the people, a thanksgiving and the dismissal. This part of the liturgy seems to have been the last part to be fixed. The thanksgiving was perhaps at first privately made by each individual for himself. At any rate the earliest form of the First Church Order does not even give a model of this concluding portion of the liturgy but leaves each individual celebrant to finish the Eucharist as he will.

The *Anamnesis* follows on the recited account of the Institution or at least some reference to Our Lord's command "Do this in remembrance of me." It occurs from the moment that definite liturgical models come into view, and probably always in this type of liturgy.

Perhaps we find a reference to it in *St Justin* (Dial. 40).

ἡ τῆς σεμιδάλεως δὲ προσφορὰ...τύπος ἦν τοῦ ἄρτου τῆς εὐχαριστίας ὃν εἰς ἀνάμνησιν τοῦ πάθους ὃ ἔπαθεν ὑπὲρ τῶν καθαιρομένων τὰς ψυχὰς ἀπὸ πάσης πονηρίας ἀνθρώπων Ἰησοῦς Χριστὸς ὁ Κύριος ἡμῶν παρέδωκε ποιεῖν.

St Irenaeus

sed et suis discipulis dans consilium primitias Deo offerre ex suis creaturis...Eum qui ex creatura est panis accepit et gratias egit dicens: Hoc est corpus meum. Et calicem similiter... et novi testamenti novam docuit oblationem; quam ecclesia ab apostolis accipiens in universo mundo offert Deo. (contr. haer. IV. xxix. 15.)

In these last words perhaps there is a reminiscence of an ἀνάμνησις.

St Cyprian's references to the liturgy, which we have seen probably imply an account of the Institution and the use of the words of institution, at the same time imply an ἀνάμνησις.

In the liturgical forms from the First Order onwards it always appears.

The ἐπίκλησις is that part of the liturgy which has undergone the greatest development. It is necessary to use the word in connexion with the primitive liturgy, but we must be careful to remember that as the form developed so did the meaning of the word, into something very different from the original signification.

Yet since the development of the ἐπίκλησις, form and word, can be traced from very early times, we can use the word in its untechnical sense of the undeveloped form.

Later word and form changed. From the fifth century onwards ἐπίκλησις may be taken to have already assumed the meaning of a prayer addressed to the Father that He would send down the Holy Spirit upon the elements that He might make them the Body and Blood of Our Lord.

The use of ποιέω in this connexion occurs in St Chrysostom (de coem. et cruce 3) and onwards, and there are earlier traces of it in St Cyril of Jerusalem. But before this such words as ἀποφαίνω[1], ἀποδείκνυμι[2] had been used.

Thus ἐπίκλησις has the sense of a "calling down upon" the elements.

In classical Greek the word has two meanings. 1. A surname. 2. Later the word gets the meaning of a "calling upon" or "appeal."

[1] ἀποφαίνω. Cyril, M. C. iv. 1 and Apost. Const. Cf. the Coptic use, liturgy of St Gregory, where the equivalent ⲟⲩⲟⲛϩ ⲉⲃⲟⲗ is used.

[2] ἀποδείκνυμι is used in this connexion by St Basil de Spir. Sanct. c. 66.

It is used twice only in the LXX and each of the classical meanings is represented. In 2 Macc. viii. 15 it is used of Israel being called by the name of God. In 2 Macc. xv. 26 it is used as more or less synonymous with εὐχή.

The verb however ἐπικαλέω, ἐπικαλοῦμαι is used very frequently in the sense of "calling upon," or "praying to," very often in address to God.

Thus it will be seen that the later use in the fifth century has a considerably developed meaning, and when the word occurs earlier in connexion with the liturgy, as it does, we must be careful not to assign to it the later technical meaning.

We shall see that the word was used at first of a prayer for the sending of the Holy Spirit, or the Divine Word, into the Church's act of communion, that the souls of the communicants might be so disposed and prepared by Him that they might receive in their communion the full grace and virtue of the Holy Sacrament. Thus St Justin tells us that the εὐχαριστία contained a petition to this effect ἀναπέμπει καὶ εὐχαριστίαν ὑπὲρ τοῦ κατηξιῶσθαι τούτων παρ' αὐτοῦ ἐπὶ πολὺ ποιεῖται (Apol. I. 65)[1]. It is the early form of ἐπίκλησις. When we come to St Irenaeus we find him actually using the word ἐπίκλησις, in connexion with the consecration of the elements. Speaking of the heretic Marcus, and his pretensions he thus

[1] It is very possible that a reminiscence of the ἐπίκλησις is contained in St Ignatius. If so it is the earliest reference. His words are ἕνα ἄρτον κλῶντες ὅς ἐστι φάρμακον ἀθανασίας ἀντίδοτος τοῦ ἀποθανεῖν ἀλλὰ ζῆν ἐν Ἰησοῦ Χριστῷ διὰ παντός. Ad Ephes. 20. Cf. the famous description of Pliny "seque sacramento non in scelus aliquod obstringere, sed ne furta, ne latrocinia, ne adulteria committerent, ne fidem fallerent, ne depositum appellati abnegarent." Ep. xcvii.

refers to his consecration of the Eucharist (contr. haer. I. vii. 2):

ἐπὶ πλέον ἐκτείνων τὸν λόγον τῆς ἐπικλήσεως πορφύρεα καὶ ἐρυθρὰ ἀναφαίνεσθαι ποιεῖ· ὡς δοκεῖν τὴν ἀπὸ τῶν ὑπὲρ τὰ ὅλα χάριν τὸ αἷμα τὸ ἑαυτῆς στάζειν ἐν ἐκείνῳ τῷ ποτηρίῳ διὰ τῆς ἐπικλήσεως αὐτοῦ.

Here St Irenaeus gives us a not very clear account of what seems to have been some sleight of hand on the part of the heretic. But it is with the use of the word ἐπίκλησις that we are concerned. ἡ ἐπίκλησις *αὐτοῦ* makes the meaning clear. It means Marcus' consecration prayer.

So Irenaeus uses λόγος ἐπικλήσεως or ἐπίκλησις simply of the consecration form generally.

He also uses as an equivalent ἡ ἐπίκλησις θεοῦ (contr. haer. IV. xxxi. 4) ὡς γὰρ ἀπὸ γῆς ἄρτος προσλαμβανόμενος τὴν ἐπίκλησιν θεοῦ οὐκέτι κοινὸς ἄρτος ἐστὶ ἀλλ' εὐχαριστία[1]. Here again he is evidently referring to the consecration form generally and his words recall the εὐχαριστηθεῖσα τροφή of Justin.

Elsewhere he uses as another equivalent ὁ λόγος τοῦ θεοῦ (c. haer. V. ii. 2), ὁ γεγονὼς ἄρτος ἐπιδέχεται τὸν λόγον τοῦ θεοῦ καὶ γίνεται εὐχαριστία, again recalling Justin's expression εὐχὴ λόγου τοῦ παρ' αὐτοῦ.

St Firmilian.

In the works of St Cyprian we come across the Latin equivalent of the word ἐπίκλησις, Invocatio, in connexion with the liturgy. It occurs in the letter of Firmilian

[1] The reading of the printed text is here ἔκκλησιν. Harnack says that this is an error and that the MS. reading is ἐπίκλησιν (Texte und Untersuch. N.F. v. 3, p. 56). This finally disposes of the Pfaffian fragment (no. xxxvii Harvey's ed.) with its ἐκκαλοῦμεν.

of Caesarea[1] to Cyprian. In this letter Firmilian gives some account of the Montanists in Phrygia and specially complains of the scandal of the Montanist prophetesses taking upon themselves the celebration of the Sacraments of Baptism and the Eucharist. Of one woman he speaks in particular.

etiam hoc frequenter ausa est, ut et invocatione non contemtibili sanctificare se panem et Eucharistiam facere simularet et sacrificium Domino non sine sacramento solitae praedicationis offerret, baptizaret quoque multos usitata et legitima verba interrogationis usurpans, et nil discrepare ab ecclesiastica regula videretur.

These words of Firmilian show:

1. That there was a regula ecclesiastica as to the Eucharistic liturgy. Evidently at least the outline is fixed.

2. That certainly the wording of most of it, if not all, was left to the celebrant is shown by the words "invocatione non contemtibili."

3. That there was a recital of some form, "solitae praedicationis"; this looks like a recital of some account of the Institution.

From this it would appear that the invocatio is not the ἐπίκλησις. By the time of Firmilian, if the First Church Order represents anything like general use, the ἐπίκλησις occurs after the account of the Institution and the ἀνάμνησις. The word seems simply to mean "prayer" or "gift of prayer."

Thus in St Irenaeus we have three equivalent expressions ἡ ἐπίκλησις, ἡ ἐπίκλησις τοῦ θεοῦ, ὁ λόγος τοῦ θεοῦ, all synonymous of the consecration generally and not referring to any particular portion of the whole εὐχαριστία.

[1] Cypr. Epist. lxxv. 10.

Acts of John.

In one of the liturgical forms in this work the ἐπίκλησις and its purpose are clearly marked. In this case it was used at the time of communion and used over each individual communicant.

c. 110. καὶ κλάσας τὸν ἄρτον ἐπέδωκεν πᾶσιν ἡμῖν, ἑκάστῳ τῶν ἀδελφῶν ἐπευχόμενος ἄξιον ἔσεσθαι αὐτὸν τῆς τοῦ Κυρίου χάριτος καὶ τῆς ἁγιωτάτης εὐχαριστίας.

In the almost contemporary Acts of Thomas the ἐπίκλησις is well marked in two cases.

A (Wright II. p. 189).

And he began to say:
Come, gift of the Exalted: come, perfect mercy; come, Holy Spirit; come, revealer of the mysteries of the chosen among the prophets; come, proclaimer by His apostles of the combats of our victorious Athlete; come, treasure of majesty; come, beloved of the mercy of the most High; come (Thou) silent (one), revealer of the mysteries of the exalted; come, utterer of hidden things, and shewer of the works of our God; come, giver of life in secret and manifest in Thy deeds; come, giver of joy and rest to all who cleave unto Thee: come, power of the Father and wisdom of the Son, for ye are one in all; come and communicate with us in this Eucharist which we celebrate and in this offering which we offer, and in this commemoration which we make.

Here is an ἐπίκλησις of the Holy Trinity in an unusual order, the Holy Spirit, the Father, and the Son. The purpose is clear that the Divine presence may be shed upon the communion of the faithful.

Also there is a simple ἀνάμνησις at the end of the ἐπίκλησις instead of the beginning.

Again in the same Acts, C (Wright, Vol. II. p. 268):

And he said:
In Thy name, Jesus, may the power of the blessing and the thanksgiving come and abide upon this bread, that all the souls

which take of it may be renewed, and their sins may be forgiven them.

The ἐπίκλησις here is addressed to Our Lord and is a simple prayer for the renewal of soul and the forgiveness of sins to those who are about to communicate.

The wording of this form is interesting for it is easy to see how readily these words "may the power of the blessing...come and abide upon this bread" would develope, when the doctrine of the Person and work of the Holy Spirit began to be defined, into the ἐπίκλησις of later days.

In another passage in the Acts of Thomas, D (Wright, II. p. 290), we have seen how the idea of the ἐπίκλησις is worked into the recital of the events of the Passion of Our Lord[1].

Origen (c. Cels. viii. 53) seems to have the ἐπίκλησις in his mind as a prayer for the good communion of those who receive, when he speaks of the Body of Christ as ἁγιάζον τοὺς μετὰ ὑγιοῦς προθέσεως αὐτῷ χρωμένους.

The First Church Order.

The Latin and Ethiopic versions of the ἀνάμνησις and ἐπίκλησις (Latin, Hauler, p. 107; Horner, p. 141).

Memores igitur mortis et resurrectionis eius (E. "Thy death and Thy resurrection") offerimus tibi panem et calicem gratias tibi agentes quia nos dignos habuisti adstare coram te et tibi ministrare. Et petimus (E. adds "Lord, we beseech Thee") ut mittas Spiritum tuum sanctum in oblationem (E. "this oblation") sanctae (E. omits) ecclesiae; in unum congregans (E. adds "that in joining them together") des omnibus qui percipiunt sanctis in repletionem Spiritus sancti ad confirmationem fidei in veritate, ut te laudemus et glorificemus (E. "they") per puerum tuum Jesum Christum, per quem tibi gloria et honor, patri et filio cum Spiritu Sancto, in sancta ecclesia tua et nunc et in saecula saeculorum. Amen.

[1] See p. 75.

Here the Latin version closes. The Ethiopic which probably represents a slightly later text goes on (Horner, pp. 141 ff.):

And the people shall say:

As it was, is and shall be to generation of generation, and to age of age. Amen.

And the bishop shall say:

And again we beseech Thee, Almighty God, the Father of the Lord and our Saviour Jesus Christ to grant us to receive with blessing this holy Mystery; and that He may not condemn any of us, but cause worthiness in all them who take the reception of the holy Mystery, the Body and the Blood of Christ, Almighty Lord our God.

And the deacon shall say: Pray ye.

And the bishop shall say: God, Almighty, grant to us the reception of Thy holy Mystery as our strengthening; nor condemn any amongst us, but bless all through Christ, through Whom to Thee with Him and with the Holy Spirit, be glory and might, now and always, and for ever and ever. Amen.

And the deacon shall say: As ye stand bow down your heads.

And the bishop shall say: Eternal God, knower of that which is secret and that which is open, to Thee Thy people bow down their heads, and to Thee they bent the hardness of heart and flesh; look from Thy worthy dwelling-place; bless them both men and women; incline Thine ear to them and hear their prayer, and strengthen (them) with the might of Thy right hand, and protect (them) from evil sickness; be their guardian for both body and soul; increase to them and to us Thy faith and Thy fear, through Thine only Son, through Whom to Thee with Him and with the Holy Spirit, be glory and might, now and always, and for ever and ever. Amen.

And the deacon shall say: Let us attend.

And the bishop shall say: Holiness to holy ones.

And the people shall say: One holy Father, One holy Son, One is the Holy Ghost.

And the bishop shall say: The Lord (be) with you all.

And the people shall say: With thy spirit.

Then follows the Communion.

The Ethiopic version is fuller than the Latin. The

three additional prayers in the Ethiopic text, "And again we beseech Thee, Almighty God," "God Almighty, grant to us," "Eternal God, knower of that which is secret," are all, it will be noticed, as to the matter contained, prayers for a good communion. Perhaps the explanation of this additional matter is that these three prayers were originally variant forms of the ἐπίκλησις, "et petimus ut mittas Spiritum tuum sanctum," which gradually all came into use in the liturgy. Such duplication of the same form is to be found elsewhere and is very likely the true explanation of certain liturgical difficulties.

The Testament of Our Lord.

And also let him (i.e. the bishop) say:

Remembering therefore Thy death and resurrection, we offer to Thee bread and cup, giving thanks to Thee who alone art God for ever and our Saviour, since Thou hast promised to us to stand before Thee and to serve Thee in priesthood. Therefore we render thanks to Thee, we Thy servants, O Lord.

And let the people say likewise.

And also let (the bishop) say:

We offer to Thee this thanksgiving, Eternal Trinity, O Lord Jesus Christ, O Lord the Father, before whom all creation and every nature trembleth fleeing into itself, O Lord the Holy Ghost; we have brought this drink and this food of Thy holiness [to Thee]; cause that it may be to us not for condemnation, not for reproach, not for destruction, but for the medicine and support of our spirit. Yea, O God, grant us that by Thy Name every thought of things displeasing to Thee may flee away. Grant, O God, that every proud conception may be driven away from us by Thy Name, which is written within the veils of Thy sanctuaries, those high ones —a Name which when Sheol heareth it is amazed, the depth is rent, the spirits are driven away, the dragon is bruised, unbelief is cast out, disobedience is subdued, anger is appeased, envy worketh not, pride is reproved, avarice rooted out, boasting taken away, arrogance humbled, [and] every root of bitterness destroyed. Grant therefore, O Lord, to our innermost eyes to see Thee, praising Thee and glorifying Thee, commemorating Thee and serving Thee, having a portion in Thee alone, O Son and Word of God, who subduest all things.

Sustain unto the end those who have gifts of revelations, confirm those who have a gift of healing. Make those courageous who have the power of tongues. Keep those who have the word of doctrine upright. Care for those who do Thy will alway. Visit the widows. Help the orphans. Remember those who have fallen asleep in the faith. And grant us an inheritance with Thy saints, and bestow [upon us] the power to please Thee as they also pleased Thee. Feed the people in uprightness: and sanctify us all, O God.

But grant that all those who partake and receive of Thy Holy Things may be made one with Thee, so that they may be filled with the Holy Ghost for the confirmation of the faith in truth that they may lift up always a doxology to Thee and to Thy beloved Son Jesus Christ, by whom praise and might [be] unto Thee with Thy Holy Spirit for ever and ever.

Let the people say: Amen.

The deacon: Earnestly let us beseech our Lord and our God that He may bestow upon us concord of spirit.

The bishop: Give us concord and the Holy Spirit, and heal our souls by this offering, that we may live in Thee in all the ages of the ages.

The people: Amen.

Let the people also pray in the same [words].

After these things the seal of thanksgiving thus: Let the Name of the Lord be blessed for ever.

The people: Amen.

The priest: Blessed is He that hath come in the Name of the Lord. Blessed [is] the name of His praise.

And let all the people say: So be it, so be it.

Let the bishop say: Send the grace of the Spirit upon us.

The Testament here as elsewhere much amplifies the form as given in the earlier forms, a Syrian characteristic.

There are certain points of interest. The Anamnesis is to be said not only by the celebrant, but by the people as well, "and let the people say likewise."

The ἐπίκλησις is addressed to the Holy Trinity. Here too the order of the Divine persons, the Son, the Father, the Holy Spirit, is a curious thing, and one which is of importance from the point of view of date. Such an order is hardly likely to have been possible after the rise of the Arian controversy.

The purpose of the ἐπίκλησις is not for the bringing about of the Sacramental change in the elements but that the partakers may duly receive the benefits of the Holy Sacrament. Into the ἐπίκλησις is inserted the Intercession[1], now appearing in a written form, or model form, for the first time.

Although the Deacon's exhortations to the people also occur and in a different form from those in the Ethiopic version, and a very short prayer for unity by the Bishop, there are no parallel forms to the three last prayers in the Ethiopic, and this confirms the view that the forms in the Ethiopic are originally alternative forms.

Immediately before the Communion the Bishop prays, "Send the grace of the Spirit upon us," again making quite clear that the ἐπίκλησις is a prayer for the people at this moment of communion, and not a summoning of the Divine power upon the elements.

It may be of interest to notice that the later Ethiopic Anaphora of Our Lord which is derived from the liturgy of the Testament inserts a developed form of ἐπίκλησις immediately after the Anamnesis.

[1] The position of the Intercession is very unnatural, thrust as it is into the middle of the ἐπίκλησις. Perhaps it is a later insertion, but probably the true explanation is that the part of the ἐπίκλησις following, "But grant that all those etc.," is really an alternative ἐπίκλησις which has, in process of copying, through the omission of mark or note, become attached to the end of the Intercession.

Therefore we also, Thy servants, O Lord, ask Thee, O Lord, and beseech Thee to send the Holy Spirit and power upon this bread and this cup, that He may make it the Body and Blood of our Lord and Saviour Jesus Christ, world without end. Amen.

Yet the earlier ἐπίκλησις of the Testament addressed to the Holy Trinity is retained as well, and occurs immediately after.

The Liturgy of Sarapion.

ἐπιδημησάτω, θεὲ τῆς ἀληθείας, ὁ ἅγιός σου Λόγος ἐπὶ τὸν ἄρτον τοῦτον ἵνα γένηται ὁ ἄρτος σῶμα τοῦ Λόγου καὶ ἐπὶ τὸ ποτήριον τοῦτο ἵνα γένηται τὸ ποτήριον αἷμα τῆς ἀληθείας. καὶ ποίησον πάντας τοὺς κοινωνοῦντας φάρμακον ζωῆς λαβεῖν εἰς θεραπείαν παντὸς νοσήματος καὶ εἰς ἐνδυνάμωσιν πάσης προκοπῆς καὶ ἀρετῆς, μὴ εἰς κατάκρισιν, θεὲ τῆς ἀληθείας, μηδὲ εἰς ἔλεγχον καὶ ὄνειδος. σὲ γὰρ τὸν ἀγένητον ἐπεκαλεσάμεθα διὰ τοῦ μονογενοῦς ἐν ἁγίῳ Πνεύματι. ἐλεηθήτω ὁ λαὸς οὗτος, προκοπῆς ἀξιωθήτω, ἀποσταλήτωσαν ἄγγελοι συμπαρόντες τῷ λαῷ εἰς κατάργησιν τοῦ πονηροῦ καὶ εἰς βεβαίωσιν τῆς ἐκκλησίας.

With Sarapion the development of the ἐπίκλησις begins. In the first place it is to be noticed that the Divine Word is invoked, not the Holy Spirit. But it is by the operation of the Word that the bread becomes the Body of the Word, the cup the Blood.

At the same time the original purpose of the ἐπίκλησις is not forgotten, and the form proceeds at once after the opening Invocation to pray for those who are about to communicate.

As in the liturgy of the Testament, the Intercession follows at once. There is no reference to the Lord's prayer, but possibly there is one slight reminiscence of it at the end, ἐλεηθήτω ὁ λαὸς οὗτος...ἀποσταλήτωσαν ἄγγελοι συμπαρόντες τῷ λαῷ εἰς κατάργησιν τοῦ πονηροῦ recalling the petitions καὶ ἄφες ἡμῖν τὰ ὀφειλήματα ἡμῶν

...καὶ μὴ εἰσενέγκῃς ἡμᾶς εἰς πειρασμὸν ἀλλὰ ῥῦσαι ἡμᾶς ἀπὸ τοῦ πονηροῦ.

St Cyril of Jerusalem.

St Cyril gives an outline of the liturgy of Jerusalem. He does not refer in any way to the occurrence of any reference to the Institution and we find in him some idea, for the first time, of a definite moment of consecration. The part of the liturgy that he regards as the "consecration form" is undoubtedly the ἐπίκλησις. Thus he can say (Cat. Myst. v. 7):

εἶτα...παρακαλοῦμεν τὸν φιλάνθρωπον Θεὸν τὸ ἅγιον Πνεῦμα ἐξαποστεῖλαι ἐπὶ τὰ προκείμενα ἵνα ποιήσῃ τὸν μὲν ἄρτον σῶμα Χριστοῦ τὸν δὲ οἶνον αἷμα Χριστοῦ.

The Invocation is on a par with that of Sarapion. The Invocation of the Divine Power, in Sarapion the Logos, in Cyril the Holy Spirit, is definitely that He may consecrate (ἵνα ποιήσῃ...).

The Second Church Order.

The last authority to be cited is the Second Church Order. But though the document itself falls within the period we are considering there can be little doubt that the passage in question has been much developed by later hands and represents a much later date. It is as follows:

§ 65. And thus let the chief priest supplicate over the oblation, that the Holy Spirit may come upon it and make the bread indeed the Body of the Christ and the cup Blood of the Christ.

The modern Coptic rite of St Mark or St Cyril has:

That He may make this bread the holy body of Christ, and this cup also His precious blood of the New Testament, even of our

Lord and our God and our Saviour and the king of us all, Jesus Christ[1].

We have now traced the ἐπίκλησις from the first occurrence of liturgical forms until the time when it attained its final development.

The chief conclusions from our consideration are as follows:

1. The name ἐπίκλησις, in the period we are treating of, is really an anachronism, the liturgy being regarded as a whole in relation to the consecration of the Eucharist, and there being no subdivision of its constituent parts beyond those of proanaphora and anaphora proper.

2. That the purpose of this portion of the liturgy did in process of time undergo a gradual and finally a very definite change until it came to all intents and purposes to be regarded in the East as the actual consecration form.

3. That the date when this change of the original purpose of the ἐπίκλησις began to become general can be placed in the middle of the fourth century, at which time the extant liturgical forms of Sarapion, St Cyril of Jerusalem, and (perhaps slightly later) such a form of liturgy as that represented by the Apostolic Constitutions, were in use.

4. The developed form of ἐπίκλησις as used even down to this present time retains unmistakable evidence of the original purpose of the ἐπίκλησις side by side with its later developed meaning.

On the other hand it is a very largely accepted theory to-day that the ἐπίκλησις was from the first regarded as the prayer for the consecration of the elements. The reference to the Institution that precedes is the recital of the Divine command, the ἐπίκλησις following at once,

[1] Brightman, p. 179.

and praying for the intervention of the Divine power to consecrate, proceeds to obey the Divine command.

Thus Mr W. C. Bishop writes[1]:

On examining these forms of consecration in the Eastern Liturgies, without any preconceived opinion or adventitious aid, it would appear that the words of institution were not recited as of themselves effecting the consecration, but rather as the authority in obedience to which the rite is performed. The priest recites the account of Our Lord's deeds and words at the Institution and then proceeds to some such effect as this: "Therefore we, according to His command, present unto Thee these gifts." Pleading thus the command of Christ, he proceeds to obey this command, at the same time designating the particular elements which are to be used for the purpose; and he then completes the action by beseeching God by His Holy Spirit to make these creatures the body and blood of Christ according to Christ's own word. The people join in his action by saying "Amen," and the consecration is accepted by faith as wrought by God in answer to priest and people. The whole action is intelligible and clear; and it would appear quite as consonant with the general dispensation of grace as set forth in the New Testament to believe that the supernatural gift is bestowed in answer to prayer as to think of it as brought about by the pronunciation of a formula—especially when the formula has no authority for this purpose from Holy Scripture, the words of institution being given in the New Testament as words of administration and not of consecration.

That this is the view of the Eastern Church from the time when the ἐπίκλησις definitely asks for the coming of the Holy Ghost or the Word, that He may make the bread and wine into the body and blood of Christ, is clear.

But in the face of the historical development of the ἐπίκλησις it is impossible to hold that this is the purpose of this form in earliest times; unless indeed the liturgical

[1] "The Primitive Form of Consecration of the Holy Eucharist." The Rev. W. C. Bishop. *C. Q. R.* July, 1908, pp. 392, 393.

remains which are still extant do not represent the general use of the Church. At the same time there is no evidence to show that any one portion of the Anaphora was regarded as effecting the Consecration, but rather the whole Canon would seem to be held as committing the effecting of the Mystery of Mysteries to God.

On the other hand we are not justified, in the face of the use of the definite baptismal formula, in holding that the idea of the Consecration of the Eucharist by a formula would be alien to the mind of the early Church. Indeed, as we have seen, there are grounds for thinking that there was a form of consecration in use which consisted of an adaptation of the baptismal formula to the Eucharist.

As we have seen, the date when the development of the *ἐπίκλησις* into a prayer for the descent of the Word or Holy Spirit for the purpose of effecting the sacramental change in the elements comes into view, is about the middle of the fourth century.

It is interesting to note that this coincides with the date of the later developments of the Arian controversy and the theological consideration of the Person and work of the Holy Spirit.

In the creeds in use after the council of Nicea we see the article of the Holy Ghost gradually developing. In the creed of Cyril of Jerusalem the Holy Spirit is associated with the effecting of the sacrament of Baptism and the function of the Church: *εἰς ἓν ἅγιον πνεῦμα, τὸν παράκλητον, τὸ λαλῆσαν ἐν τοῖς προφήταις. καὶ εἰς ἓν βάπτισμα μετανοίας εἰς ἄφεσιν ἁμαρτιῶν, καὶ εἰς μίαν ἁγίαν καὶ καθολικὴν ἐκκλησίαν κ.τ.λ.*, and the work of the Holy Spirit is more clearly than ever declared as the Giver of spiritual life and grace in the so-called creed of Constantinople, which at any rate may be taken as a representative creed of the Eastern churches at that time.

St Cyril of Jerusalem is enlightening on the subject. It is the Holy Spirit who effects the change in the elements.

παρακαλοῦμεν τὸν φιλάνθρωπον Θεὸν τὸ ἅγιον Πνεῦμα ἐξαποστεῖλαι ἐπὶ τὰ προκείμενα, ἵνα ποιήσῃ τὸν μὲν ἄρτον σῶμα Χριστοῦ, τὸν δὲ οἶνον αἷμα Χριστοῦ. πάντως γὰρ οὗ ἂν ἐφάψηται τὸ ἅγιον Πνεῦμα, τοῦτο ἡγίασται καὶ μεταβέβληται. (C. M. v. 7.)

In the same way St Cyril explains the use of the unction at Baptism. The Holy Spirit sanctifies the oil to this special use. He even ventures to compare this sanctification of the oil with the consecration of the Eucharist.

ὥσπερ γὰρ ὁ ἄρτος τῆς εὐχαριστίας μετὰ τὴν ἐπίκλησιν τοῦ ἁγίου Πνεύματος οὐκ ἔτι ἄρτος λιτὸς ἀλλὰ σῶμα Χριστοῦ, οὕτω καὶ τὸ ἅγιον τοῦτο μύρον οὐκ ἔτι ψιλὸν, οὐδ' ὡς ἂν εἴποι τις κοινὸν μετ' ἐπίκλησιν, ἀλλὰ Χριστοῦ χάρισμα καὶ Πνεύματος παρουσίᾳ τῆς τοῦ θεότητος ἐνεργητικὸν γινόμενον. (C. M. III. 3.)

Also on the water of Baptism[1],

μὴ ὡς ὕδατι λιτῷ πρόσεχε τῷ λουτρῷ...τὸ λιτὸν ὕδωρ Πνεύματος ἁγίου καὶ Χριστοῦ καὶ Πατρὸς τὴν ἐπίκλησιν λαβὸν, δύναμιν ἁγιότητος ἐπικτᾶται. (III. 3.)

An ἐπίκλησις of the Holy Spirit upon the waters of Baptism was probably used from very early times. Scriptural warrant for it would be found in the hovering of the Holy Spirit over the waters at Creation, and in the descent of the Holy Spirit at the Baptism of Our Lord.

Also the doctrinal settlement of the fourth century most probably did much in the developing of the ἐπί-

[1] Tertullian says much the same: "supervenit enim statim Spiritus de caelis et aquis superest, sanctificans eas de semetipso et ita sanctificatae vim sanctificandi combibunt." De bapt. 4.

κλησις. The last phase of the Arian controversy finally resulted in the doctrinal definition of the Person and work of the Holy Spirit.

It is only natural that this doctrinal settlement should have had some influence on that part of the liturgy which deals with the work of the Holy Spirit, with the result that the old prayer for a worthy communion was enlarged by the addition of a direct reference to the sanctifying work of the Holy Spirit in the consecration of the elements, and this addition speedily became the most prominent feature of the prayer, thus effecting the development of the ἐπίκλησις from its primitive purpose into the actual consecrating formula.

And lastly we see even in the developed forms evidences of the original purpose of the ἐπίκλησις.

In the form of Sarapion, which may be taken perhaps as a transitional form, it is true that it is the Λόγος and not the Holy Spirit for whose descent on the elements petition is made. But immediately Sarapion's liturgy proceeds to pray for a good communion of the partakers of the Blessed Sacrament.

St Cyril does not give us the words of the ἐπίκλησις of the liturgy used at Jerusalem. It is true that he regards the prayer for the descent of the Holy Spirit to consecrate the gifts as the essence of it. Still we may perhaps be permitted to believe that if he had given us the words we should have found an equally definite petition contained in them for the communicants.

To pass on to the liturgy of the Apostolic Constitutions[1].

[1] It is very generally held that the liturgy of the A.C. was never a living rite. Whether this is the case or not is not of very great importance. If it is only an example or model it is certainly representative of the actual uses of its time.

ἀξιοῦμέν σε ὅπως...καταπέμψῃς τὸ ἅγιόν σου Πνεῦμα ἐπὶ τὴν θυσίαν ταύτην...ὅπως ἀποφήνῃ[1] τὸν ἄρτον τοῦτον σῶμα τοῦ Χριστοῦ σου καὶ τὸ ποτήριον τοῦτο αἷμα τοῦ Χριστοῦ σου· ἵνα οἱ μεταλαβόντες αὐτοῦ βεβαιωθῶσι πρὸς εὐσέβειαν κ.τ.λ. (VIII. 12.)

Not even here as in Sarapion *ἵνα ποιήσῃ*, but still the chief purpose of the descent of the Holy Spirit *ἵνα οἱ μεταλαβόντες αὐτοῦ βεβαιωθῶσι*. The distinction is clearly marked by the use of *ὅπως* and *ἵνα*.

But indeed when we pass on to the finally developed liturgies, even to those of the present day in the Eastern Church, we find the evidence of the primitive object of the *ἐπίκλησις*, the communicant.

Thus in St James:

τὸ Πνεῦμά σου τὸ πανάγιον κατάπεμψον, δέσποτα, ἐφ' ἡμᾶς καὶ ἐπὶ τὰ προκείμενα ἅγια δῶρα ταῦτα, ἵνα ἐπιφοιτῆσαν τῇ ἁγίᾳ καὶ ἀγαθῇ καὶ ἐνδόξῳ αὐτοῦ παρουσίᾳ ἁγιάσῃ καὶ ποιῇ τὸν μὲν ἄρτον τοῦτον σῶμα ἅγιον Χριστοῦ, καὶ τὸ ποτήριον τοῦτο αἷμα τίμιον Χριστοῦ, ἵνα γένηται πᾶσι τοῖς ἐξ αὐτῶν μεταλαμβάνουσιν εἰς ἄφεσιν ἁμαρτιῶν καὶ εἰς ζωὴν αἰώνιον, εἰς ἁγιασμὸν ψυχῶν καὶ σωμάτων κ.τ.λ.

Here the presence of the Holy Spirit is sought on the people equally as on the gifts. The original sole purpose of the *ἐπίκλησις* and the later development are placed side by side.

In the liturgy of the Nestorians, probably as old as that of St James, owing to the omission, in text at least, of the words of institution[2], one might have expected a great development of the *ἐπίκλησις*.

[1] In connexion with this use of *ἀποφαίνω* it is interesting to compare the apparently Antiochene Coptic Liturgy of St Basil. There, in the words "that He may...manifest them," ⲛ̄ⲧⲉϥⲟⲩⲟⲛϩⲟⲩ ⲉⲃⲟⲗ represent exactly *ἵνα ἀποφήνῃ*.

[2] I may be perhaps permitted to state my own view in this matter. That is, that the omission of the words of institution from this liturgy is of comparatively recent date.

And may there come, O my Lord, Thine Holy Spirit, and rest upon this offering of Thy servants, and bless it and hallow it, that it be to us, O my Lord, for the pardon of offences, and the remission of sins, etc.[1]

Here the ἐπίκλησις reminds us of that in the liturgy of the First Church Order, "et petimus ut mittas Spiritum tuum sanctum in oblationem sanctae ecclesiae, in unum congregans des omnibus qui percipiunt, etc."

There is no reference even to the Holy Spirit effecting the sacramental change in the elements.

In the liturgies of St Basil and St Chrysostom in the ninth century[2] it is the same:

St Basil

δεόμεθα καὶ σὲ παρακαλοῦμεν ἅγιε ἁγίων εὐδοκίᾳ τῆς σῆς ἀγαθότητος ἐλθεῖν τὸ Πνεῦμά σου τὸ Παναγιον ἐφ' ἡμᾶς καὶ ἐπὶ τὰ προκείμενα δῶρα ταῦτα καὶ εὐλογῆσαι αὐτὰ καὶ ἁγιάσαι καὶ ἀναδεῖξαι τὸν μὲν ἄρτον τοῦτον αὐτὸ τὸ τίμιον σῶμα τοῦ Κυρίου...τὸ δὲ ποτήριον τοῦτο αὐτὸ τὸ τίμιον αἷμα τοῦ Κυρίου...ἡμᾶς δὲ πάντας τοὺς ἐκ τοῦ ἑνὸς ἄρτου καὶ τοῦ ποτηρίου μετέχοντας ἑνῶσαι ἀλλήλοις εἰς ἑνὸς Πνεύματος ἁγίου κοινωνίαν καὶ μηδένα ἡμῶν εἰς κρίμα ἢ εἰς κατάκριμα κ.τ.λ.

St Chrysostom

παρακαλοῦμεν καὶ δεόμεθα καὶ ἱκετεύομεν κατάπεμψον τὸ Πνεῦμά σου τὸ Ἅγιον ἐφ' ἡμᾶς καὶ ἐπὶ τὰ προκείμενα ταῦτα καὶ ποίησον τὸν μὲν ἄρτον τοῦτον τίμιον σῶμα Χριστοῦ σου μεταβαλὼν τῷ πνεύματί σου τῷ ἁγίῳ, τὸ δὲ ἐν τῷ ποτηρίῳ τούτῳ τίμιον αἷμα τοῦ Χριστοῦ σου μεταβαλὼν τῷ πνεύματί σου τῷ ἁγίῳ, ὥστε γενέσθαι τοῖς μεταλαμβάνουσιν εἰς νῆψιν ψυχῆς κ.τ.λ.

In both of these late liturgies the purpose of the ἐπίκλησις is twofold. In St Basil the *τὸν μὲν ἄρτον... ἡμᾶς δὲ πάντας*, in St Chrysostom the *τὸν μὲν ἄρτον...ὥστε γενέσθαι τοῖς μεταλαμβάνουσιν*, show that the ἐπίκλησις is a prayer for the presence of the Holy Spirit in the

[1] Brightman, p. 287.

[2] Brightman, pp. 329, 330.

communion of the people as much as for the consecration of the elements. The liturgy of St Chrysostom in use at the present day[1] has in the ἐπίκλησις almost the same words as in the ninth century.

Note A. St Paul 1 *Cor. xi.*

It would appear from St Paul's words that in celebrating the Eucharist he referred to the Institution and most probably recited the words of institution, a use not of his own invention but a *παράδοσις* which he received.

His solemn words of warning as to the disposition of the communicant are very like a reminiscence of a following *ἐπίκλησις* or prayer for the communicants:

v. 27. *ὥστε ὃς ἂν ἐσθίῃ τὸν ἄρτον ἢ πίνῃ τὸ ποτήριον ἀναξίως ἔνοχος ἔσται τοῦ σώματος καὶ τοῦ αἵματος τοῦ Κυρίου.*

28. *δοκιμαζέτω δὲ ἄνθρωπος ἑαυτὸν καὶ οὕτως ἐκ τοῦ ἄρτου ἐσθιέτω καὶ ἐκ τοῦ ποτηρίου πινέτω.*

29. *ὁ γὰρ ἐσθίων καὶ πίνων, κρίμα ἑαυτῷ ἐσθίει καὶ πίνει μὴ διακρίνων τὸ σῶμα.*

Compare Justin's words (Apol. I. 65) *ἀναπέμπει καὶ εὐχαριστίαν ὑπὲρ τοῦ κατηξιῶσθαι τούτων παρ' αὐτοῦ ἐπὶ πολὺ ποιεῖται*, and the Acta Johannis c. 110 *ἐπέδωκεν πᾶσιν ἡμῖν ἑκάστῳ τῶν ἀδελφῶν ἐπευχόμενος ἄξιον ἔσεσθαι αὐτὸν τῆς τοῦ Κυρίου χάριτος καὶ τῆς ἁγιωτάτης εὐχαριστίας.*

v. 30. *διὰ τοῦτο ἐν ὑμῖν πολλοὶ ἀσθενεῖς καὶ ἄρρωστοι.* Compare "ad confirmationem fidei in veritate" of the First Church Order (Veron. fragments) and similar words in the *ἐπίκλησις* generally.

We have seen that there were probably at the first several divergent uses in the consecration of the Eucharist, and of these the Scriptural use (*i.e.* that containing at least a reference to the words of institution and followed by an *ἐπίκλησις*) had by the end of the second century displaced entirely the other uses.

This Scriptural use in its entirety, reference to the Institution and *ἐπίκλησις*, was it would seem the apostolic use, or at least the use of the apostle Paul.

[1] Brightman, p. 387.

Note B. The ἐπίκλησις in the Roman rite

"It is very commonly said that there is a radical difference of opinion between the eastern and western portions of the church as to the 'form,' i.e. the form of words, that must be used in the consecration of the holy Eucharist, the west in general regarding the consecration as effected by the use of the words of institution, the east regarding it as an answer to the prayer of invocation[1]."

Perhaps it may also be said that it is commonly believed that there is a radical difference in the structure of the Roman and Eastern rites underlying this difference of opinion as to the consecrating form, the Eastern liturgies all containing an ἐπίκλησις and the Roman none. It is true that in the later Eastern sense there is no invocation in the Latin rite, but there still remains in that rite, imbedded in other matter, the ancient ἐπίκλησις of the primitive Church. The chief distinction between the Alexandrian and Antiochene families of the Eastern rite lies in the fact that in the former of these two families the intercession for the living and the dead occurs before the consecration, in the latter after the consecration. In the Latin rite the intercession is divided into two parts, of which the "commemoratio pro vivis" occurs before, the "commemoratio pro defunctis" after the consecration. Between the Anamnesis and the "commemoratio pro defunctis," that is between the Anamnesis and (part of) the Intercession, in the place where the primitive ἐπίκλησις occurs, the following obscure form appears:

"supra quae propitio ac sereno vultu respicere digneris: et accepta habere, sicuti accepta habere dignatus es munera pueri tui iusti Abel et sacrificium patriarchae nostri Abrahae, et quod tibi obtulit summus sacerdos tuus Melchisedech, sanctum sacrificium, immaculatam hostiam. Supplices te rogamus, Omnipotens Deus: iube haec perferri per manus Angeli tui in sublime altare tuum, in conspectu divinae Maiestatis tuae: ut quotquot ex hac altaris participatione sacrosanctum Filii tui Corpus et Sanguinem sumpserimus, omni benedictione caelesti et gratia repleamur. Per eundem Christum Dominum nostrum."

From this form we can extract the ancient ἐπίκλησις:

[1] "The Primitive Form of Consecration of the Holy Eucharist." W. C. Bishop. *C. Q. R.* no. 132, p. 385.

"Supplices te rogamus, Omnipotens Deus, ut quotquot ex hac altaris participatione sacrosanctum Filii tui Corpus et Sanguinem sumpserimus, omni benedictione caelesti et gratia repleamur, per eundem Christum Dominum nostrum."

In the oldest known form of the Roman Canon, that contained in the de Sacramentis, of the part of this form that is given the only differences are "ut hanc oblationem suscipias" for "iube haec perferri" and "angelorum tuorum" for "Angeli tui."

The Alexandrian liturgy of St Mark throws light on the curious arrangement and obscurity of this Roman form. In the intercession in St Mark's liturgy, following on that part of the Intercession which is the "commemoratio pro defunctis," the "commemoratio pro vivis" commences thus:

τῶν προσφερόντων τὰς θυσίας, τὰς προσφορὰς, τὰ εὐχαριστήρια πρόσδεξαι, ὁ Θεὸς; εἰς τὸ ἅγιον καὶ ἐπουράνιον καὶ νοερόν σου θυσιαστήριον εἰς τὰ μεγέθη τῶν οὐρανῶν διὰ τῆς ἀρχαγγελικῆς σου λειτουργίας τῶν τὸ πολὺ καὶ ὀλίγον, κρύφα καὶ παρρησίᾳ, βουλομένων καὶ οὐκ ἐχόντων καὶ τῶν ἐν τῇ σήμερον ἡμέρᾳ τὰς προσφορὰς προσενεγκάντων, ὡς προσεδέξω τὰ δῶρα τοῦ δικαίου σου Ἄβελ, τὴν θυσίαν τοῦ πατρὸς ἡμῶν Ἀβραάμ, Ζαχαρίου τὸ θυμίαμα, Κορνηλίου τὰς ἐλεημοσύνας κ.τ.λ.

In a much simpler and shorter form the same petition for the offerers occurs in the "commemoratio pro vivis" in the Intercession of Sarapion's liturgy.

δέξαι δὲ καὶ τὴν εὐχαριστίαν τοῦ λαοῦ καὶ εὐλόγησον τοὺς προσενεγκόντας τὰ πρόσφορα καὶ τὰς εὐχαριστίας.

Here we have the explanation of the submersion of the Roman *ἐπίκλησις*. It has been thrust almost out of sight by the rearrangement of the dislocated Intercession. Once the Intercession "pro vivis" (closing with a petition for those who offer) and "pro defunctis" occurred in the earlier part of the Canon before the consecration. In the rearrangement, from whatever motive, the "commemoratio pro vivis" was left in its place, except for the prayer for those who offered, which with the "commemoratio pro defunctis" was put after the *ἐπίκλησις*. Then it seems that the petition for the offerers was taken to refer to the consecrated elements and it was worked into the *ἐπίκλησις*, quite obscuring the latter.

In the Mozarabic liturgy which is probably at least influenced by the early Roman liturgy, we find the petition for offerers apparently already almost incomprehensible, but still before the consecration.

"Adesto, adesto, Jesu bone pontifex, in medio nostri sicut fuisti in medio discipulorum tuorum: sanctifica hanc oblationem (cf. form in the de Sacramentis) ut sanctificata sumamus per manus sancti Angeli tui, sancte Domine ac Redemptor Eterne."

And then follows at once the consecration.

In the Liturgy of St Mark there is no doubt as to the meaning of this petition for the offerers, but in its present position in the Roman Mass it is almost unintelligible and has long been a difficulty to explain[1]. It is probably based on the passage in the Apocalypse (viii. 3, 4) *καὶ ἄλλος ἄγγελος ἦλθεν καὶ ἐστάθη ἐπὶ τοῦ θυσιαστηρίου ἔχων λιβανωτὸν χρυσοῦν, καὶ ἐδόθη αὐτῷ θυμιάματα πολλά, ἵνα δώσει ταῖς προσευχαῖς τῶν ἁγίων πάντων ἐπὶ τὸ θυσιαστήριον τὸ χρυσοῦν τὸ ἐνώπιον τοῦ θρόνου.*

Thus the Roman rite far from being radically different from the Eastern rites in having no ἐπίκλησις, not only has an ἐπίκλησις, though unfortunately much obscured in its present position, but a form much older and more primitive than any Eastern liturgy that has been used later than the fourth century.

Additional Note

In his appendix to Dom Conolly's "Homilies of Narsai" Mr Edmund Bishop deals with the Epiklesis in the Roman rite (pp. 129 ff.). He is not willing to see in the "supplices te rogamus" the parallel form to the Eastern Invocation, inasmuch as there is no invocation on the elements in the Latin form. On the other hand there is such an invocation on the elements in the prayer preceding the words of Institution, "quam oblationem tu Deus in omnibus, quaesumus, benedictam adscriptam, ratam, rationabilem acceptabilemque facere digneris: ut nobis Corpus et Sanguis fiat dilectissimi Filii tui Domini nostri Jesu Christi." In this he would see the parallel to the Eastern Epiklesis. Of this form Mr Bishop says (p. 133) that it is "a passage which, turn it as we will, is an invocation, and even its object is expressly stated." "Benedictam... facere" he points out = "to bless," though the next four words he admits to be unintelligible.

[1] For example, in the eighteenth century Le Brun shows from his language that he is not at all certain of the meaning of it, though he offers an explanation. "On a été fort longtemps," he says, "sans développer le sens de cette admirable prière." Explic. de la Messe, I. 515.

But as a matter of fact does not the "nobis" point to the object of the prayer? May not the insertion of this one word make the whole passage refer not to the Consecration but to the communion of the people? As has been pointed out, even in the developed Epiklesis of the Eastern churches the ἐφ' ἡμᾶς lingering on before the elements are mentioned seems to be the last sign of the original purpose of the Epiklesis. Is not the "nobis" in this form parallel to the ἐφ' ἡμᾶς in the Eastern form?[1]

But we have tried to show in tracing the development of the Epiklesis that the present form and purpose of the Eastern prayer is fundamentally different from what it was originally. And so in one way the use of the technical name Epiklesis for this part of the liturgy is really inconvenient. If by "Epiklesis" we confine ourselves to the later Eastern view and mean Invocation of the Holy Spirit, or of the Power of God in any way, on the elements for the effecting of the sacramental change, then the "supplices te rogamus" is not an Epiklesis at all, while the "quam oblationem" perhaps is.

But if we can disabuse our minds of the later Eastern meaning, and still use the word Epiklesis (and there is no other term) of this form which in the East has in process of time undergone such a great transformation; then we find in the Roman rite two such forms, one before the words of institution, and one in the position it occupies in the Eastern rite. This reduplicated Epiklesis already appears in the liturgy by the time of Pseudo-Ambrose. We can only conjecture that, originally alternative forms, both at length became absorbed into the rite. We have seen that in the liturgies of the Ethiopic Church Order and of the Testamentum Domini there appear to be alternative forms of Epiklesis actually side by side and regarded as one. In the Roman rite the fact that the alternative forms have come to occupy different positions makes the adoption of the two together more easy to understand and explain.

[1] So Billot (de Eccles. Sacramentis) whom Mr Bishop quotes (p. 152). The Eastern Epiklesis is found in the Roman Canon "aequipollenter," *viz.* in the Quam oblationem... Nor in our "quam oblationem" do we pray "ut oblatio fiat corpus et sanguis, sed ut *nobis* fiat, scilicet cum effectu salutari...per Dei gratiam......." The effect of the prayer "quam oblationem" then is: "uti...impleatur Eucharistiae mysterium non in eorum (sc. fidelium) judicium et condemnationem, sed in salutem atque utilitatem."

Note C. On the position of the ἐπίκλησις

The normal position of the ἐπίκλησις is after the reference to the Institution and the anamnesis.

There are some grounds for believing that this was not the invariable position. If the purpose of the form was to pray for a good communion of the faithful there is no reason why it should not precede the recital of the account of the Institution, as does our prayer of humble access which has the same object.

In the εὐχὴ of Sarapion just before the account of the Institution occur these words: Κύριε τῶν δυνάμεων, πλήρωσον καὶ τὴν θυσίαν ταύτην τῆς σῆς δυνάμεως καὶ τῆς σῆς μεταλήψεως. Is this the remnant of an ἐπίκλησις occurring before the recital of the words of Institution, and alternative to the ἐπίκλησις of the Logos which follows them?

In the same way do the words of the Roman liturgy, "quam oblationem tu Deus in omnibus, quaesumus, benedictam adscriptam, ratam, rationabilem acceptabilemque facere digneris: ut nobis Corpus et Sanguis fiat dilectissimi Filii tui Domini nostri Jesu Christi," hint at a form of ἐπίκλησις occurring here, as an alternative or earlier use? Such alternative forms or at least positions for the form might explain the almost disappearance of the ἐπίκλησις at the time of the new arrangement of the Intercession.

But most marked is the passage[1] immediately preceding the words of institution in that same Liturgy of St Mark which throws such light on the Roman rite:

πλήρωσον ὁ Θεὸς καὶ ταύτην τὴν θυσίαν τῆς παρὰ σοῦ εὐλογίας διὰ τῆς ἐπιφοιτήσεως τοῦ παναγίου σου πνεύματος.

These words recall at once the words of Sarapion.

In some recently discovered fragments[2] of an Alexandrian liturgy the fact of the occurrence of the ἐπίκλησις before the words of institution in some liturgies seems to have been settled beyond

[1] Brightman, p. 132.

[2] Fragments inédits d'une liturgie égyptienne écrits sur papyrus, par Dom Pierre de Puniet. These texts were first published in the Report of the nineteenth Eucharistic Congress, 1909. The text is also to be found in the "Dictionnaire d'archéologie chrétienne et de liturgie," s. v. Canon.

question, that is, if these fragments have been paged in the right order[1].

The fragment is as follows:

Recto.]a

...σοὶ παραστήκουσιν κ[ύκλῳ τὰ σεραφὶμ ἓξ πτέρυγ]ες τῷ ἑνὶ κ[αὶ ἓ]ξ [πτέρυγες τῷ ἑνί]. καὶ ταῖς μὲν δυσὶ[ν κατεκά]λυπτον τὸ πρόσωπον καὶ τ[αῖς δυσὶ]ν τοὺς πόδας καὶ ταῖς δυσὶ[ν ἐπέτα]ντο. πάντα δὲ πάντοτε σὲ ἁγ[ιάζει]. ἀλλὰ μετὰ πάντων σὲ τῶν ἁγιαζόντων δέξαι καὶ τὸν ἡμέτερον ἁγιασμὸν λε[γ]όντων σοὶ Ἅγιος ἅγιος ἅγιος Κύριος σαβαώθ, πλήρης ὁ οὐρανὸς καὶ ἡ γῆ τῆς δόξ[η]ς σου. πλήρωσον καὶ ἡμᾶς τῆς παρ[ὰ σοὶ] δόξης. [κα]ὶ καταξίωσον κατ[απ]έμψαι τὸ πνεῦμα τ[ὸ ἅ]γιόν σου ἐπὶ τὰ κτίσματα ταῦτα [καὶ ποίησ]ον τὸν μὲν ἄρτον σῶμα τ[οῦ κυρίου καὶ] σωτῆρος ἡμῶν Ἰησοῦ Χριστοῦ [τὸ] δὲ π[οτήριον α]ἷμα τῆς καινῆς...

Verso.

[διαθήκης. ὅτι ὁ κύριος ἡμῶν Ἰησοῦς Χριστὸς τῇ νυκ]τ[ὶ ᾗ παρεδίδοτο λαβὼν ἄρτον εὐχαρισ]τήσα[ς] κ[αὶ εὐλογήσας ἔκλασεν καὶ ἔδωκεν] τοῖς μα[θηταῖς αὐτοῦ καὶ ἀποστό]λοι[ς] εἰπὼν λ[άβετε φάγετε πάντες ἐ]ξ αὐτοῦ. τοῦτό μ[ου ἐστὶν] τὸ σῶμα τὸ ὑπὲρ ὑμῶν διδ[όμενο]ν εἰς ἄφεσιν ἁμαρτιῶν. ὁμο[ίως με]τὰ τὸ δειπνῆσαι λαβὼν ποτήριο[ν] κ[αὶ ε]ὐλογήσας καὶ πιὼν ἔδωκεν αὐτοῖς εἰπὼν λάβετε πίετε πάντες ἐξ αὐτοῦ τοῦτό μου ἐστὶν τὸ αἷμα τὸ ὑπὲρ ὑμῶν ἐκχυννόμενον εἰς ἄφεσιν ἁμαρτιῶν. ὁ[σάκις] ἐὰν ἐσθίητε τὸν ἄρτον τοῦτον πί[νη]τε δὲ τὸ ποτήριον [το]ῖτο τὸν ἐμὸν θάνατον καταγ[γέλ]λεται τὴν ἐμὴν ἀνάμν[ησιν ὁμολογ]εῖτε. τὸν θάνατόν σου κ[αταγγέλλ]ομεν τὴν ἀνάστασίν [σου ὁμολογοῦμ]εν καὶ δεόμεθα τ...

This fragment seems to settle the question definitely and to show that even in times no longer primitive the order of the component parts of the liturgy may not have been so definitely fixed as we are in the habit of thinking[2].

[1] Dom Puniet says: "le texte permet ici de discerner avec certitude le recto du feuillet: le trisagion transcrit de ce côté doit sûrement précéder les paroles d'institution reproduites au verso; l'ordre inverse serait inadmissible." Report, p. 397.

[2] Also it is a curious vindication of the correct liturgical instinct of the English reformers. The position of the invocation in the contemned first Prayer Book has after all ancient precedent.

The Intercession

In earliest days the ἐπίκλησις closed with an intercession for all members of the Church and for the departed, and then followed the communion.

Owing to its varying character, according to the needs and circumstances of each church locally, we find that the form is left unfixed for some time after the rest of the Canon.

Thus in the earliest state of the First Church Order the model Canon stops short at the end of the ἐπίκλησις.

In the somewhat later form of the First Church Order the Testament of Our Lord, the Intercession appears for the first time, and is inserted into the middle of the ἐπίκλησις, if the concluding part of the ἐπίκλησις is not really an alternative form[1]. It is as follows:

> Sustain unto the end those who have gifts of revelations. Confirm those who have a gift of healing. Make those courageous who have the power of tongues. Keep those who have the word of doctrine upright. Care for those who do Thy will alway. Visit the widows. Help the orphans. Remember those who have fallen asleep in the faith. And grant us an inheritance with Thy saints, and bestow [upon us] the power to please Thee as they also pleased Thee. Feed the people in uprightness: and sanctify us all, O God.

This is the earliest intercession that we know. It seems to be a general or model type. There is no special or local need or circumstance of the Christian Community referred to. Such needs or circumstances would be temporary and variable and the celebrant would insert such petitions in his own words. But it is only the Christian Community that is prayed for. There is no mention of Emperors or governors or of any civil officials.

[1] See p. 104 note.

Sarapion.

The Intercession in Sarapion's liturgy follows immediately after the *ἐπίκλησις*.

παρακαλοῦμεν δὲ καὶ ὑπὲρ πάντων τῶν κεκοιμημένων, ὧν ἐστιν καὶ ἡ ἀνάμνησις... (μετὰ τὴν ὑποβολὴν τῶν ὀνομάτων.) ἁγίασον τὰς ψυχὰς ταύτας· σὺ γὰρ πάσας γινώσκεις. ἁγίασον πάσας τὰς ἐν Κυρίῳ κοιμηθείσας. καὶ συγκαταρίθμησον πάσαις ταῖς ἁγίαις σου δυνάμεσιν καὶ δὸς αὐτοῖς τόπον καὶ μονὴν ἐν τῇ βασιλείᾳ σου· δέξαι δὲ καὶ τὴν εὐχαριστίαν τοῦ λαοῦ καὶ εὐλόγησον τοὺς προσενεγκόντας τὰ πρόσφορα καὶ τὰς εὐχαριστίας, καὶ χάρισαι ὑγείαν καὶ ὁλοκληρίαν καὶ εὐθυμίαν καὶ πᾶσαν προκοπὴν ψυχῆς καὶ σώματος ὅλῳ τῷ λαῷ τούτῳ διὰ τοῦ μονογενοῦς σου Ἰησοῦ Χριστοῦ ἐν ἁγίῳ Πνεύματι. ὥσπερ ἦν καὶ ἐστὶν καὶ ἔσται εἰς γενεὰς γενεῶν καὶ εἰς τοὺς σύμπαντας αἰῶνας τῶν αἰώνων. ἀμήν.

Here we find prayer for the departed, with a recital of the names of those remembered. Prayer for the acceptance of the worship of the people. For those who have provided the elements of bread and wine for use in the Eucharist. For the spiritual well-being of the Christian Community generally.

Here again there is no sign of prayer for the Emperor or public officials, but only for the Christian Church.

St Cyril of Jerusalem describes the Intercession of the Church of Jerusalem.

παρακαλοῦμεν τὸν θεὸν ὑπὲρ κοινῆς τῶν ἐκκλησιῶν εἰρήνης, ὑπὲρ τῆς τοῦ κόσμου εὐσταθείας, ὑπὲρ βασιλέων, ὑπὲρ στρατιωτῶν καὶ συμμάχων, ὑπὲρ τῶν ἐν ἀσθενείαις, ὑπὲρ τῶν καταπονουμένων, καὶ ἁπαξαπλῶς ὑπὲρ πάντων βοηθείας δεομένων δεόμεθα πάντες ἡμεῖς καὶ ταύτην προσφέρομεν τὴν θυσίαν. εἶτα μνημονεύομεν καὶ τῶν κεκοιμημένων, πρῶτον πατριαρχῶν προφητῶν ἀποστόλων μαρτύρων, ὅπως ὁ Θεὸς ταῖς εὐχαῖς αὐτῶν καὶ πρεσβείαις προσδέξηται ἡμῶν τὴν δέησιν. εἶτα καὶ ὑπὲρ τῶν προκεκοιμημένων ἁγίων πατέρων καὶ ἐπισκόπων καὶ πάντων ἁπλῶς τῶν ἐν ἡμῖν προκεκοιμημένων, μεγίστην ὄνησιν πιστεύοντες ἔσεσθαι ταῖς ψυχαῖς ὑπὲρ ὧν ἡ δέησις ἀναφέρεται τῆς ἁγίας καὶ φρικωδεστάτης προκειμένης θυσίας.

Here we have the first reference to the Emperors since Justin and Tertullian refer to the custom of the Christians of praying for the Emperor. Indeed Cyril's language is very close to Tertullian's[1]:

"precantes sumus omnes semper pro omnibus imperatoribus, vitam illis prolixam, imperium securum, domum tutam, exercitus fortes, senatum fidelem, populum probum, orbem quietum."

Next the intercession includes petitions for special cases (*ὑπὲρ πάντων βοηθείας δεομένων*)[2].

Then the Saints and Martyrs are commemorated, then Bishops and clergy, then the faithful departed of the local community (*ἐν ἡμῖν*).

The Intercession, then, on the evidence of the earliest documents, came originally after the *ἐπίκλησις*.

In the Testament of Our Lord and in Sarapion it is noticeable that it is only the Christian Community that is prayed for. In St Cyril the names of the Emperors appear and the Church prays for the peace of the Empire and all things connected with it.

Probably the explanation is that Cyril's liturgy, so far as the Intercession is concerned, shows the use of the Church after the time of the Christian Emperors, while certainly the Testament of our Lord, and perhaps the liturgy of Sarapion, represent a period before this time. If so, in the Eucharist the Christian Community only was prayed for. Now Tertullian and Justin both tell us that Christians prayed for the Emperor. If so, are they referring to the Intercession in the Eucharist or not? Probably not.

As we have seen, in early times the Sunday Morning

[1] Apol. 30.

[2] Was the next sentence originally a petition for the offerers? Perhaps it was originally *καὶ ὑπὲρ τῶν ταύτην προσφερομένων τὴν θυσίαν*.

Service was distinct from the Eucharist, though probably it normally preceded it. The "Morning Service" always concludes with prayers or intercessions. It is probably these prayers and intercessions to which Justin and Tertullian refer when asserting that the Church prayed for the Emperors. The Eucharist was distinctively the Christian service for Christians only, and the exclusion of the Emperor and civil power from the Eucharistic Intercession would be in keeping with the exclusiveness, so far as the heathen were concerned, of the early Church[1].

But when in process of time the "Morning Service" became attached to the Eucharistic liturgy and became the Proanaphora, as a consequence there appeared two Intercessions in the liturgy, the first coming at the end of the Proanaphora the second in the old place after the *ἐπίκλησις*.

Perhaps here may be found an explanation of the difference of position of the Intercession in the Alexandrian and Antiochene families of the Eastern rite.

The liturgy proper began with the kiss of peace, but after the union of the Morning Service with the Eucharist the commencement of the Anaphora is not clearly marked. Thus in the liturgy of the Apostolic Constitutions the beginning of the Anaphora is put back into the middle of the Intercessions which form the concluding portion of the old "Morning Service." The intercessions for the catechumens, for the energumens, for the *φωτιζόμενοι*, for the

[1] As all non-Christians were permitted to be present at the "Morning Service" or missa catechumenorum, but were rigidly excluded from the Eucharist, so it would seem that even prayers for those who were not Christians were excluded from the Christian Mysteries. I think it would not be hard to find parallels to such a spirit of exclusiveness (if our view is correct) elsewhere in the history of the Early Church.

penitents still remain in the Proanaphora, while the general intercessions for the faithful are drawn into the Anaphora. The liturgy of the Apostolic Constitutions is content with this duplication of the Intercession.

In St James the Intercessions of the old morning service have all been drawn into the "Missa fidelium" though in a very much shortened form. They have also lost something of their character as Intercessions and assumed something of the nature of a preparation for the Eucharist. The full Eucharistic Intercession remains in its proper position after the ἐπίκλησις. In the Alexandrian rite the intercesssions of the old morning service are also drawn into the "Missa fidelium," yet they are short and the Eucharistic Intercession proper is transferred from the ancient position into the preface or thanksgiving. Probably this is due to an attempt to unite the two intercessions into one though the union has been left incomplete.

In the Roman rite the Alexandrian use seems to have been carried out and the Eucharistic Intercession transferred and placed before the Consecration, to the exclusion altogether of the proanaphoral intercessions. Or perhaps it was for this purpose that the separation of the Intercession in that rite was made, and the "commemoratio pro vivis" was brought to the earlier part of the Canon while the remaining "Commemoratio pro defunctis" was left in its old place, with the unfortunate result, as we have seen, of submerging and obscuring altogether the ancient ἐπίκλησις of the Roman liturgy.

It is probably the presence of the Intercessions in the original Proanaphora that have caused the transference of the Eucharistic intercession into the preface or thanksgiving of the Alexandrian rite, though not altogether doing away with the proanaphoral Intercessions, while the Antiochene liturgies were content to have the double intercession each in its original place, though the proanaphoral Intercessions have tended to become much shorter and unimportant.

(3) *The Communion and Dismissal*

The communion of the people with a thanksgiving and dismissal followed after the Intercession.

This concluding part of the liturgy was perhaps the last portion to be fixed.

The words of administration seem to have been on the one hand based on Our Lord's own words of administration and on the other hand to have been a personal application of the prayer of the ἐπίκλησις to each particular communicant.

The words of St Paul, "whosoever shall eat this bread and drink this cup of the Lord unworthily shall be guilty of the body and blood of the Lord," seem to point to such words of administration as "the Body of the Lord," "the Blood" or "cup of the Lord."

In the Acts of John (c. 110) there is on the other hand a sort of combination of the ἐπίκλησις with the words of administration whatever they were, or as I have said a sort of personal application of the prayer of the ἐπίκλησις to the individual communicant.

καὶ κλάσας τὸν ἄρτον ἐπέδωκεν πᾶσιν ἡμῖν, ἑκάστῳ τῶν ἀδελφῶν ἐπευχόμενος ἄξιον ἔσεσθαι αὐτὸν τῆς τοῦ Κυρίου χάριτος καὶ τῆς ἁγιωτάτης εὐχαριστίας. γευσάμενος δὲ καὶ αὐτὸς ὁμοίως καὶ εἰρηκὼς Κἀμοὶ μέρος ἔστω μεθ' ὑμῶν...

Then immediately the Eucharist seems to end with the dismissal εἰρήνη μεθ' ὑμῶν ἀγαπητοί.

This passage shows that there were some words of administration though they are not given.

We find the words of administration in the Acts of Thomas to be of the same character as in the Acts of John, namely a personal application of the ἐπίκλησις.

And he gave first to the woman and said to her: "Let it be unto thee for remission of transgressions and sins, and for the everlasting resurrection."

And after her he gave to the persons who were baptized with her. Then he gave to every one, and said: "Let this Eucharist be unto you for life and rest and not for judgement and vengeance."

And they said "Amen[1]."

Then two varying forms of administration are given at the same celebration of the Eucharist, an example of the freedom that was given to the celebrant.

Again in the same Acts:

He laid his hand on them, and broke the Eucharist, and gave unto all of them, and said unto them: "Let this Eucharist be unto you for grace and mercy, and not for judgement and vengeance."

And they said, "Amen[2]."

And much the same in another passage:

And he brake the Eucharist and gave...and said:

"Let this Eucharist be to you for life and rest and joy and health and for the healing of your souls and bodies."

And they said "Amen."

The liturgical forms of the earliest text of the First Church Order stop short, as we have seen, with the ἐπίκλησις. In the description a little later in the Baptismal ceremonies the words of administration in the Eucharist that follows are given. It must be borne in mind that this is not a normal case, and there is certainly

[1] Act. Thom. A in app. of texts. Wright II. p. 190.

[2] Ib. B. Wright, p. 169.

some confusion of the sacramental cup with the milk and honey which was given to the newly baptized.

And when the Bishop therefore has now broken the bread, let him give a piece to each one of them saying: "This is the bread of heaven, the Body of the Christ Jesus." Let him who receives answer "Hamen."... Let him who gives the cup say: "This is the blood of Jesus Christ Our Lord." And he who receives also shall answer "Hamen[1]."

In the somewhat later Ethiopic text of the First Order, the Communion is considerably amplified and more fixed.

And the deacon shall say: Let us attend.

And the bishop shall say: Holiness to holy ones.

And the people shall say: One Holy Father, one Holy Son, one is the Holy Spirit[2].

The bishop shall say: The Lord (be) with you all.

And the people shall say: With thy spirit.

And then they shall lift up their hands for glorifying, and the people shall come in for the salvation of their souls, in order that their sin may be remitted.

The prayer after that they have communicated.

God Almighty, the Father of the Lord and our Saviour Jesus Christ, we give Thee thanks, because Thou hast imparted to us the reception of the Holy Mystery; let it not be for guilt or condemnation, but for the renewal of soul and body and spirit, through Thine only Son, through Whom to Thee with Him and with the Holy Spirit (be) glory and might now and always and for ever and ever. Amen.

And the people shall say: Amen.

And the presbyter shall say (the prayer of) laying on of hands after they have received.

Eternal God, Almighty, the Father of the Lord and our Saviour Jesus Christ, bless Thy servants and Thy handmaids; protect and help and prosper (them) by the power of Thine Archangel. Keep and confirm in them Thy fear by[3] Thy greatness. Provide[3] that they shall both think what is Thine, and believe what is Thine,

[1] Horner, p. 319. For variations of text see Appendix of texts.

[2] *Or* "the Father is Holy, the Son Holy, and the Spirit Holy."

[3–3] The text is probably corrupt and the meaning is doubtful.

and will what is Thine. Grant to them peace without sin and anger: through Thine only Son, through Whom to Thee with Him and with the Holy Spirit be glory and might, now and always, and for ever and ever. Amen.

And the people shall say: Amen.

And the bishop shall say: The Lord (be) with you all.

And the people shall say: With thy spirit.

And the deacon shall say: Go in peace.

The most noticeable point in this form of communion is that there are no words of administration given. These are perhaps referred to in the rubric, "the people shall come in for the salvation of their souls, in order that their sin may be remitted," and presuppose some such form as "Let this be unto thee for the salvation of thy soul and for remission of sins."

But more probably there were no words of administration properly speaking, but the prayer "after that they have communicated," following immediately on the delivery of the Sacrament, supplies their place.

The Testament of Our Lord.

The deacon: Earnestly let us beseech our Lord and our God that He may bestow upon us concord of spirit.

The bishop. Give us concord in the Holy Spirit and heal our souls by this offering, that we may live in Thee in all the ages of the ages.

The people: Amen.

Let the people also pray in the same [words].

After these things the seal of the thanksgiving thus: Let the name of the Lord be blessed for ever.

The people: Amen.

The priest: Blessed is He that hath come (*or* cometh B) in the name of the Lord. Blessed [is] the name of His praise.

And let all the people say: So be it, so be it.

Let the bishop say: Send the grace of the Spirit upon us.

....

Let each one when he receiveth the thanksgiving, say before he partaketh: Amen

After that let him pray thus; after[1] *that he receiveth the Eucharist let him say*:

Holy, Holy, Holy, Trinity ineffable, grant me to receive unto life this Body, [and] not unto condemnation. And grant me to bring forth the fruits that are pleasing to Thee, so that when I shall be shown to be pleasing to Thee, I may live in Thee, doing Thy commandments; and [that] with boldness I may call Thee Father, when I call for Thy kingdom, and Thy will [to come] to me. May Thy name be hallowed in me, O Lord; for Thou art mighty and [to be] praised, and to Thee be praise for ever and ever. Amen.

After the prayer let him receive.

When he taketh of the cup let him say twice "Amen" *for a complete symbol of the Body and Blood.*

After all receive, let them pray, giving and rendering thanks for the reception, the deacon saying:

Let us give thanks unto the Lord, receiving His Holy Things, so that the reception [of them] may be for the life and salvation of our souls. Let us beg and beseech [His grace], raising a doxology to the Lord our God.

After that let the bishop say:

O Lord, giver of light eternal, the Helmsman of our souls, the guide of saints; give us understanding eyes which always look to Thee, and ears which hear Thee only, so that our soul may be filled with grace. Create in us a clean heart, O God; so that we may alway comprehend Thy greatness. O God, Wonderful, who lovest man, make our souls better, and by this Eucharist which we Thy servants who fail in much, have [now] received, form our thoughts so that they shall not swerve: for Thy kingdom is blessed, O Lord God, [who art] glorified and praised in Father and in Son and in Holy Ghost, both before the worlds, and now and alway, and for the ages, and for ever and ever without end.

The people. Amen.

The liturgy of the Testament is most important in this portion of it. We have seen that in the prayer after

[1] B in a recent hand "before."

communion in the Didache there is almost certainly a reminiscence of the "Our Father." Here in the Testament there is no doubt of the occurrence of the Lord's Prayer.

One of the most striking facts in connexion with the earlier liturgical forms, even including the liturgy of the Apostolic Constitutions, is the absence of the Lord's Prayer. It is hardly credible that it should not have occurred in the liturgy, and the explanation of its apparent absence is probably the simple one that, being known to everyone and its position in the Eucharist being equally familiar, it was not considered necessary to insert it in writing.

But here in the Testament we get at least a hint as to where it did occur.

Unfortunately there is some slight confusion and contradiction in the text.

A prayer is given for each communicant to say "after[1] that he receiveth the Eucharist." This prayer concludes

> Grant......that with boldness I may call Thee Father, when I call for Thy kingdom and Thy will to come to me. May Thy name be hallowed in me, O Lord, for Thou art mighty and to be praised and to Thee be praise for ever and ever.

Here evidently *after* communion the Lord's Prayer occurred; not said by the celebrant alone but by the people as well, if not by the people individually as an act of thanksgiving after their communion. While in the later uses it was the universal custom for priest and people together to say the Our Father before communion, there

[1] It is true that in another MS. this is corrected by a late hand to "before," and that after this prayer comes the rubric "after the prayer let him receive." But this is most probably a later addition, and there seems to be here an attempt to bring an early use into line with a later use by a slight alteration, though the rubric preceding the prayer has been overlooked.

is on the other hand the "de Sacramentis" which seems to treat the Lord's Prayer, as in the Testament, as coming after the Communion and forming part of the thanksgiving of the people, as well as coming immediately after the ἐπίκλησις. That the Lord's Prayer was said privately, if not in common by the people after communion, seems clear from the writer's language.

He says (v. iv. 12):

> ergo venisti ad altare, accepisti Corpus Christi. Audi iterum quae sacramenta es consecutus.

Then he goes on (v. iv. 18):

> nunc quid superest nisi oratio? Et nolite putare mediocris virtutis esse quemadmodum oretis. Apostoli sancti dicebant ad dominum Jesum: "Domine doce nos orare"... Tunc ait Dominus orationem "Pater noster...."
>
> ...19. Ergo attolle oculos ad Patrem...qui te per Filium redemit, et dic "Pater noster."

The liturgy of the "de Sacramentis," then, seems to contain the Lord's Prayer in two places, first immediately after the ἐπίκλησις said by the priest alone, and secondly after the Communion said by the communicants.

Probably this is not the original use of the Prayer, but it was used, as apparently in the Testament, as an act of thanksgiving after communion. Later it became the climax of the Canon in the East, said by priest and people together. In the Roman Church in St Gregory's time it was said by the priest alone. In the liturgy of the "de Sacramentis" we seem to see the transitional stage, when it was already the climax of the Canon, but was at the same time still used as a thanksgiving after communion.

In Sarapion the Communion and dismissal are represented by three short prayers:

μετὰ τὴν εὐχὴν ἡ κλάσις καὶ ἐν τῇ κλάσει εὐχή.

καταξίωσον ἡμᾶς τῆς κοινωνίας καὶ ταύτης, Θεὲ τῆς ἀληθείας, καὶ ποίησον σώματα ἡμῶν χωρῆσαι ἁγνείαν καὶ τὰς ψυχὰς φρόνησιν καὶ γνῶσιν. καὶ σόφισον ἡμᾶς, Θεὲ τῶν οἰκτιρμῶν, διὰ τῆς μεταλήψεως τοῦ σώματος καὶ αἵματος, ὅτι διὰ τοῦ μονογενοῦς σοὶ ἡ δόξα καὶ τὸ κράτος ἐν ἁγίῳ Πνεύματι, νῦν καὶ εἰς τοὺς σύμπαντας αἰῶνας τῶν αἰώνων. ἀμήν.

μετὰ τὸ διδόναι τὴν κλάσιν τοῖς κληρικοῖς χειροθεσία λαοῦ.

ἐκτείνω τὴν χεῖρα ἐπὶ τὸν λαὸν τοῦτον καὶ δέομαι ἐκταθῆναι τὴν τῆς ἀληθείας χεῖρα, καὶ δοθῆναι εὐλογίαν τῷ λαῷ τούτῳ διὰ τὴν σὴν φιλανθρωπίαν, Θεὲ τῶν οἰκτιρμῶν, καὶ τὰ μυστήρια τὰ παρόντα· χεὶρ εὐλαβείας καὶ δυνάμεως καὶ σωφρονισμοῦ καὶ καθαρότητος καὶ πάσης ὁσιότητος εὐλογησάτω τὸν λαὸν τοῦτον καὶ διατηρησάτω εἰς προκοπὴν καὶ βελτίωσιν διὰ τοῦ μονογενοῦς σου Ἰησοῦ Χριστοῦ ἐν ἁγίῳ Πνεύματι καὶ νῦν καὶ εἰς σύμπαντας αἰῶνας τῶν αἰώνων. ἀμήν.

μετὰ τὴν διάδοσιν τοῦ λαοῦ εὐχή.

εὐχαριστοῦμέν σοι, δέσποτα, ὅτι ἐσφαλμένους ἐκάλεσας καὶ ἡμαρτηκότας προσεποιήσω καὶ ὑπερτέθεισαι τὴν καθ᾽ ἡμῶν ἀπειλὴν φιλανθρωπίᾳ τῇ σῇ συγχωρήσας καὶ τῇ μετανοίᾳ ἀπαλείψας καὶ τῇ πρὸς σὲ γνώσει ἀποβαλών. εὐχαριστοῦμέν σοι ὅτι δέδωκας ἡμῖν κοινωνίαν σώματος καὶ αἵματος· εὐλόγησον ἡμᾶς, εὐλόγησον τὸν λαὸν τοῦτον, ποίησον ἡμᾶς μέρος ἔχειν μετὰ τοῦ σώματος καὶ τοῦ αἵματος, διὰ τοῦ μονογενοῦς σου Υἱοῦ, δι᾽ οὗ σοὶ ἡ δόξα καὶ τὸ κράτος ἐν ἁγίῳ Πνεύματι καὶ νῦν καὶ ἀεὶ καὶ εἰς τοὺς σύμπαντας αἰῶνας τῶν αἰώνων. ἀμήν.

Here again no words of administration are given. It may be that the second prayer, the χειροθεσία λαοῦ is to be regarded as the equivalent. But it is more likely that some short form was used, and was too well known to be given among these forms.

St Cyril gives us the use of the Church of Jerusalem. Immediately after the Lord's Prayer comes the Communion. The priest says:

τὰ ἅγια τοῖς ἁγίοις.

and the people reply:

εἷς ἅγιος, εἷς κύριος Ἰησοῦς Χριστός.

Then during the singing of the Psalm "Taste and see" the people receive the Holy Communion. Cyril bids them say "Amen" after receiving the Body and the Blood. Doubtless he means that they are to make this response to the words of administration, though he gives no such words.

Then apparently the dismissal takes place at once. He refers to a prayer of Blessing and dismissal with the words *εἶτα ἀναμείνας τὴν εὐχὴν εὐχαριστεῖ τῷ θεῷ τῷ καταξιώσαντί σε τῶν τηλικούτων μυστηρίων.*

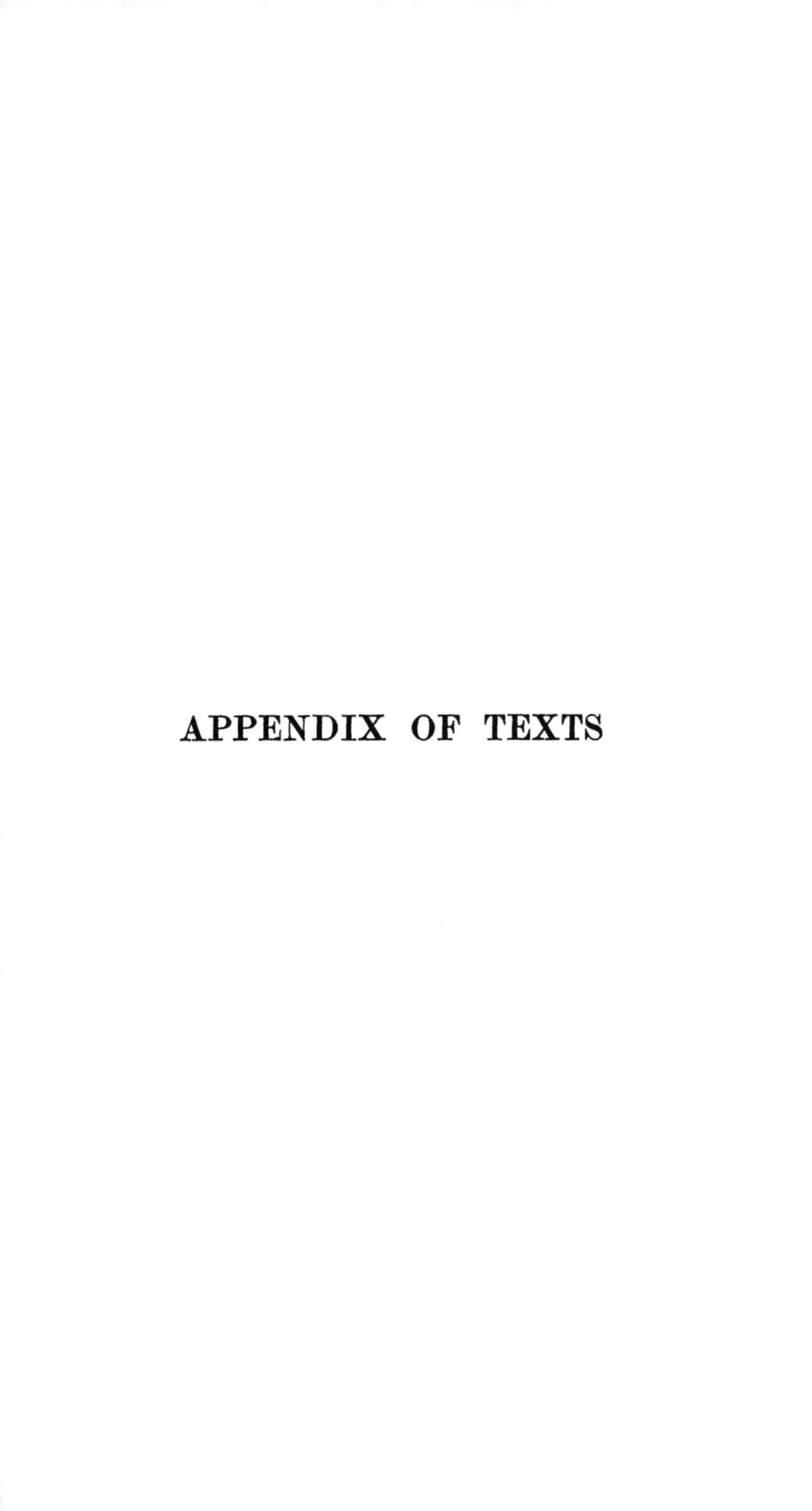

APPENDIX OF TEXTS

I. Liturgical forms from *Didache* (ed. Hoole).

II. Forms from *Acta Johannis* (ed. Lipsius and Bonnet).

III. Forms, Syriac and English, from *Acta Thomae* (Text and transl. Wright *Apocryph. Acts of the Apostles*).

IV. *Sursum Corda* and description of liturgy from the First Church Order. Coptic text and translation. Text, de Lagarde's *Aegyptiaca* Sahidic, with lacunae filled up from the late Bohairic version publ. by Tattam. With variants of the Verona fragments and the Canons of Hippolytus. Translation from G. Horner's *Statutes of the Apostles.*

V. Another description of liturgy from First Church Order. Coptic text and translation (Horner) with Verona and C. H. variants.

VI. The liturgy from the *Verona Latin Version* of First Church Order, with variants from the Ethiopic version; and the Ethiopic text and translation of the post-communion forms.

Latin version from Hauler's *Didascaliae apostolorum fragmenta Veronensia Latina.*

Ethiopic text and translation from G. Horner's *Statutes of the Apostles.*

VII. Liturgy from the *Testamentum Domini Nostri.* Syriac text from Rahmani's edition, translation from Cooper and Maclean's *Testament of Our Lord.*

VIII. Description of liturgy from Second Church Order. Coptic text from de Lagarde's *Aegyptiaca*, translation G. Horner's.

IX. Sarapion's liturgy. Text from G. Wobbermin's *Altchristliche liturgische Stücke.*

X. Description of liturgy from *Catechesis Mystagogica* v. of St Cyril of Jerusalem. (Text, J. Rupp.)

Didache.

c. ix. περὶ τῆς εὐχαριστίας οὕτως εὐχαριστήσατε· πρῶτον περὶ τοῦ ποτηρίου·

Εὐχαριστοῦμέν σοι, πάτερ ἡμῶν, ὑπὲρ τῆς ἁγίας ἀμπέλου Δαβὶδ τοῦ παιδός σου, ἧς ἐγνώρισας ἡμῖν διὰ Ἰησοῦ τοῦ παιδός σου· σοὶ ἡ δόξα εἰς τοὺς αἰῶνας.

περὶ δὲ τοῦ κλάσματος·

Εὐχαριστοῦμέν σοι, πάτερ ἡμῶν, ὑπὲρ τῆς ζωῆς καὶ γνώσεως ἧς ἐγνώρισας ἡμῖν διὰ Ἰησοῦ τοῦ παιδός σου· σοὶ ἡ δόξα εἰς τοὺς αἰῶνας· ὥσπερ ἦν τοῦτο κλάσμα διεσκορπισμένον ἐπάνω τῶν ὀρέων καὶ συναχθὲν ἐγένετο ἕν, οὕτω συναχθήτω σοῦ ἡ ἐκκλησία ἀπὸ τῶν περάτων τῆς γῆς εἰς τὴν σὴν βασιλείαν· ὅτι σοῦ ἐστὶν ἡ δόξα καὶ ἡ δύναμις διὰ Ἰησοῦ Χριστοῦ εἰς τοὺς αἰῶνας.

c. x. μετὰ δὲ τὸ ἐμπλησθῆναι οὕτως εὐχαριστήσατε· Εὐχαριστοῦμέν σοι, πάτερ ἅγιε, ὑπὲρ τοῦ ἁγίου ὀνόματός σου οὗ κατεσκήνωσας ἐν ταῖς καρδίαις ἡμῶν, καὶ ὑπὲρ τῆς γνώσεως καὶ πίστεως καὶ ἀθανασίας ἧς ἐγνώρισας ἡμῖν διὰ Ἰησοῦ τοῦ παιδός σου· σοὶ ἡ δόξα εἰς τοὺς αἰῶνας. σύ, Δέσποτα, παντόκρατορ, ἔκτισας τὰ πάντα ἕνεκεν τοῦ ὀνόματός σου τροφήν τε καὶ πότον ἔδωκας τοῖς ἀνθρώποις εἰς ἀπόλαυσιν, ἵνα σοι εὐχαριστήσωσιν, ἡμῖν δὲ ἐχαρίσω πνευματικὴν τροφὴν καὶ πότον καὶ ζωὴν αἰώνιον διὰ τοῦ παιδός σου. πρὸ πάντων εὐχαριστοῦμέν σοι ὅτι δύνατος εἶ· σοὶ ἡ δόξα εἰς τοὺς αἰῶνας.

μνήσθητι, κύριε, τῆς ἐκκλησίας σου τοῦ ῥύσασθαι αὐτὴν ἀπὸ παντὸς πονηροῦ καὶ τελειῶσαι αὐτὴν ἐν τῇ ἀγάπῃ σου, καὶ σύναξον αὐτὴν ἀπὸ τῶν τεσσάρων ἀνέμων, τὴν ἁγιασθεῖσαν εἰς τὴν σὴν βασιλείαν ἣν ἡτοίμασας αὐτῇ· ὅτι σοῦ ἐστὶν ἡ δύναμις καὶ ἡ δόξα εἰς τοὺς αἰῶνας.

ἐλθέτω χάρις καὶ παρελθέτω ὁ κόσμος οὗτος. ὡσαννὰ τῷ υἱῷ Δαβίδ.

εἴ τις ἅγιός ἐστιν, ἐρχέσθω· εἴ τις οὐκ ἔστι, μετανοείτω. μαραναθά. ἀμήν.

τοῖς δὲ προφηταῖς ἐπιτρέπετε εὐχαριστεῖν ὅσα θέλουσιν.

Acta Johannis cc. 85, 86. (Lipsius and Bonnet.)

85. καὶ ταῦτα εἰπὼν ὁ Ἰωάννης ἐπευξάμενος καὶ λαβὼν ἄρτον ἐκόμισεν εἰς τὸ μνῆμα κλάσαι· καὶ εἶπε·

Δοξάζομέν σου τὸ ὄνομα τὸ ἐπιστρέφον ἡμᾶς ἐκ τῆς πλάνης καὶ ἀνηλεοῦς ἀπάτης· Δοξάζομέν σε τὸν παρ' ὀφθαλμοῖς δείξαντα ἡμῖν ἃ εἴδομεν· μαρτυροῦμέν σου τῇ χρηστότητι ποικίλαις φάνισιν· αἰνοῦμέν σου τὸ ἀγαθὸν ὄνομα, κύριε, ἐλέγξαντι τοὺς ὑπὸ σοῦ ἐλεγχομένους· εὐχαριστοῦμέν σε, κύριε Ἰησοῦ Χριστέ, ὅτι πεπείσμεθα ἀμετάβολον οὖσαν· εὐχαριστοῦμέν σοι τῷ χρήσαντι φύσιν φύσεως σῳζομένης·

εὐχαριστοῦμέν σοι τῷ τὴν ἀπαραίτητον ἡμῖν δεδωκότι ταύτην ὅτι σὺ μόνος καὶ νῦν καὶ ἀεί· οἱ σοὶ δοῦλοι εὐχαριστοῦμέν σοι μετὰ προφάσεως συλλεγόμενοι καὶ ἀναλεγόμενοι, ἅγιε.

86. καὶ εὐξάμενος οὕτως καὶ δοξάσας ἐξῄει τοῦ μνήματος, κοινωνήσας τοῖς ἀδελφοῖς πᾶσι τῆς τοῦ κυρίου εὐχαριστίας.

Acta Johannis cc. 109, 110.

c. 109. καὶ αἰτήσας ἄρτον εὐχαρίστησεν οὕτως·

Τίνα αἶνον, ἢ ποίαν προσφορὰν ἢ τίνα εὐχαριστίαν κλῶντες τὸν ἄρτον τοῦτον ἐπονομάσωμεν ἀλλ' ἢ σὲ μόνον, κύριε Ἰησοῦ; δοξάζομέν σου τὸ λεχθὲν ὑπὸ τοῦ πατρὸς ὄνομα. δοξάζομέν σου τὸ λεχθὲν διὰ υἱοῦ ὄνομα. δοξάζομέν σου τὴν εἴσοδον τῆς θύρας. δοξάζομέν σου τὴν δειχθεῖσαν ἡμῖν διὰ σοῦ ἀνάστασιν[1]. δοξάζομέν σου τὴν ὁδόν. δοξάζομέν σου τὸν σπόρον, τὸν λόγον[2], τὴν χάριν, τὴν πίστιν, τὸ ἅλας, τὸν ἄλεκτον μαργαρίτην, τὸν θησαυρὸν, τὸ ἄροτρον, τὴν σαγήνην, τὸ μέγεθος, τὸ διάδημα, τὸν δι' ἡμᾶς λεχθέντα υἱὸν ἀνθρώπου, τὸν χαρισάμενον ἡμῖν τὴν ἀλήθειαν, τὴν ἀνάπαυσιν, τὴν γνῶσιν, τὴν δύναμιν, τὴν ἐντολὴν, τὴν παρρησίαν, τὴν ἐλπίδα, τὴν ἀγάπην, τὴν ἐλευθερίαν, τὴν εἰς σὲ καταφυγήν. σὺ γὰρ εἶ μόνος, κύριε[3], ἡ ῥίζα τῆς ἀθανασίας καὶ ἡ πηγὴ τῆς ἀφθαρσίας καὶ ἡ ἕδρα τῶν αἰώνων, λεχθεὶς ταῦτα πάντα δι' ἡμᾶς νῦν ὅπως καλοῦντές σε διὰ τούτων γνωρίζομέν σου τὸ μέγεθος ἀθεώρητον ἡμῖν ἐπὶ τοῦ παρόντος ὑπάρχον, καθαροῖς δὲ θεωρητὸν μόνον ἐν τῷ μόνῳ σου ἀνθρώπῳ εἰκονιζόμενον[4].

c. 110. καὶ κλάσας τὸν ἄρτον ἐπέδωκεν πᾶσιν ἡμῖν, ἑκάστῳ τῶν ἀδελφῶν ἐπευχόμενος ἄξιον ἔσεσθαι αὐτὸν τῆς τοῦ κυρίου χάριτος καὶ τῆς ἁγιωτάτης εὐχαριστίας. γευσάμενος δὲ καὶ αὐτὸς ὁμοίως καὶ εἰρηκὼς, Κἀμοὶ μέρος ἔστω μεθ' ὑμῶν, καὶ, Εἰρήνη μεθ' ὑμῶν ἀγαπητοί, ...

1 ἀνάστασιν τοῦ σοῦ σώματος ἐκ νεκρῶν B.

2 τῶν λογίων V, R.

3 Add. Ἰησοῦ λόγε τοῦ θεοῦ B.

4 θεωρούμενον Γ. ἔπιδε ἐπὶ τοὺς σοὶ πεπιστευκότας ἐν ἀληθείᾳ add. Δ, dein εὐλόγησον τὸν ἄρτον τοῦτον καὶ ἡμᾶς δι' αὐτοῦ add. R, U, B, et ὅτι σε δοξάζομεν μόνον τὸν ὄντως ὄντα θεὸν add. V, B, ὅτι σοῦ ἐστιν ἡ δόξα καὶ τὸ κράτος σὺν τῷ πατρὶ καὶ τῷ (τ. π. κ. τ. om. U) ἁγίῳ πνεύματι add. R, U, εἰς τοὺς αἰῶνας (τῶν αἰώνων add. U) ἀμὴν add. Δ.

Wright, *Apoc. Acts of the Apostles*, vol. I. p. ܪܢܚ.

Greek Version (ed. Bonnet), cc. 49, 50.

A.

ܘܦܩܕ ܗܘܐ ܫܠܝܚܐ ܠܡܫܡܫܢܘܗܝ ܕܢܣܝܡܘܢ ܦܬܘܪܐ ܘܐܝܬܝܘ
ܣܦܣܠܐ ܠܬܡܢ: ܘܦܪܣܘ ܥܠܘܗܝ ܟܬܢܐ. ܘܐܝܬܝ ܣܡ
ܥܠܘܗܝ ܠܚܡܐ ܕܒܘܪܟܬܐ. ܘܐܬܐ ܫܠܝܚܐ ܩܡ ܠܘܬ
ܦܬܘܪܐ ܘܐܡܪ ܗܘܐ.
ܝܫܘܥ ܕܐܫܘܝܬܢ ܕܢܬܩܪܒ ܠܦܓܪܟ ܩܕܝܫܐ ܘܠܫܘܬܦܘܬ
ܠܕܡܟ ܡܚܝܢܐ ܘܡܛܠ ܬܘܟܠܢ ܕܥܠܝܟ ܡܡܪܚܝܢ ܘܡܩܪܒܝܢ
ܘܩܪܝܢ ܠܫܡܟ ܩܕܝܫܐ ܗܘ ܕܐܬܐܡܪ ܒܝܕ ܢܒ̈ܝܐ ܐܝܟ ܕܨܒܬ
ܐܠܗܘܬܟ. ܘܡܫܬܡܥ ܐܢܬ ܒܝܕ ܫ̈ܠܝܚܝܟ ܒܟܠܗ ܥܠܡܐ
ܐܝܟ ܛܝܒܘܬܟ. ܘܐܬܓܠܝܬ ܒܪ̈ܚܡܝܟ ܠܙܕ̈ܝܩܐ. ܒܚܝܠ
ܕܝܠܟ ܕܐܬܐܬܐ ܘܬܕܡܪ̈ܬܐ ܥܒܕܬ ܠܥܘܕܪܐ ܘܠܢ̈ܫܐ.
ܘܠܡܬܚܣܢܘܬܗܘܢ ܕܡܫ̈ܒܚܝܢ ܠܟ. ܕܐܬܓܠܠܬ ܒܣܪܢ
ܒܡܫܟܢܐ ܘܒܚܝܠܢ ܐܒܝܐ. ܘܝܗܒܐ ܠܗܘܢ ܠܫܘܠܛܢܐ
ܕܢܬܦܨܘܢ ܘܠܢ̈ܫܐ ܕܦܓܪ̈ܝܗܘܢ ܡܟܠܗܝܢ ܒܝܫܐ ⁘
ܘܫܪܝ ܗܘܐ ܕܢܐܡܪ:
ܬܐ ܡܘܗܒܬܗ ܕܪܡܐ. ܬܘ ܪ̈ܚܡܐ ܡ̈ܫܡܠܝܐ. ܬܐ ܪܘܚܐ
ܩܕܝܫܬܐ. ܬܐ ܓܠܝܬ ܐ̈ܪܙܘܗܝ ܕܓܒܝܐ ܩ̈ܕܝܫܐ. ܬܐ
ܫܘܬܦܬ ܒܟܠܗܘܢ ܐ̈ܓܘܢܘܗܝ ܕܐܬܠܝܛܐ ܛܒܐ. ܬܐ
ܫܝܢܬܗ ܕܪܘܡܐ. ܬܐ ܫܠܝܬܐ ܕܓܠܝܐ ܪ̈ܘܪܒܘܗܝ ܕܟܠܐ. ܬܐ
ܥܡܘܩܬܐ ܓܠܝܬ ܐ̈ܪܙܘܗܝ ܕܪܡܐ. ܬܐ ܡܩܕܫܢܝܬܐ
ܕܦܘܪܩܢܐ. ܘܫܘܝܬ ܚ̈ܕܘܘܗܝ ܕܐܠܗܐ. ܬܐ ܫܠܝܬ ܢ̈ܫܐ

WRIGHT, *Apoc. Acts*, vol. II. pp. 180—190.

A.

And the Apostle ordered his deacon to make ready the Eucharist; and he brought a bench thither, and spread over it a linen cloth; and he brought (and) placed on it the bread of blessing. And the Apostle came (and) stood beside it, and said:

Jesus, who hast deemed us worthy to draw nigh unto Thy holy Body, and to partake of Thy life-giving Blood; and because of our reliance upon Thee we are bold and draw nigh, and invoke Thy holy Name, which has been proclaimed by the prophets as Thy Godhead willed; and Thou art preached by Thy Apostles through the whole world according to Thy Grace, and art revealed by Thy mercy to the just; we beg of Thee that Thou wouldest come and communicate with us for help and for life, and for the conversion of Thy servants unto Thee, that they may go under Thy pleasant yoke and under Thy victorious power, and that it may be unto them for the health of their souls and for the life of their bodies in Thy living world[1].

And he began to say:

Come, gift of the Exalted; come, perfect mercy; come, holy Spirit; come, revealer of the mysteries of the chosen among the Prophets; come, proclaimer by His Apostles of the combats of our victorious Athlete; come, treasure of majesty; come, beloved of the mercy of the most High; come, (thou) silent (one), revealer of the mysteries of the Exalted; come, utterer of hidden things and shewer of the works of our God; come, giver of life in secret and manifest

[1] The Greek version is much shorter (c. 49) Ἰησοῦ ὁ καταξιώσας ἡμᾶς τῆς εὐχαριστίας τοῦ σώματός σου τοῦ ἁγίου καὶ τοῦ αἵματος κοινωνῆσαι, ἰδοὺ τολμῶμεν προσέρχεσθαι τῇ σῇ εὐχαριστίᾳ καὶ ἐπικαλεῖσθαί σου τὸ ἅγιον ὄνομα· ἐλθὲ καὶ κοινώνησον ἡμῖν.

ܒܡܫܘܬܗ̇. ܘܒܠܚܘܕܐ ܒܡܫܒܚܘܬܗ̇. ܬܐ ܢܡܫܚ ܚܘܬܡܐ ܘܚܢܢܐ
ܠܟܠܗܘܢ ܐܝܠܝܢ ܕܡܫܬܡܥܝܢ ܠܗ̇. ܬܐ ܚܝܠܗ ܕܐܒܐ ܘܚܟܡܬܐ
ܕܒܪܐ. ܕܗܘ ܐܝܬܘܗܝ ܒܟܠ. ܬܐ ܘܐܫܬܘܬܦ ܥܡܢ ܒܗܕܐ
ܐܘܟܪܝܣܛܝܐ ܕܥܒܕܝܢ. ܘܒܫܡܐ ܡܘܗܒܬܐ ܕܡܩܪܒܝܢ.
ܘܒܫܘܡܐ ܕܡܦܪܫܐ ܕܥܒܕܝܢ.

ܘܪܫܡ ܨܠܝܒܐ ܥܠ ܠܚܡܐ. ܘܩܨܐ ܗܘܐ ܕܢܬܠ. ܘܫܪܝ
ܠܡܦܠܓ ܠܗ̇. ܐܢܬܬܐ ܘܐܡܪ ܠܗ̇.
ܕܬܗܘܐ ܠܟܝ ܠܫܘܒܩܢ ܚܘܒܐ ܘܚܛܗܐ ܘܠܚܝܘܬܐ ܕܠܥܠܡ.
ܘܡܢ ܒܬܪܗ̇ ܦܠܓ ܠܟܠܗܘܢ ܐܚܐ ܕܐܬܛܥܢܘ ܒܒܗ̇.
ܗ̇ܕܝܢ ܦܠܓ ܠܟܠܢܫ ܘܐܡܪ ܠܗܘܢ.
ܬܗܘܐ ܠܟܘܢ ܐܘܟܪܝܣܛܝܐ ܗܕܐ ܠܚܢܢܐ ܘܠܪܚܡܐ. ܘܠܐ
ܠܕܝܢܐ ܘܠܬܒܥܬܐ.
ܘܥܢܘ ܐܡܪܘ ܐܡܝܢ ܀

WRIGHT, p. ܣܘ (Greek c. 29).

B.

ܘܡܢ ܐܡܪ ܗܠܝܢ. ܩܡ ܐܦܝܗ ܠܟܠܗܘܢ. ܘܩܨܐ
ܐܘܟܪܝܣܛܝܐ ܘܦܠܓ ܠܟܠܗܘܢ ܘܐܡܪ ܠܗܘܢ.
ܬܗܘܐ ܠܟܘܢ ܗܕܐ ܐܘܟܪܝܣܛܝܐ. ܠܚܝܐ ܘܠܪܘܚܐ. ܘܠܐ
ܠܕܝܢܐ ܘܬܒܥܬܐ.
ܘܥܢܘ ܐܡܪܘ ܐܡܝܢ ܀

in Thy deeds[1]; come, giver of joy and rest to all who cleave unto Thee; come, power of the Father, and wisdom of the Son, for Ye are one in all; come and communicate with us in this Eucharist which we celebrate[2], and in this offering which we offer, and in this commemoration which we make.

And he made the sign of the Cross upon the bread, and began to give (it). And he gave first to the woman, and said to her:

Let it be unto thee for remission of transgressions and sins, and for the everlasting resurrection.

And after her he gave to the persons who were baptized[3] *with her. Then he gave to every one and said to them:*

Let this Eucharist be unto you for life and rest, and not for judgment and vengeance.

And they said: Amen.

[1] The Syriac has: *and (giver of) manifest things in her (thy) deeds;* but as the corresponding Greek words are ἡ φανερὰ ἐν ταῖς πράξεσιν αὐτῆς, I suppose that we should read ܘܓܠܝܬܐ ܒܣܘܥܪ̈ܢܝܟ.

[2] Which we are making, ἣν ποιοῦμεν (ἐπὶ τῷ ὀνόματί σου).

[3] Or, whom he had baptized.

WRIGHT, vol. II. p. 169.

B.

And when he had spoken thus, he laid his hand on them, and broke the Eucharist, and gave unto all of them, and said unto them:

Let this Eucharist be unto you for grace and mercy, and not for judgment and vengeance.

And they said: Amen.

WRIGHT, vol. I. pp. ܟܐ and ܟܒ. Greek, c. 133.

C.

ܘܒܬܪ ܕܥܡܕܗ ܘܠܒܫܗ ܐܝܬܝ ܠܚܡܐ ܘܚܡܪܐ ܘܣܡ ܗܘܐ ܥܠ
ܦܬܘܪܐ. ܘܫܪܝ ܗܘܐ ܕܢܒܪܟ ܥܠܘܗܝ ܘܐܡܪ ܗܘܐ.
ܠܚܡܐ ܚܝܐ ܕܐܟ̈ܠܘܗܝ ܠܐ ܡܝܬܝܢ. ܠܚܡܐ ܕܠܢܦ̈ܫܬܐ
ܟܦ̈ܢܬܐ ܡܣܒܥ ܡܢ ܒܘܣܡܗ. ܐܢܬ ܕܐܫܬܘܝܬ ܕܬܩܒܠ
ܡܘܗܒܬܐ. ܘܬܗܘܐ ܠܫܘܒܩܢ ܚܛ̈ܗܐ ܕܐܟ̈ܠܝܢ ܠܟ ܠܐ
ܢܡܘܬܘܢ. ܫܡܐ ܕܐܒܐ ܐܬܩܪܝ ܥܠܝܟ. ܫܡܐ ܕܒܪܐ
ܐܬܩܪܝ ܥܠܝܟ. ܫܡܐ ܕܪܘܚܐ ܐܬܩܪܝ ܥܠܝܟ. ܫܡܐ
ܪܡܐ ܕܟܣܐ ܡܢ ܟܠ.

ܘܐܡܪ.

ܒܫܡܟ ܝܫܘܥ ܬܐܬܐ ܚܝܠܐ ܕܒܘܪܟܬܐ ܘܬܘܕܝܬܐ
ܘܬܫܪܐ ܥܠ ܗܢܐ ܠܚܡܐ ܕܟܠܗܘܢ ܢܦ̈ܫܬܐ ܕܢܣܒܝܢ ܡܢܗ
ܢܬܚ̈ܕܬܢ ܘܢܫ̈ܬܒܩܘܢ ܠܗܘܢ ܚܛ̈ܗܝܗܘܢ.
ܘܩܨܐ ܘܝܗܒ ܠܗ ܠܣܝܦܘܪ ܘܠܐܢܬܬܗ ܘܠܒܪܬܗ ܀

WRIGHT, vol. II. p. 268.

C.

And when they were baptized and had put on their clothes, he brought bread and wine, and placed it on the table, and began to bless it, and said:

Living bread, the eaters of which die not! Bread, that fillest hungry souls with thy blessing! Thou that art worthy to receive the gift and to be for the remission of sins, that those who eat thee may not die! [1]We name the name of the Father over thee; we name the name of the Son over thee; we name the name of the Spirit over thee, the exalted name that is hidden from all[1].

And he said:

In Thy name, Jesus, may the power of the blessing and the thanksgiving come and abide upon this bread, that all the souls which take of it may be renewed, and their sins may be forgiven them[2].

And he brake and gave to Ṣîfûr and to his wife, and to his daughter.

[1–1] The Greek is different, *ἐπιφημίζομέν σε τὸ τῆς μητρὸς ὄνομα, ἀπορρήτου μυστηρίου ἀρχῶν τε καὶ ἐξουσιῶν κεκρυμμένων· ἐπιφημίζομέν σου ὀνόματί σου Ἰησοῦ.*

[2] The Greek is shorter, *ἐλθάτω δύναμις εὐλογίας καὶ ἐνιδρύσθω ὁ ἄρτος, ἵνα πᾶσαι αἱ μεταλαμβάνουσαι ψυχαὶ ἀπὸ τῶν ἁμαρτιῶν ἀπολούσονται.*

WRIGHT, vol. I. p. ܫܟܒ. Greek c. 158.

D.

ܘܟܕ ܥܡܕܗ ܘܠܒܫܗ. ܐܝܬܝ ܠܚܡܐ ܘܣܡܗ ܥܠ ܦܬܘܪܐ:
ܘܒܪܟ ܥܠܘܗܝ ܘܐܡܪ.

ܦܓܪܟ ܩܕܝܫܐ ܕܐܙܕܩܦ ܥܠ ܚܛܗܝܢ ܐܟܠܝܢ. ܘܕܡܟ ܡܚܝܢܐ ܕܐܬܐܫܕ ܥܠ ܚܛܗܝܢ ܫܬܝܢ. ܢܗܘܐ ܠܢ ܦܓܪܟ ܠܚܝܐ. ܘܕܡܟ ܠܫܘܒܩܢ ܚܛܗܐ. ܘܚܠܦ ܡܪܝܪܘܬܐ ܕܐܫܬܝܬ ܚܠܦܝܢ: ܬܫܬܩܠ ܡܢ ܡܪܝܪܘܬܗ ܕܒܥܠܕܒܒܢ. ܘܚܠܦ ܕܐܫܬܝܬ ܚܠܐ ܡܛܠܬܢ ܬܬܚܝܠ ܡܚܝܠܘܬܢ. ܘܪܘܩܐ ܕܩܒܠܬ ܡܛܠܬܢ ܢܩܒܠ ܚܝ̈ܝ ܡܫ̈ܠܡܢܐ. ܘܕܩܒܠܬ ܟܠܝܠܐ ܕܟܘ̈ܒܐ ܚܠܦܝܢ: ܢܩܒܠ ܡܢܟ ܟܠܝܠܐ ܕܠܐ ܚܒܠܐ. ܘܕܐܬܟܪܟܬ ܒܣܕܢܐ ܡܛܠܬܢ. ܢܬܚܝܠ ܡܢ ܚܝܠܟ ܪܒܐ ܕܠܐ ܡܬܙܟܐ. ܘܕܐܬܩܒܪܬ ܒܝܬ ܩܒܘܪܐ ܚܕܬܐ ܚܠܦ ܡܛܠܬܢ: ܢܩܒܠ ܐܦ ܚܢ ܚܘܕܬܐ ܕܢܦܫܐ. ܘܐܝܟ ܕܩܡܬ ܢܬܚܝܐ ܚܢ. ܘܢܩܘܡ ܩܕܡܝܟ ܒܕܝܢܐ ܕܩܘܫܬܐ.

ܘܩܪܐ ܐܘܢܓܠܝܘܢ ܘܫܪܝ........ ܘܐܡܪ.

ܬܗܘܐ ܠܟܘܢ ܐܘܢܓܠܝܘܢܐ ܗܕܐ ܠܚ̈ܝܐ ܘܠܚܝܠܐ ܘܠܚܕܘܬܐ ܘܠܚܘܠܡܢܐ. ܘܠܐܣܝܘܬܐ ܕܢܦ̈ܫܬܟܘܢ ܘܦܓ̈ܪܝܟܘܢ.

ܘܥܢܘ ܐܡܪܘ ܐܡܝܢ.

WRIGHT, vol. II. p. 290.

D.

And after they had been baptized and were come up, he brought bread and the mingled cup, and spake a blessing over it and said:

Thy holy Body, which was crucified for our sake, we eat, and Thy life-giving Blood, which was shed for our sake, we drink. Let Thy Body be to us for life, and Thy Blood for the remission of sins. For the gall which Thou drankest for us, let the bitterness of our enemy be taken away from us. And for Thy drinking vinegar for our sake, let our weakness be strengthened. And (for) the spit which Thou didst receive for us[1], let us receive Thy perfect life[2]. And because Thou didst receive the crown of thorns for us, let us receive from Thee the crown that withereth not. And because Thou wast wrapped in a linen cloth for us, let us be girt with Thy mighty strength, which cannot be overcome. And because Thou wast buried in a new sepulchre for our mortality, let us too receive intercourse[3] with Thee in Heaven. And as Thou didst arise, let us be raised, and let us stand before Thee at the Judgment of truth.

And he brake the Eucharist and gave......and said:

Let this Eucharist be to you for life and rest and joy and health, and for the healing of your souls and of your bodies.

And they said: Amen.

[1] G. adds δεξώμεθα δρόσον τῆς σῆς χρηστότητος· καὶ ἐν τῷ καλάμῳ ᾧ ἔτυψάν σε δι' ἡμᾶς.

[2] G. οἶκον.

[3] ἀνακαινισμὸν τῆς ψυχῆς δεξώμεθα καὶ τοῦ σώματος.

First Church Order.

De Lagarde, *Aegyptiaca.* Can. Eccles. p. 250, § 31.

ⲙⲁⲣⲉ ⲟⲩⲟⲛ ⲛⲓⲙ ϯⲉⲓⲣⲏⲛⲏ ⲛⲁϥ ϩⲛ̄ ⲧⲉⲩⲧⲁⲡⲣⲟ ⲉⲩⲁⲥⲡⲁⲍⲉ ⲙ̄ⲙⲟϥ.

ⲙⲁⲣⲉ ⲛ̄ⲇⲓⲁⲕⲟⲛⲟⲥ ⲇⲉ ⲉⲛ ⲧⲡⲣⲟⲥⲫⲟⲣⲁ ⲉϩⲟⲩⲛ ⲛⲁϥ. ⲡⲁⲓ ⲇⲉ ⲉϥϣⲁⲛⲕⲱ ⲛ̄ⲧⲉϥϭⲓϫ ⲉϫⲛ̄ ⲧⲡⲣⲟⲥⲫⲟⲣⲁ ⲙⲛ̄ ⲛⲉⲡⲣⲉⲥⲃⲩⲧⲉⲣⲟⲥ ⲙⲁⲣⲉϥϫⲟⲟⲥ ⲉϥⲉⲩⲭⲁⲣⲓⲥⲧⲟⲩ ϫⲉ

ⲟ ⲕⲩⲣⲓⲟⲥ ⲙⲉⲧⲁ ⲡⲁⲛⲧⲱⲛ ⲩⲙⲱⲛ

ⲛ̄ⲧⲉ ⲡⲗⲁⲟⲥ ⲧⲏⲣϥ ϫⲟⲟⲥ ϫⲉ

ⲙⲉⲧⲁ ⲧⲟⲩ ⲡⲛⲉⲩⲙⲁⲧⲟⲥ ⲥⲟⲩ

ⲛ̄ϥϫⲟⲟⲥ ϫⲉ

ⲁⲛⲱ ⲩⲙⲱⲛ ⲧⲁⲥ ⲭⲁⲣⲧⲓⲁⲥ

ⲛ̄ⲧⲉ ⲗⲁⲟⲥ ϫⲉ

ⲉⲭⲱⲙⲉⲛ ⲡⲣⲟⲥ ⲧⲟⲛ ⲕⲩⲣⲓⲟⲛ

ⲛ̄ϥϫⲟⲟⲥ ⲟⲛ ϫⲉ

ⲉⲩⲭⲁⲣⲓⲥⲧⲏⲥⲱⲙⲉⲛ ⲧⲟⲛ ⲕⲩⲣⲓⲟⲛ

ⲛ̄ⲧⲉ ⲡⲗⲁⲟⲥ ⲧⲏⲣϥ ϫⲟⲟⲥ ϫⲉ

ⲁⲝⲓⲟⲛ ⲕⲁⲓ ⲇⲓⲕⲁⲓⲟⲛ

ⲁⲩⲱ ⲙⲁⲣⲉϥϣⲗⲏⲗ ⲟⲛ ⲛ̄ⲧⲉⲓϩⲉ ⲛ̄ϥϫⲱ ⲛ̄ⲛⲉⲧⲛⲏⲩ ⲙⲛ̄ⲛ̄ⲥⲁ ⲛⲁⲓ ⲕⲁⲧⲁ ⲡⲥⲱⲛⲧ ⲛ̄ⲧⲉⲡⲣⲟⲥⲫⲟⲣⲁ ⲉⲧⲟⲩⲁⲁⲃ.

G. Horner, *Statutes of the Apostles*, p. 307.

Let everyone give peace to him (i.e. the newly ordained bishop) with their mouth, saluting him[1].

Let the deacons then offer to him the oblation. And[2] *having put his hand upon the oblation with the presbyters let him say in giving thanks*[3]*:*

The Lord with you all[4].

And all the people say:

With thy spirit.

And he says:

Lift up your hearts.

And the people say:

We have them with the Lord.

And he says again:

Let us give thanks to the Lord.

And all the people say:

Meet and right.

And[5] *let him pray also thus and say the things which come after these according to the custom of the holy Oblation.*

[1] Veron. Fragm. add quia dignus effectus est. So C. H.

[2] C. H. add He who has been made bishop.

[3] The Bohairic text has: a thanksgiving (*εὐχαριστία*), C. H. omit.

[4] C. H. omit 'all,' transliterating the Greek in the Copt. text.

[5] C. H.: and after this let him say the prayer and finish the Quddash.

DE LAGARDE, *Aegyptiaca.* Can. Eccles. 46, p. 257.

ⲙⲁⲣⲉ ⲛⲓⲇⲓⲁⲕⲟⲛⲟⲥ ⲉⲛ ϯⲡⲣⲟⲥⲫⲟⲣⲁ ⲙ̄ⲡⲓⲉⲡⲓⲥⲕⲟⲡⲟⲥ ⲟⲩⲟϩ ⲛⲑⲟϥ ⲉϥϣⲉⲡϩⲙⲟⲧ ⲉϫⲉⲛ ⲟⲩⲱⲓⲕ ⲉⲑⲃⲉ ϫⲉ ⲡⲥⲙⲟⲧ ⲛ̄ⲧⲥⲁⲣⲝ ⲙ̄ⲡⲭⲣⲓⲥⲧⲟⲥ ⲛⲉⲙ ⲟⲩⲁⲫⲟⲧ ⲛ̄ⲏⲣⲡ, ϫⲉ ⲛ̄ⲑⲟϥ ⲡⲉ ⲡⲥⲛⲟϥ ⲙ̄ⲡⲭⲣⲓⲥⲧⲟⲥ ⸢ⲉⲧⲟⲩⲛⲁⲫⲟⲛϥ ⲉⲃⲟⲗ⸣ ⲉϫⲉⲛ ⲟⲩⲟⲛ ⲛⲓⲃⲉⲛ ⲉⲑⲛⲁϩϯ ⲉⲣⲟϥ, ⲟⲩⲟϩ ⲟⲩⲉⲣⲱϯ ⲛⲉⲙ ⲟⲩⲉⲃⲓⲱ ⲉⲩⲑⲏⲧ ⲉⲛϫⲓⲛⲙⲟϩ ⲛ̄ⲛⲓⲱϣ ⲛ̄ⲧⲉ ⲛⲓⲟϯ ϫⲉ ⲁϥϫⲟⲥ ϫⲉ ϯⲛⲁϯ ⲛⲱⲧⲉⲛ ⲛ̄ⲟⲩⲕⲁϩⲓ ⲉϥⲍⲁⲧⲓ ⲛ̄ⲉⲣⲱϯ ϩⲓ ⲉⲃⲓⲱ.

ⲧⲁⲓ ⲧⲉ ⲧⲥⲁⲣⲝ ⲙ̄ⲡⲉⲭⲣⲓⲥⲧⲟⲥ ⲛ̄ⲧⲁϥⲧⲁⲁⲥ ⲛⲁⲛ ⲉⲧⲣⲉⲛⲥⲁⲁⲛϣ ⲉⲃⲟⲗ ⲛ̄ϩⲏⲧⲥ ⲛ̄ⲑⲉ ⲛ̄ϩⲉⲛϣⲏⲣⲉϣⲏⲙ ⲛ̄ϭⲓⲛⲉⲧⲛⲓⲥⲧⲉⲩⲉ ⲉⲣⲟϥ. ⲥⲛⲁⲧⲣⲉ ⲛ̄ⲥⲓϣⲉ ⲙ̄ⲡϩⲏⲧ ⲃⲱⲗ ⲉⲃⲟⲗ ϩⲓⲧⲙ̄ ⲡⲉϩⲗⲟϭ ⲙ̄ⲡⲗⲟⲅⲟⲥ. ⲛⲁⲓ ϭⲉ ⲧⲏⲣⲟⲩ ⲉⲣⲉ ⲡⲉⲡⲓⲥⲕⲟⲡⲟⲥ ϯⲗⲟⲅⲟⲥ ⲙ̄ⲙⲟⲟⲩ ⲙ̄ⲡⲉⲧⲛⲁϫⲓ ⲃⲁⲡⲧⲓⲥⲙⲁ.

ⲉⲣϣⲁⲛ ⲡⲉⲡⲓⲥⲕⲟⲡⲟⲥ ϭⲉ ⲧⲉⲛⲟⲩ ⲡⲉϣ ⲡⲟⲉⲓⲕ ⲙⲁⲣⲉϥϯ ⲛ̄ⲟⲩⲕⲗⲁⲥⲙⲁ ⲙ̄ⲡⲟⲩⲁ ⲡⲟⲩⲁ ⲙ̄ⲙⲟⲟⲩ ⲉϥϫⲱ ⲙ̄ⲙⲟⲥ ϫⲉ

ⲡⲁⲓ ⲡⲉ ⲡⲟⲉⲓⲕ ⲛ̄ⲧⲡⲉ ⲡⲥⲱⲙⲁ ⲙ̄ⲡⲉⲭⲣⲓⲥⲧⲟⲥ ⲓⲏⲥⲟⲩⲥ

ⲙⲁⲣⲉ ⲡⲉⲧϫⲓ ϩⲱⲱϥ ⲟⲩⲱϣⲃ ϫⲉ, ϩⲁⲙⲏⲛ.

ⲉϣⲱⲡⲉ ⲇⲉ ⲙⲛ̄ ϩⲟⲩⲟ ⲡⲣⲉⲥⲃⲩⲧⲉⲣⲟⲥ ⲙ̄ⲙⲁⲩ ⲙⲁⲣⲉ ⲛ̄ⲇⲓⲁⲕⲟⲛⲟⲥ ⲁⲙⲁϩⲧⲉ ⲙ̄ⲡⲡⲟⲧⲏⲣⲓⲟⲛ ⲛ̄ⲥⲉⲁϩⲉⲣⲁⲧⲟⲩ ϩⲛ̄ ⲟⲩⲉⲩⲧⲁⲝⲓⲁ ⲛ̄ⲥⲉϯ ⲛⲁⲩ ⲙ̄ⲡⲉⲥⲛⲟϥ ⲙ̄ⲡⲉⲭⲣⲓⲥⲧⲟⲥ ⲓⲏⲥⲟⲩⲥ ⲡⲉⲛϫⲟⲉⲓⲥ ⲁⲩⲱ ⲡⲁⲡⲉⲣⲱⲧⲉ ⲙⲛ̄ ⲡⲁⲡⲉⲃⲓⲱ. ⲙⲁⲣⲉϥϫⲟⲟⲥ ⲛ̄ϭⲓ ⲡⲉⲧϯ ⲙ̄ⲡⲡⲟⲧⲏⲣⲓⲟⲛ ϫⲉ

ⲡⲁⲓ ⲡⲉ ⲡⲉⲥⲛⲟϥ ⲛ̄ⲓⲏⲥⲟⲩⲥ ⲡⲉⲭⲣⲓⲥⲧⲟⲥ ⲡⲉⲛϫⲟⲉⲓⲥ

ⲛ̄ⲧⲉ ⲡⲉⲧϫⲓ ϩⲱⲱϥ ⲟⲛ ⲟⲩⲱϣⲃ ϫⲉ ϩⲁⲙⲏⲛ.

HORNER, *Statutes of the Apostles*, p. 319.

[1]Let the deacons bring the Oblation to the Bishop, and he shall give thanks[2] over bread because that (it is) the form of the Flesh of the Christ; and a cup of wine because it is the Blood of the Christ which will be shed for all who believe Him; and milk and honey mingled in fulfilment of the promises of the fathers, because He said: I will give to you a land flowing with milk and honey[1].

This is the Flesh of the Christ, which He gave to us to nourish us with it like children, namely we who believe Him; It will cause the bitterness of the heart to be dissolved by the sweetness of the word[3]. All these things shall the bishop recount to him who shall be baptized. And when the bishop therefore has now broken the bread, let him give a piece to each one of them saying:

This is the bread of heaven, the Body of the Christ Jesus.

Let him who receives answer—Hamen.

Further if there is no [more] priest let the deacons take hold of the cup, and stand in right order and give to them the Blood of the Christ Jesus our Lord: and he who has the milk and the honey. Let him who gives the cup say:

This is the Blood of Jesus the Christ our Lord.

And he who receives also shall answer—Hamen.

1–1 The text here is supplied from Tattam's Bohairic version, as there are two folios missing in the Sahidic text.

2 The Ethiopic and C. H. appear to be from a later recension here:

E. He shall give thanks over the bread and the cup; and the bread that it may become the Body of our Lord Christ, and the cup, the wine mixed, that it may become the Blood of our Lord Christ.

C. H. Deinde diaconus incipit sacrificare, episcopus autem defert reliquias mysteriales corporis et sanguinis domini nostri. quando autem finivit, communicat populum stans ad mensam corporis et sanguinis domini.

The rest of the section is different in arrangement in C. H. and is evidently a later arrangement than that of the Coptic.

3 Verona vers. adds 'aquam vero in oblationem in iudicium lavacri ut et interior homo, quod est animale, similia consequatur sicut et corpus.' E. to same effect. Probably this was once in the Coptic; if the sentence ended ⲡⲥⲱⲙⲁ, the similarity to the ending of the previous sentence ⲃⲁⲡⲧⲓⲥⲙⲁ would account for the accidental omission.

HAULER, *Didascaliae Apost. fragmenta Veronensia Latina*, pp. 106, 107.

Illi (*episcopo*) *vero offerant diacones oblationem, qui imponens manus in eam cum omni presbyterio dicat gratias agens:*

Dominus vobiscum.

Et omnes dicant: Et[1] cum spiritu tuo.

Sursum corda.

Habemus ad Dominum[2].

Gratias agamus Domino.

Dignum[3] et iustum est.

Et sic iam prosequatur:

Gratias tibi referimus, Deus, per dilectum puerum tuum Jesum Christum, quem in ultimis temporibus misisti nobis, salvatorem et redemptorem, et angelum voluntatis tuae; qui est verbum tuum inseparabile, per quem omnia fecisti et beneplacitum tibi fuit; misisti de caelo[4] in matricem virginis; qui in utero habitus incarnatus est et filius tibi ostensus est ex spiritu sancto et virgine natus; qui voluntatem tuam complens et populum sanctum tibi acquirens, extendit manus cum pateretur[5], ut a passione[6] liberaret eos qui in te crediderunt; qui cum traderetur voluntariae passioni, ut mortem solvat, et vincula diaboli dirumpat, et infernum calcet, et iustos illuminet[7], et terminum figat et resurrectionem manifestet, accipiens[8] panem gratias tibi agens dixit: Accipite, manducate; hoc est corpus meum quod pro vobis confringitur. Similiter et calicem dicens[9]: Hic est sanguis meus qui pro vobis effunditur[10]; quando hoc facitis meam commemorationem facitis[11].

Memores igitur mortis et resurrectionis eius[12] offerimus tibi panem et calicem gratias tibi agentes quia nos dignos habuisti

[1] E. 'perfectly.' Prof. Burkitt suggests that ፍጹመ should be ፍጹሞ, i.e. all (the people).

[2] E. The Lord our God.

[3] E. praemitt. [it is] right.

[4] E. add. Thy Son.

[5] E. for suffering (cf. Testament of O. L.).

[6] E. the sufferers.

[7] E. lead forth.

[8] E. praemitt. on that night in which He was betrayed.

[9] E. having given thanks He said.

[10] Perhaps both confringitur and effunditur should be future, as in E.

[11] E. imperative.

[12] E. Thy death and Thy resurrection.

adstare coram te et tibi ministrare. Et petimus[1] ut mittas spiritum tuum sanctum in oblationem[2] sanctae[3] ecclesiae; in unum congregans[4] des omnibus qui percipiunt, sanctis in repletionem spiritus sancti ad confirmationem fidei in veritate, ut te [5]laudemus et glorificemus[5] per puerum tuum Jesum Christum, per quem tibi gloria et honor, patri et filio cum spiritu sancto, in sancta ecclesia tua et nunc et in saecula saeculorum. Amen.

[Here the Latin version ends with directions for blessing oil, cheese and olives.] The Eth. version however proceeds (Horner, pp. 12—14, and pp. 141—143):—

[1] E. add. Lord, we beseech Thee. [2] E. this oblation.
[3] Om. E. [4] E. that in joining them together.
[5–5] E. they may glorify and praise.

ወሕዝብ ይበሉ

በከመ፡ ሀሎ፡ ህልወ፡ ወይሄሉ፡ ለትወልደ፡ ትዉልድ፡ ወልዓለመ፡ ዓለመ፡ አሜን።

ይበል፡ አጹሰቆጰስ፡

ወካዕበ፡ ናስተበቍዕ፡ ዘኵሎ፡ ይእኅዝ፡ እግዚአብሔር፡ አብ፡ ለእግዚእ፡ ወመድኀኒነ፡ ኢየሱስ፡ ክርስቶስ፡ ከመ፡ የሀበነ፡ በበረከት፡ ንንሢእ፡ ዘቅዱስ፡ መሠጢረ። ወሊመንሃ፡ እመውስቴትነ፡ ኢያርስሕ፡ አላ፡ ለኵሉ፡ ተድላሆሙ፡ ይረሲ፡ ለእለ፡ ይትሜጠው፡ ንሠአተ፡ ዘቅዱስ፡ መሠጢር፡ ሠጋሁ፡ ወደሙ፡ ለክርስቶስ፡ ዘኵሎ፡ ይእኅዝ፡ እግዚአብሔር፡ አመላክነ።

ይበል፡ ዲያቆን፡ ጸልዩ፡

ወይበል፡ ኤጲስቆጶስ፡ እግዚአብሒር፡ ዘኵሎ፡ ትእኅዝ፡ ንሠአተ፡ ዘቅዱስ፡ መሠጢርከ፡ ጽንዓተ፡ ለነ፡ በሀነ፡ ወሊመነሂ፡ እመውስቴትነ፡ ኢታርስሕ፡ አላ፡ ኵሎ፡ ባርክ፡ በክርስቶስ፡ ዘቦቱ፡ ለከ፡ መስሴሁ፡ ወመስለ፡ ቅዲስ፡ መንፈስ፡ ስብሐት፡ ወእኂዝ፡ ይእዜኒ፡ ወዘልፈኒ፡ ወለዓመ፡ ዓለመ፡ ስሜን።

ይበል፡ ዲያቆን፡ እንዘ፡ ትቀውሙ፡ ርእሰክሙ።

ይበል፡ ኤጱስቆጶስ፡ እግዚአብሒር፡ ዘለዓለመ፡ ሚእመር፡ ዘኅቡእ፡ ወዘገሂድ፡ ለከ፡ አትሐቱ፡ ርእሶሙ፡ ሕዝብከ፡ ወለከ፡ አግረረ፡ ቀፈተ፡ ልብ፡ ወሠጋ፡ ርሲ፡ እመድልው፡ ሚኂደርከ፡ ባርክ፡ ኪያሆሙ፡ ወኪያሆመነ፡ አጽመእ፡ ሎሙ፡ እዝነከ፡ ወስመዓሙ፡ ጸሎቶሙ፡ ወአጽንዕ፡ በኃይለ፡ የሚነከ፡ ወክድን፡ እመሕመሜ፡ እኩይ፡ ዓቃቤ፡ ሎሙ፡ ኩን፡ ለሠጋ፡ ወለነፍስኒ፡ ወስክ፡ ሎሙ፡ ወለነኒ፡ ሃይሚናተከ፡ ወፈረሆተከ፡ በወልድከ፡ ዘቦቱ፡ ለከ፡ መስሴሁ፡ ወመስለ፡ ቅዲስ፡ መንፈስ፡ ስብሐት፡ ወእኅዝ፡ ይእዜኒ፡ ወዘልፈኒ፡ ወለዓለመ፡ ዓለመ፡ አሚን።

ወይበል፡ ዲያቆን፡ ንነጽር።

ወኤጲስቆጶስ፡ ይበል፡ ቅድሳት፡ ለቅዲሳን፡

HORNER, pp. 141—143.

And the people shall say:

As it was, is, and shall be to generation of generation, and to age of age. Amen.

The bishop shall say:

And again we beseech Thee, Almighty God, the Father of the Lord, and our Saviour Jesus Christ, to grant us to receive with blessing this holy Mystery; and that He may not condemn any of us, but cause worthiness in all them who take the reception of the holy Mystery, the Body and the Blood of Christ, Almighty Lord our God.

And the deacon shall say: Pray ye.

And the bishop shall say: God, Almighty, grant to us the reception of Thy holy Mystery as our strengthening; nor condemn any amongst us, but bless all through Christ, through Whom to Thee with Him, and with the Holy Spirit, be glory and might, now and always, and for ever and ever. Amen.

The deacon shall say: As ye stand bow down your heads.

The bishop shall say: Eternal God, knower of that which is secret, and that which is open, to Thee Thy people bowed down their heads, and to Thee they bent the hardness of heart and flesh; look from Thy worthy dwelling-place; bless them, both men and women; incline Thine ear to them and hear their prayer, and strengthen (them) with the might of Thy right hand, and protect (them) from evil sickness; be their guardian for both body and soul; increase to them and to us also Thy faith and Thy fear; through Thine only Son, through Whom to Thee with Him and with the Holy Spirit, be glory and might, now and always, and for ever and ever. Amen.

And the deacon shall say: Let us attend.

And the bishop shall say: Holiness to holy ones.

ወይበሉ፡ ሕዝብ፡ አብ፡ ቅዱሳ፡ ወልድ፡ ቅዱስ፡ ውእቱ፡ መንፈስ፡ ቅዱ ።

ኤጲስቆጶስ፡ ይበል፡ እግዚአብሔር፡ ምስለ፡ ኵልክሙ።

ወይበሉ፡ ሕዝብ፡ ምስለ፡ መንፈስከ።

ወእምዝ፡ ያንሥኡ፡ እደዊሆሙ፡ ለስብሐት፡ ወይባኡ፡ ሕዝብ፡ በእንተ፡ መድኃኒተ፡ ነፍሶሙ፡ በዘይትኃደግ፡ ኃጢአቶሙ፡ ይንሥኡ።

ጸሎት፡ እምድኅረ፡ ተመጠው፡

እግዚአብሔር፡ ዘኵሎ፡ ትእኅዝ፡ አብ፡ ለእግዚእ፡ ወመድኃኒነ፡ ሊየሱስ፡ ክርስቶስ፡ ነአኵተከ፡ እስመ፡ ከፈልከነ፡ ንንሣእ፡ እምቅዱስ፡ ምሥጢር፡ ሊይኩን፡ ለርስሐት፡ ወሊለኵነኒ፡ እላ፡ ለሐድሶ፡ ነፍስ፡ ወሥጋ፡ ወመንፈስ፡ በወልድከ፡ ዘቦቱ፡ ለከ፡ ምስሌሁ፡ ወምስለ፡ ቅዱስ፡ መንፈስ፡ ስብሐት፡ ወእኂዝ፡ ይእዜኒ፡ ወዘልፈኒ፡ ወለዓለም፡ ዓለመ፡ አሜን።

ወይበሉ፡ ሕዝብ፡ አሜን።

ወቀሲስ፡ ይበል፡ እንብር፡ እድ፡ እምድኅረ፡ ነሥኡ።

እግዚአብሔር፡ ዘለዓለም፡ ዘኵሎ፡ ትእኅዝ፡ አብ፡ ለእግዚእ፡ ወመድኃኒነ፡ ሊየሱስ፡ ክርስቶስ፡ ባርክ አግብርቲከ፡ ወአእማቱከ፡ ክድን፡ ወደእ፡ ወሠርሕ፡ በኃይለ፡ ሊቃነ፡ መላእክቲከ፡ ዕቀብ፡ ወአጽንዕ፡ ላዕሌሆሙ፡ ፈርሃተከ፡ በዘዚአከ፡ ዕበይ፡ አሰርጕ፡ ወዘዚአከ፡ የሐልዩ፡ ወዘዚአከ፡ ይዕመኑ፡ ወዘዚአከ፡ ይፍቅዱ፡ ጸጕ፡ ሎሙ፡ ሰላሜ፡ ዘእንበለ፡ አበሳ፡ ወመዓት፡ በወልድከ፡ ዋህድ፡ ዘቦቱ፡ ለከ፡ መሰሌሁ፡ ወምስለ፡ ቅዱስ፡ መንፈስ፡ ስብሐት፡ ወእኂዝ፡ ይእዜኒ፡ ወዘልፈኒ፡ ወለዓለም፡ ዓለመ፡ አሜን።

ይበሉ፡ ሕዝብ፡ አሜን።

ወይበል፡ ኤጲስቆጶስ፡ እግዚአብሔር፡ ምስለ፡ ኵልክሙ፡

ወይበሉ፡ ሕዝብ፡ ምስለ፡ መንፈስከ።

ወይበል፡ ዲያቆን፡ እተው፡ በሰባመ።

And the people shall say: One Holy Father, one Holy Son, one is the Holy Spirit[1].

The bishop shall say: The Lord (be) with you all.

And the people shall say: With thy spirit.

And then they shall lift up their hands for glorifying, and the people shall come in for the salvation of their souls, in order that their sin may be remitted.

THE PRAYER AFTER THAT THEY HAVE COMMUNICATED.

God, Almighty, the Father of the Lord and our Saviour Jesus Christ, we give Thee thanks, because Thou hast imparted to us the reception of the holy Mystery: let it not be for guilt or condemnation, but for the renewal of soul and body and spirit; through Thine only Son, through Whom to Thee with Him, and with the Holy Spirit (be) glory and might, now and always, and for ever and ever. Amen.

And the people shall say: Amen.

And the presbyter shall say (the prayer) laying on of hand after they have received:

Eternal God, Almighty, the Father of the Lord and our Saviour Jesus Christ, bless Thy servants and Thy handmaids; protect and help and prosper (them) by the power of Thine Archangel. Keep and confirm in them Thy fear by [2] Thy greatness. Provide that [2] they shall both think what is Thine and believe what is Thine and will what is Thine. Grant to them peace without sin and anger: through Thine only Son, through Whom to Thee with Him, and with the Holy Spirit be glory and might, now and always, and for ever and ever. Amen.

The people shall say: Amen.

And the bishop shall say: The Lord (be) with you all.

And the people shall say: With thy spirit.

And the deacon shall say: Go in peace.

[1] *Or* 'The Father is Holy, the Son Holy, and the Spirit Holy.'

[2–2] The Eth. text is corrupt, and the meaning is uncertain. The translation given here is a conjecture by Mr Horner.

Testamentum Domini Jesu Christi, Lib. I. c. XXIII.
Ed. Rahmani, pp. 36 ff.

ܡܢܟ ܕܝܢ ܢܒܕܘܩ ܐܦܝܣܩܘܦܐ ܐܘ ܡܫܡܫܢܐ ܒܒܟܐ ܠܫܪܪܐ
ܟܠ ܫܠܝܐ ·:· ܒܬܪܟܢ ܒܗ ܫܠܝܐ ܡܫܡܫܢܐ ܗܘܐ
ܡܫܡܫܢܐ ܕܐܡܪ ܗܟܢܐ ·:·

ܡܘܕܥܢܘܬܐ ܕܡܫܡܫܢܐ ܥܠ ܐܘܪܟܣܛܝܐ

ܡܫܡܫܢܐ ܠܟܘܠܟܘܢ ·:·
ܐܢ ܐܢܫ ܥܠ ܢܟܙܗ ܐܝܬ ܠܗ ܐܟܠܐ ܢܛܪܟܐ ·:·
ܐܢ ܐܢܫ ܒܬܐܪܬܐ ܕܠܐ ܡܗܝܡܢܘܬܐ ܢܩܕܐ ·:·
ܐܢ ܐܢܫ ܬܪܥܘܬܐ ܐܪܡܝܘܬܐ ܕܡܘܫܐ ܐܝܬ ܠܗ ܢܥܪܐ ·:·
ܐܢ ܐܢܫ ܒܒܛܠܢܘܬܐ ܕܣܛܢܐ ܐܝܬܘܗܝ ܠܐ ܢܬܩܪܐ
ܠܒܬܩܪܒ ܠܗ ܠܗ ·:·
ܐܢ ܐܢܫ ܡܫܬܥܝܢܘܬܐ ܐܝܬܘܗܝ ܒܪܗܐ ܠܐ ܢܬܩܒܠ ·:·
ܐܢ ܐܢܫ ܡܫܡܥܐ. ܐܢ ܐܢܫ ܠܐ ܡܫܪܪܐ. ܟܠ ܐܬܪܐ ·:·
ܐܢ ܐܢܫ ܢܟܙܝ ܠܚܘܪܢܝܗܘܢ ܕܡܦܠܒ ܢܫܒܐ ·:·
ܐܢ ܐܢܫ ܠܢܒܝܐ ܡܨܝܕ ܢܦܘܫ ܢܦܫܗ ܡܢ ܚܛܗ ܕܡܫܝܚܐ
ܢܦܘܩ ܗܘ ܠܗ ·:·
ܠܝܛܒܐ ܠܐ ܢܣܒ ·:·
ܢܦܘܩ ܡܢ ܥܕܬܐ ·:·
ܡܢܝ ܚܙܐ ܐܝܬ ܠܝ ܐܒܐ ܕܢܗܘܐ ܡܢ ܒܪܐ ܡ̈ܠܐܟܐ
ܕܫܡܝܐ ·:·
ܚܘ ܢܫ̈ܬܘܢ. ܠܐ ܒܗ ܐܝܟܢ ܐܢܬܘܢ ܐܟܬܐ ܒܠ
ܦ̈ܪܝܫܝܢ ·:·
ܚܘ ܕܠܟܐ ܐܢܫ ܒܪܘܚܐ ܐܢܬܘܢ. ܐܠܗܐ ܚܝܐ ·:·
ܠܟܠ ܠܟܘܬܟܘܢ ܠܡܦܪܥ ܠܦܘܪܥܢܐ ܕܚܝܐ ܘܡܫܡܫܢܘܬܐ ·:·
ܒܡܫܡܫܢܘܬܐ ܕܐܠܗܐ ܢܦܩ ܠܛܝܒܘܬܐ ܗܘ ܕܐܫܬܡܫܬ ܠܝ ·:·

The Testament of our Lord, translated by A. J. Maclean, p. 70.

Before the bishop or presbyter offereth, let the people give the Peace to one another.

Then a great silence being made let the deacon say thus:

ADMONITION OF THE DEACON ON THE EUCHARIST.

[Lift up] your hearts to[1] heaven.

If any man have wrath against his companion let him be reconciled.

If any man have[2] a conscience without faith, let him confess [it].

If any man have a thought foreign to the commandments let him depart.

If any man have fallen into sin, let him not hide himself: he may[3] not hide himself.

If any man have a disordered reason, let him not draw near.

If any man be defiled, if any man be not firm, let him give place.

If any man be a stranger to the commandments of Jesus let him depart.

If any man despise the prophets, let him separate himself: from the wrath of the Only-Begotten let him deliver himself.

Let us not despise the cross.

Let us flee from threatening.

We have our Lord as onlooker, the Father of Lights[4] with the Son, [and] the angels who visit [us].

See to yourselves that ye be not in[5] anger against your neighbours.

See that no man be in wrath: God seeth.

[Lift] up your hearts to offer for the salvation of Life and holiness.

In the wisdom of God let us receive the grace which hath been bestowed upon us.

[1] Lit. be in. [2] Lit. be in. [3] Or, can.

[4] B. Let us flee from the threatening of the Lord. We have an onlooker, the Father of lights.

[5] Lit. keep not.

ܒܬܪܟܢ ܐܦܝܣܩܘܦܐ ܢܐܡܪ ܟܕ ܡܘܕܐ ܘܡܫܡܠ ܬܫܡܫܬܐ
ܥܡ ܒܪܬ ܩܠܐ ܕܫܠܡܬܐ ܀

ܡܪܝ ܒܪܟܢܝ.

ܘܥܡܐ ܢܐܡܪ: ܘܥܡ ܪܘܚܐ ܕܝܠܟ ܀

ܐܦܝܣܩܘܦܐ ܢܐܡܪ: ܠܥܠ ܠܥܠܡܝܢ ܀

ܥܡܐ ܢܐܡܪ: ܐܬܬܣܝܡܝ ܠܘܬ ܡܪܝܐ ܀

ܐܦܝܣܩܘܦܐ ܢܐܡܪ: ܢܘܕܐ ܠܡܪܝܐ ܀

ܘܟܠܗ ܥܡܐ ܢܐܡܪ: ܫܘܐ ܘܙܕܩ ܀

ܘܐܦܝܣܩܘܦܐ ܢܩܥܐ: ܩܕܝܫܐ ܒܩܕܝܫܐ ܀

ܘܥܡܐ ܢܥܢܘܢ: ܒܫܡܝܐ ܘܥܠ ܐܪܥܐ ܕܠܐ ܫܠܝܐ ܀

ܐܘܟܪܣܛܝܐ ܐܘܚܪܢܬܐ ܡܛܠ ܬܫܡܫܬܐ ܥܠ ܡܘܪܢܐ.

ܐܦܝܣܩܘܦܐ ܡܚܕܐ ܢܐܡܪ:

ܡܫܡܠܝܢ ܬܫܡܫܬܟ ܐܠܗܐ ܗܘ ܩܕܝܫܐ ܘܡܫܪܪܐ ܕܠܒܘ̈ܬܢ
ܘܢܘܗܪܐ ܕܚܝܝܢ ܒܗ ܕܠܐ ܐܬ ܡܬܚܠܦܢܘܬܐ ܘܐܒܐ ܕܚܝܐ
ܕܝܠܟ ܦܪܘܩܐ ܕܝܠܝ. ܗܘ ܕܒܪܝܬܐ ܐܚܪܢܐ ܫܪܪܬ ܠܝ ܦܪܘܩܐ
ܘܡܫܡܪܢܐ ܕܬܪܒܝܬܐ ܕܝܠܝ. ܬܪܒܝܬܟ ܒܪܐ ܐܬܝܬܝܗ
ܕܬܦܪܘܩ ܒܝ. ܡܘܕܐ ܠܟ ܠܟܐ ܕܝܠܝ ܡܪܝܐ ܗܘܝܐ ܢܦܫܐ
ܥܡ ܟܠܗ ܚܘܫܒܐ. ܐܡܝܢܐ ܕܬܐܬܐ ܒܠܝ ܬܫܡܫܬܟ
ܡܪܝܐ ܐܡܝܢܐ ܕܡܫܝܚ ܐܡܝܢܐܝܬ ܘܠܡܫܝܚܐ ܒܪܟ
ܘܠܪܘܚܐ ܩܕܝܫܐ ܗܫܐ ܘܒܟܠܙܒܢ ܘܠܥܠܡ ܥܠܡܝܢ. ܐܡܝܢ.
ܐܝܬ ܚܝܠܐ ܕܐܒܐ ܬܫܡܫܬܐ ܕܒܢ̈ܝܢܐ ܡܫܡܠܝܬܐ ܫܡܠܝܬܐ
ܫܪܝܪܬܐ ܐܝܩܘܬܐ ܕܡܢܝܢܐ ܘܡܫܪܪܐ ܕܠܒ̈ܘܬܐ
ܦܪܘܩܐ ܕܝܠܝ ܘܡܫܝܚܢܐ. ܐܢܬ ܒܪܐ ܐܬܝܬܝܗ ܫܘܪܪܐ
ܕܢܘܗܪܐ ܡܫܪܪܐ ܕܢܘ̈ܗܪܐ. ܕܡܬܪܕܦܝܢ ܠܡܐܡܢܐ ܕܝܠܟ
ܕܡܬܛܪܦܝܢ ܒܢܘܗܪܐ ܕܡܫܝܚܐ ܒܪܐ ܕܐܠܗܐ ܚܝܐ
ܐܕܝܢ ܟܠܝ ܡܢ ܡܫܡܫܬܟ ܗܝ ܠܐ ܡܬܡܢܝܢܬܐ
ܠܡܥܡܘܕܝܬܐ ܟܢܘܫܬܐ ܬܫܡܫܬܐ ܫܡܠܬܐ ܡܫܪܪܬܐ
ܫܒܝܚܘܬܐ ܠܐ ܡܬܡܠܠܢܝܬܐ ܫܪܝܪܐ ܠܐ ܡܬܒܕܩܢܐ

Then let the bishop say, giving and rendering thanks with an awed voice:

Our Lord [be] with you.

And let the people say: And with thy spirit.

Let the bishop say: [Lift] up your hearts.

Let the people say: They are [lifted up] unto the Lord.

Let the bishop say: Let us give thanks unto the Lord.

And let all the people say: It is meet and right.

And let the bishop cry: Holy things in holy [persons].

And let the people call out: In heaven and on earth without ceasing.

EUCHARIST[1] OR THANKSGIVING OVER THE OFFERING[2].

Let the bishop immediately say:

We render thanks to Thee, O God, the Holy One, Confirmer of our souls, and Giver of our life, the Treasure of incorruptibility, and Father of Thy Only-begotten, Our Saviour, whom in the latter times Thou didst send to us as a Saviour and Proclaimer of Thy purpose[3]. For it is Thy purpose[3] that we should be saved in Thee. Our heart giveth thanks unto Thee, O Lord, [our] mind, [our] soul, with all its thinking[4], that Thy grace may come upon us, O Lord, so that we may continually praise Thee, and Thy Only-begotten Son, and Thy Holy Ghost, now and alway, and for ever and ever. Amen.

O Thou Power of the Father, the Grace of the nations, Knowledge, true Wisdom, the Exaltation of the meek, the Medicine of souls[5], the Confidence of us who believe[6], for Thou art the Strength of the righteous, the Hope of the persecuted, the Haven of those who are buffeted, the Illuminator of the perfect, the Son of the living God, make to arise on us, out of Thy gift which cannot be searched into, courage, might, reliance, wisdom, strength, unlapsing faith, unshaken

[1] εὐχαριστία transliterated. [2] M. offerings.

[3] Or, thought. [4] Or, intelligence.

[5] So Rahmani conjectures from the Ethiopic translation; M. and B. read: Medicine of the meek, Exaltation of souls.

[6] Lit. of us believers.

ܒܕܚܠܬܐ ܕܪܘܚܐ ܕܝܠܟ. ܘܡܫܡܫܢܘܬܐ ܬܪܝܨܘܬܐ ܐܡܝܢܐ
ܕܒܟܠܗܘܢ ܚܝ ܒܒܢܝܐ ܕܝܠܟ ܡܪܝܐ ܘܟܠܗ ܥܡܐ ܠܟ
ܕܐܝܬܝܟ ܢܫܒܚ. ܠܟ ܢܫܒܚ ܠܟ ܢܘܕܐ ܡܪܝܐ ܒܟܠܙܒܢ ܘܠܟ
ܢܣܓܘܕ ܀

ܘܬܘܒ ܐܦܝܣܩܘܦܐ ܢܐܡܪ:

ܐܢܬ ܡܪܝܐ ܡܬܐܡܢܐ ܕܪ̈ܘܚܐ ܘܡܠܟܐ ܕܟܠܗ ܒܪ̈ܝܐ
ܢܘܗܪ̈ܢܐ ܦܩܘܕܐ ܕܝܗܒ ܡܫܝܚܘܬܐ [ܐܠܗܝܬܐ ܕܐܦܝ̈ܣܩܘܦܐ
ܪܫ ܡܠ̈ܐܟܐ ܕܚܝ̈ܘܬܐ ܕܫܘܒܚܐ ܕܟܘܪ̈ܣܘܬܐ ܕܠܒܘ̈ܫܐ
ܕܢܘܗܪ̈ܐ ܕܫܘ̈ܘܬܐ ܕܒܘܣܡܐ. ܐܒܐ ܕܡ̈ܠܟܐ ܗܘ ܕܠܟܠ
ܐܚܝܕ ܐܢܬ ܒܐܝܕܟ ܘܡܦܪܢܣ ܐܢܬ ܒܡܫܝܚܘܬܟ ܒܗ
ܒܪܐ ܕܝܠܟ ܚܒܝܒܐ ܗܘ ܕܝܠܗ ܡܫܠܡ ܐܝܠܝܢ. ܐܢܬ
ܡܪܝܐ ܠܡܠܬܐ ܕܝܠܟ ܗܘ ܕܐܫܬܪܪܘܗܝ ܠܟܠܗܘܢ ܒܪܘܬ
ܒܗ ܐܬܓܠܝܬ ܒܗ ܫܕܪܬܘܗܝ ܠܟܪܣܐ ܕܒܬܘܠܬܐ ܗܘ
ܕܒܗ ܐܬܒܣܪ ܒܪܐ ܕܝܠܟ ܐܬܚܘܝ ܒܗ ܡܢ ܪܘܚܐ
ܩܕܝܫܐ ܘܡܢ ܒܬܘܠܬܐ ܐܬܝܠܕ. ܗܘ ܕܟܕ ܨܒܝܢܐ ܕܝܠܟ
ܡܫܡܠܐ ܘܥܡܐ ܩܕܝܫܐ ܡܩܢܐ ܦܫܛ ܐܝܕܘܗܝ ܠܚܫܐ
ܕܡܢ ܚܫܐ ܘܚܒܠܐ ܘܡܘܬܐ ܢܦܪܘܩ ܠܗܠܝܢ ܕܒܟ ܣܒܪܘ.
ܗܘ ܕܟܕ ܡܫܬܠܡ ܗܘܐ ܠܚܫܐ ܨܒܝܢܝܐ ܐܝܟܢܐ ܠܡܫܪܐ
ܕܥܒܕܗ ܢܬܪܝ ܠܐܣ̈ܘܪܐ ܢܟܣ ܘܠܫܝܘܠ ܢܫܐ ܘܠܡܘܬܐ
ܢܒܛܠ ܘܠܐܣܘܪ̈ܐ ܕܐܦܠܝܐ ܢܫܪܐ ܘܠܬܪܥܝܬܐ ܕܐܒܕܐ
ܢܥܠܐ ܘܠܫܝܘܠ ܢܕܘܫ ܘܐܘܪܚܐ ܕܚ̈ܝܐ ܢܚܘܐ ܘܠܙ̈ܕܝܩܐ
ܠܘܬ ܢܘܗܪܐ ܢܕܒܪ ܘܬܚܘܡܐ ܢܩܒܥ ܘܠܫܘܒܚܐ ܢܢܗܪ
ܘܠܥܒ̈ܕܐ ܢܪܡܐ ܘܠܡܝܬܘܬܐ ܢܚܠܐ. ܟܕ ܢܣܒ ܠܚܡܐ ܗܒ
ܠܬܠܡܝ̈ܕܘܗܝ ܟܕ ܐܡܪ ܣܒܘ ܐܟܘܠܘ ܗܢܐ ܕܝܠܝ ܐܝܬܘܗܝ
ܦܓܪܐ ܗܘ ܕܥܠܝܟܘܢ ܡܬܩܨܐ ܠܫܘܒܩܢܐ ܕܚܛ̈ܗܐ.
ܐܡܬܝ ܕܗܕܐ ܬܥܒܕܘܢ ܩܝܡܬܐ ܕܝܠܝ ܥܒܕܝܢ ܐܢܬܘܢ ܀
ܐܦ ܟܣܐ ܕܚܡܪܐ ܕܡܙܝܓ ܡܙܓ ܠܛܘܦܣܐ ܕܕܡܐ ܗܘ
ܕܐܬܐܫܕ ܚܠܦܝܢ ܀

hope, the knowledge of Thy Spirit, meekness [and] uprightness, so that alway, O Lord, we Thy servants, and all the people, may praise Thee purely, may bless Thee, may give thanks unto Thee, Lord, at all times, and may beseech Thee.

And also let the bishop say:

Thou, Lord, the Founder of the heights, and King of the treasuries of light, Visitor of the heavenly Sion, King of the orders of Archangels[1], of Dominions, Praises, Thrones, Raiments, Lights, Joys, Delights, the Father of kings, who holdest all in Thy hands, and suppliest[2] all by Thy reason, through Thine Only-begotten Son, who was crucified for our sins: Thou, Lord, didst send Thy Word, who is of Thy counsel and covenant[3], by whom Thou madest all things, being well pleased with Him, into a virgin womb; who, when He was conceived [and] made flesh, was shown to be Thy Son, being born of the Holy Ghost and the Virgin[4]: who fulfilling Thy will and preparing a holy people, stretched forth His hands to suffering, that He might loose from sufferings and corruption and death those who have hoped in Thee; who, when He was betrayed to voluntary suffering that He might raise up those who had slipped, and find those who were lost, and give life to the dead, and loose [the pains of] death, and rend the bonds of the Devil, and fulfil the counsel of the Father, and tread down Sheol, and open the way of life, and guide the righteous to light, and fix the boundary, and lighten the darkness, and nurture the babes, and reveal the resurrection; taking bread, gave it to His disciples, saying, Take, eat, this is My Body which is broken for you for the forgiveness of sins. When ye do[5] this, ye make[5] My resurrection. Also the cup of wine which He mixed He gave for a type of the Blood which was shed for us.

[1] Lit. of the Archangelic orders, of Dominions, etc.

[2] Or, managest.

[3] Lit. Son of [Thy] counsel and Son of Thy promise.

[4] Or, a virgin.

[5] The Syriac does equally well for 'offer,' in both cases.

ܘܬܘܒ ܢܐܡܪ܆
ܒܗ ܒܙܒܢ ܗܫܐ ܠܒܪܟܬܟ ܘܠܫܘܒܚܟ ܡܦܪܫܝܢ ܠܟ
ܠܝܚܝܕܐ ܘܫܡܫܐ ܒܗ ܕܒܗܘܢ ܠܟ ܠܗܘ ܕܒܠܥܕܝܟ ܐܠܗܐ
ܕܠܥܠܡ ܘܦܪܘܩܐ ܕܝܠܢ ܒܠ ܗܠܝܢ ܕܐܫܬܘܕܝܬ ܠܗ ܠܒܢܝܟ
ܡܕܒܪܝܢ ܘܠܡܫܡܫܘ ܠܟ. ܒܟܠ ܗܕܐ ܡܫܒܠܝܢ ܠܫܘܒܚܟ
ܥܡ ܒܢܝܐ ܕܝܠܟ ܡܪܢܐ ܀
ܘܒܬܪܐ ܢܐܡܪ ܒܗ ܒܕܡܘܬܐ ܀
ܘܬܘܒ ܢܐܡܪ܆
ܠܟ ܡܣܪܒܝܢ ܗܢܐ ܫܘܒܠܢܘܬܐ ܬܠܝܬܝܘܬܐ ܕܠܥܠܡ
ܡܪܢܐ ܝܫܘܥ ܡܫܝܚܐ ܡܪܢܐ ܐܠܗܐ ܡܢ ܗܘ ܕܐܒܘܗ
ܒܪܬܐ ܘܟܠ ܒܢܝܐ ܢܒܠܐ ܒܗ ܠܗܬ ܢܦܫܗ ܦܪܘܩܐ ܡܪܢܐ
ܢܘܗܪܐ ܡܫܝܚܐ ܐܝܬܝܟ (Cod. M ܐܝܬܘܗܝ) ܠܫܡܝܐ ܗܘܐ
ܘܠܐܒܘܠܘܬܐ ܗܕܐ ܕܡܫܝܚܘܬܐ ܕܝܠܟ. ܒܒܗ ܕܢܘܗܪܐ
ܠܐ ܠܚܘܫܒܐ ܠܐ ܠܚܙܝܐ ܠܐ ܠܐܡܒܢܐ ܐܝܠܐ
ܠܐܡܣܘܬܐ ܠܡܘܟܟܐ ܕܢܘܗܪܐ ܕܝܠܟ. ܐܝܟ ܐܠܗܐ ܗܒ
ܠܢ ܕܒܗ ܢܫܒܚ ܬܒܪܘܟ ܒܠ ܡܫܝܚܘܬܐ ܕܗܠܝܢ ܕܠܐ
ܢܫܒܩܘܢ ܠܟ. ܡܪܝܐ ܗܒ ܕܬܬܦܪܫ ܡܢ ܟܠ ܬܪܥܝܬܐ
ܪܥܘܬܐ ܒܗ ܢܫܒܚ ܗܘ ܕܐܒܘܬܟ ܠܟܘ ܡܢ ܐܒܝ ܬܪ̈ܥܐ
ܕܡܫܪ̈ܝܐ ܕܝܠܟ ܡܪܢ ܪ̈ܒܐ. ܗܘ ܕܒܗ ܫܩܠܬܐ ܫܦܠ
ܕܬܬܘܗܐ. ܬܡܪܘܟܐ ܕܡܫܬܪܡ. ܪ̈ܘܚܐ ܕܬܬܛܪ̈ܕܢ. ܬܒܝܢܐ
ܕܬܬܪ̈ܝ. ܠܐ ܡܫܒܚܘܬܐ ܕܬܬܪܕܦܐ. ܠܐ ܕܬܬܦܣܝܘܬܐ
ܕܬܬܒܒܫܐ. ܪܘܚܐ ܕܬܬܪܓܫ. ܛܝܢܐ ܠܐ ܕܒܒܒ.
ܕܫܬܟܠܝܘܬܐ ܕܬܬܒܣܣܐ. ܪܘܚܬ ܒܣܡܐ ܕܬܬܒܣܪܐ.
ܫܒܗܪܘܬܐ ܕܬܬܬܪܥܐ. ܪܚܡܘܬܐ ܕܬܬܒܒܒܐ. ܦܠ ܒܢܝܐ
ܕܟܠܗ ܒܪܢܐ ܕܡܫܬܬܪ. ܗܒ ܫܒܠ ܒܪܢܐ ܠܒܢܝܐ ܕܝܠ ܗܠܝܢ
ܕܡܢ ܠܟܘ ܕܝܠܟ ܚܝܝܢ ܒܗ ܒܡܫܒܚܝܢ ܘܒܡܗܕ̈ܝܢ ܠܟ ܒܗ ܕܬܫܒܘܚ̈ܢ
ܠܟ ܒܗ ܦܠܛܝܢ ܠܟ ܒܗ ܒܟ ܟܠܝܘܡ ܡܢܬܐ ܐܝܬ ܠܗܘܢ ܒܪܐ
ܘܓܠܬܐ ܕܐܠܗܐ ܠܗܘ ܠܥܠܡܝܢ ܕܥܠܡܝܢ.
ܠܫܘܒ̈ܚܐ ܕܫܘܒܚܐ ܕܟܠܝܢܐ ܒܗܒܐ ܠܫܘܠܛܢܐ ܫܡܝܢ.
ܠܫܘܒ̈ܚܐ ܕܫܒܚܐ ܕܐܡܘܢܬܐ ܫܪܪ. ܠܫܘܒ̈ܚܐ ܕܚܝܠܐ ܕ̈ܠܝܫܐ

And also let him say:

Remembering[1] therefore Thy death and resurrection, we offer to Thee bread and cup, giving thanks to Thee who alone art God for ever, and our Saviour, since Thou hast promised[2] to us to stand before Thee and to serve Thee in priesthood. Therefore we render thanks to Thee, we Thy servants, O Lord.

And let the people say likewise.

And also let [the bishop] say:

We offer to Thee this thanksgiving, Eternal Trinity, O Lord Jesus Christ, O Lord the Father, before[3] whom all creation and every nature trembleth fleeing into itself, O Lord the Holy Ghost; we have brought[4] this drink and this food of Thy holiness [to Thee]; cause that it may be to us not for condemnation, not for reproach, not for destruction, but for the medicine and support of our spirit. Yea, O God, grant us that by Thy Name every thought of things displeasing to Thee may flee away. Grant, O Lord, that every proud conception may be driven away from us by Thy Name, which is written within the veils[5] of Thy sanctuaries, those high ones—a Name which, when Sheol heareth, it is amazed, the depth is rent, the spirits are driven away, the dragon is bruised, unbelief is cast out, disobedience is subdued, anger is appeased, envy worketh not, pride is reproved, avarice rooted out, boasting taken away, arrogance humbled, [and] every root of bitterness[6] destroyed. Grant, therefore, O Lord, to our innermost eyes to see Thee, praising Thee and glorifying Thee, commemorating[7] Thee and serving Thee, having a portion in Thee alone, O Son and Word of God, who subduest[8] all things.

Sustain unto the end those who have gifts of revelations. Confirm those who have a gift of healing. Make those courageous

[1] Or, commemorating.

[2] Rahmani conjectures 'hast made us worthy.'

[3] Lit. from.

[4] M reads 'bring.'

[5] Lit. faces of the doors.

[6] Lit. every nature that begetteth bitterness.

[7] Or, remembering.

[8] Or, possibly: to whom all things are subdued.

ܠܒܢ̈ܝܐ ܒܟܗ. ܠܗܠܝܢ ܕܩܒܠܬܐ ܕܠܒܫܘܬܐ ܬܪܬܝ.
ܕܗܠܝܢ ܕܒܟܗܝܢ ܙܒܢܐ ܕܠܝܟ ܒܟܠܗܝܢ ܐܝܟ. ܠܐܪ̈ܡܠܬܐ
ܘܒܬܪ. ܠܝܬܡ̈ܐ ܥܡܟ. ܠܗܠܝܢ ܕܒܡܣܟܢܘܬܐ ܥܒܕܘ
ܐܬܕܒܪ. ܘܗܟܠ ܡܪܬܘܬܐ ܒܗ ܡܢ̈ܟܝܢ ܘܥܡ ܚܝܠܐ
ܠܡܥܒܪ ܠܝ ܐܝܟܢܐ ܕܐܦ ܗܠܝܢ ܥܒܪܘ ܠܝ. ܠܒܢܝܐ ܪܒ
ܒܬܪܝܨܘܬܐ. ܡܛܠ ܠܟ ܠܟܠ ܐܠܗܐ.
ܗܒ ܕܝܢ ܕܢܬܚܙܘܢ ܠܝ ܒܟܠܗܘܢ ܗܠܝܢ ܕܡܫܬܘܬܦܝܢ ܘܢܣܒܝܢ
ܡܢ ܡܘܗܒܬܐ ܕܠܝ ܠܘܬ ܗܢ ܕܢܬܒܠܥܘܢ ܡܢ ܪܘܚܐ ܡܩܕܫܐ
ܠܫܘܪܪܐ ܕܡܗܝܡܢܘܬܐ ܒܫܪܪܐ ܕܢܫܒܚܘܢ ܠܝ ܕܟܠܠܘܬ
ܫܘܒܚܐ ܒܟܠܙܒܢ ܘܠܒܪܟ ܝܚܝܕܝܐ ܥܡܗ ܕܩܕܝܫܐ
ܕܐܝܬܘܗܝ ܠܝ ܬܫܒܘܚܬܐ ܘܐܘܚܕܢܐ ܥܡ ܪܘܚܟ
ܩܕܝܫܐ ܠܥܠܡܥܠܡܝܢ ܀
ܥܡܐ ܢܐܡܪ: ܐܡܝܢ.
ܡܫܡܫܢܐ: ܣܓܝܐܝܬ ܬܒܥܘ ܠܡܪܢ ܘܐܠܗܐ ܐܝܟܢܐ
ܕܫܘܘܬ ܬܪܥܝܬܐ ܕܪܘܚܐ ܢܬܠ ܠܢ ܀
ܐܦܝܣܩܘܦܐ: ܗܒ ܠܢ ܫܘܘܬ ܬܪܥܝܬܐ ܒܪܘܚܐ ܩܕܝܫܐ.
ܘܐܣܐ ܢܦ̈ܫܬܢ ܒܗ ܡܘܪܒܐ ܗܢܐ ܐܝܟܢܐ ܕܒܟ ܚܝܐ
ܒܟܠܗܘܢ ܥ̈ܠܡܐ ܕܥ̈ܠܡܝܢ ܀
ܥܡܐ: ܐܡܝܢ ܀
ܦܝܫ ܒܗ ܦܝܫ ܚܝܠܐ ܐܦ ܥܡܐ.
ܘܡܢ ܒܬܪ ܗܠܝܢ ܫܡܥܐ ܕܡܘܟܠܣܘܬܐ ܗܟܢܐ:
ܢܗܘܐ ܫܡܗ ܕܡܪܝܐ ܡܒܪܟ ܠܥܠܡܝܢ.
ܥܡܐ: ܐܡܝܢ ܀
ܟܗܢܐ: ܡܒܪܟ ܗܘ ܗܘ ܕܐܬܐ ܒܫܡܗ ܕܡܪܝܐ. ܡܒܪܟ
ܫܡܐ ܕܬܫܒܘܚܬܗ ܀
ܘܢܐܡܪ ܟܠܗ ܥܡܐ: ܢܗܘܐ ܢܗܘܐ ܀
ܐܦܝܣܩܘܦܐ ܢܐܡܪ: ܫܕܪ ܛܝܒܘܬܐ ܕܪܘܚܐ ܥܠܝܢ ܀

. . . .

. . . .

who have the power of tongues. Keep those who have the word of doctrine upright. Care for those who do Thy will alway. Visit the widows. Help the orphans. Remember those who have fallen asleep in the faith. And[1] grant us an inheritance with Thy saints, and bestow [upon us] the power to please Thee as they also pleased Thee. Feed the people in uprightness: and sanctify us all, O God.

But grant that all those who partake and receive of Thy Holy Things may be made one with Thee, so that they may be filled with the Holy Ghost, for the confirmation of the faith in truth, that they may lift up always a doxology to Thee, and to Thy beloved Son Jesus Christ, by whom praise and might [be] unto Thee, with Thy Holy Spirit for ever and ever.

Let the people say: Amen.

The deacon: Earnestly let us beseech our Lord and our God that He may bestow upon us concord[2] of spirit[3].

The bishop: Give us concord[2] in the Holy Spirit, and heal our souls by this offering, that we may live in Thee in all the ages of the ages.

The people: Amen.

Let the people also pray in the same [words].

After these things the seal of thanksgiving thus: Let the Name of the Lord be blessed for ever.

The people: Amen.

The priest: Blessed is He that hath come[4] in the Name of the Lord. Blessed [is] the Name of His praise.

And let all the people say: So be it, so be it.

Let the bishop say: Send the grace of the Spirit upon us.

....

[1] B. omits 'and.'

[2] ὁμόνοια translated.

[3] Or, of the Spirit.

[4] B. cometh.

ܟܠܝܢܗ ܕܝܢ ܒܗ ܢܦܫܗ ܩܘܒܠ ܛܝܒܘܬܐ ܢܐܡܪ ܩܕܡ
ܕܡܫܬܘܬܦ: ܐܡܝܢ ܀

ܒܬܪܟܢ ܚܝܠܐ ܗܟܢܐ ܡܢ ܒܬܪ ܕܢܦܩ ܡܢ ܐܘܟܪܣܛܝܐ
ܢܐܡܪ:

ܩܕܝܫܐ ܩܕܝܫܐ ܬܠܝܬܝܘܬܐ ܠܐ ܡܬܡܠܠܢܝܬܐ.
ܗܒ ܠܝ ܕܐܣܒ ܠܚܝܐ ܦܓܪܐ ܗܢܐ ܠܐ ܠܚܘܒܠܐ ܘܗܒ
ܠܝ ܕܐܟܪܙ ܒܐܦܝܐ ܕܫܦܝܪ ܠܟ. ܐܡܝܢܐ ܕܒܗ ܐܬܚܙܐ
ܕܫܦܪ ܐܦܢܐ ܠܝ ܐܝܢܐ ܕܝ ܒܗ ܟܪܒܗ ܐܝܟܐ ܦܘܩܕܢܝ. ܘܗܟܢ
ܠܡܥܒܕܘܬܐ ܐܘܪܚܝ ܐܝܟܐ ܒܗ ܦܪܐ ܐܝܟܐ ܒܠܝ ܡܠܟܘܬܝ
ܘܪܚܡܝ. ܬܦܩܘܣ ܒܝ ܕܝܢ ܫܡܝ ܡܪܝܐ. ܡܛܠ ܕܫܠܝܛܐ
ܐܢܬܝ ܘܡܫܒܚܐ ܘܠܝ ܬܫܒܘܚܬܐ ܠܥܠܡܥܠܡܝܢ. ܐܡܝܢ܀
ܟܕ ܒܬܪ ܕܝܢ ܨܠܘܬܐ ܢܦܩ.

ܒܗ ܫܥܬ ܕܝܢ ܡܢ ܚܘܒܐ ܢܐܡܪ ܬܪܬܝܢ ܙܒܢܝܢ ܐܡܝܢ ܠܥܘܠܡܐ
ܕܦܓܪܐ ܘܕܡܐ ܀

ܟܕ ܡܬܪ ܕܝܢ ܕܢܣܒܝܢ ܟܠܗܘܢ ܚܕ ܠܗܘܢ ܒܗ ܡܗܕܝܢ ܘܡܫܬܒܚܝܢ
ܛܝܒܘܬܐ ܚܠܦ ܢܦܝܩܘܬܐ ܒܗ ܡܫܡܫܢܐ ܐܡܪ:

ܢܗܘܐ ܠܡܪܢܐ ܒܗ ܡܢ ܩܘܪܒܢܐ ܕܝܠܗ ܢܦܩܝܢ ܐܝܟܢܐ ܕܠܝܬܐ
ܘܠܦܘܪܩܢܐ ܕܢܦܫܬܗܘܢ ܬܗܘܐ ܗܢ ܢܦܝܩܘܬܐ. ܢܒܥܐ
ܬܒܥܐ ܒܗ ܡܫܡܫܝܢ ܡܢܠܠܬ ܫܘܒܚܐ ܠܡܪܢܐ ܐܠܗܢ ܀

ܒܬܪܟܢ ܐܦܝܣܩܘܦܐ:

ܡܪܢܐ ܢܦܘܫܐ ܕܢܗܘܪܐ ܡܬܘܡܝܐ ܡܢܠܝܐ ܕܡܫܬܐ
ܡܗܕܝܐ ܕܡܕܒܚܐ. ܗܒܠ ܒܢܝܐ ܡܬܗܘܢܝܬܐ ܕܒܟܠ ܙܒܢ
ܒܝ ܫܒܩ ܘܐܬܪܐ ܕܠܝ ܒܠܒܗ ܫܦܝܪ ܐܝܟܢܐ ܕܬܬܒܠܐ
ܢܦܫܝ ܡܢ ܛܝܒܘܬܐ. ܠܒܐ ܕܝܢ ܕܒܢܐ ܬܘܒ ܡܢ ܐܠܗܐ

Let each one when he receiveth the thanksgiving[1] *say before he partaketh:* Amen.

After that let him pray thus: after that[2] *he receiveth the Eucharist*[3] *let him say:*

Holy, Holy, Holy, Trinity ineffable, grant me to receive unto life[4] this Body, [and] not unto condemnation. And grant me to bring forth the fruits that are pleasing to Thee, so that when I shall be shown to be pleasing to Thee I may live in Thee doing Thy commandments: and [that] with boldness I may call Thee Father[5], when I call for Thy kingdom and Thy will [to come] to me. May Thy Name be hallowed in me, O Lord; for Thou art mighty and [to be] praised, and to Thee be praise for ever and ever. Amen.

After the prayer let him receive.

When he taketh of the cup, let him say twice, Amen, *for a complete symbol of the Body and Blood.*

After all receive, let them pray, giving and rendering thanks for the reception, the deacon saying:

Let us give thanks unto the Lord, receiving His Holy Things, so that the reception [of them] may be for the life and salvation of our souls. Let us beg and beseech [His grace], raising a doxology to the Lord our God.

After that let the bishop [*say*]*:*

O Lord, Giver of light eternal[6], the Helmsman of souls, the Guide of saints; give us understanding eyes which always look to Thee, and ears which hear Thee only, so that our soul may be filled with grace. Create[7] in us a clean heart, O God; so that we may

[1] εὐχαριστία is here *translated* from the Greek, not transliterated as before.

[2] B (recent hand): before that.

[3] εὐχαριστία transliterated.

[4] Or, salvation.

[5] Or, call on Thee, O Father.

[6] Or, Eternal Giver of light.

[7] Lit. form.

ܐܝܟܢܐ ܕܟܠܗܘܢ ܢܫܬܡܥ ܪܒܘܬܟ. ܐܠܗܐ ܬܫܒܘܚܬܐ
ܘܪܘܚܐ ܐܝܟܐ ܐܬܐܡܪ ܢܬܩ̈ܠܣܢ ܘܬܫܒ̈ܚܢ ܬܗܘܐ ܠܟ
ܡܢ ܬܠܡܝܕܘܬܐ ܟܕ ܐܘܪܫܠܡ ܗܘܐ ܕܢܦܩܘܢ ܚܕ ܟܬ̈ܒܐ
ܕܝܠܟ ܡܢܝ̈ܐ. ܡܛܠ ܕܡܬܪܥܝܬܐ ܐܝܬܘܗ̇ ܡܠܟܘܬܐ ܕܝܠܟ
ܡܪܝܐ ܐܠܗܐ ܘܡܫܝܚܐ ܘܡܗܕܪܐ ܒܐܒܐ ܘܒܒܪܐ
ܘܒܪܘܚܐ ܩܕܝܫܐ ܐܝܟ ܡܢ ܩܕܡ ܥ̈ܠܡܐ ܐܦ ܗܫܐ
ܘܒܟܠܙܒܢ ܘܠܕܪ̈ܕܪܝܢ ܘܠܥ̈ܠܡܐ ܠܐ ܡܫܬܠܡ̈ܢܐ ܕܥ̈ܠܡܐ ܀
ܠܥܠܐ: ܐܡܝܢ ܀

alway comprehend Thy greatness. O God, Wonderful, who lovest man[1], make our souls better, and by this Eucharist[2], which we Thy servants who fail in much[3], have [now] received, form our thoughts so that they shall not swerve : for Thy Kingdom is blessed, O Lord God, [who art] glorified and praised in Father and in Son and in Holy Ghost, both before the worlds, and now, and alway, and for the ages, and for ever and ever without end.

The people: Amen.

[1] φιλάνθρωπος translated. [2] εὐχαριστία transliterated.

[3] Lit. Thy deficient servants.

Second Church Order.

De Lagarde, *Aegyptiaca*, p. 274. Canones Eccles. § 64.

ⲁⲩⲱ ⲉⲩϣⲁⲛⲁⲥⲡⲁⲍⲉ ⲙ̄ⲙⲟϥ ϩⲙ̄ ⲁⲥⲡⲁⲥⲙⲟⲥ ⲉⲧϩⲙ̄ ⲡϫⲟⲉⲓⲥ ⲙⲁⲣⲟⲩⲱϣ ϩⲛ̄ ⲡⲉⲩⲁⲅⲅⲉⲗⲓⲟⲛ ⲉⲧⲟⲩⲁⲁⲃ. ⲁⲩⲱ ⲉⲩϣⲁⲛⲟⲩⲱ ⲉⲩⲱϣ ⲙ̄ⲡⲉⲩⲁⲅⲅⲉⲗⲓⲟⲛ ⲙⲁⲣⲉ ⲡⲉⲡⲓⲥⲕⲟⲡⲟⲥ ⲛ̄ⲧⲁⲩⲭⲓⲣⲟⲇⲟⲛⲉⲓ ⲙ̄ⲙⲟϥ ⲁⲥⲡⲁⲍⲉ ⲛ̄ⲧⲉⲕⲕⲗⲏⲥⲓⲁ ⲧⲏⲣⲥ ⲉϥϫⲱ ⲙ̄ⲙⲟⲥ ϫⲉ ⲧⲉⲭⲁⲣⲓⲥ ⲙ̄ⲡⲉⲛϫⲟⲉⲓⲥ ⲓⲏⲥⲟⲩⲥ ⲡⲉⲭⲣⲓⲥⲧⲟⲥ ⲁⲩⲱ ⲧⲁⲅⲁⲡⲏ ⲙ̄ⲡⲛⲟⲩⲧⲉ ⲡⲉⲓⲱⲧ ⲙⲛ̄ ⲧⲕⲟⲓⲛⲱⲛⲓⲁ ⲙ̄ⲡⲉⲡⲛⲉⲩⲙⲁ ⲉⲧⲟⲩⲁⲁⲃ ⲛⲙ̄ⲙⲏⲧⲛ̄ ⲧⲏⲣⲧⲛ̄. ⲁⲩⲱ ⲙⲁⲣⲟⲩⲟⲩⲱϣⲃ ⲧⲏⲣⲟⲩ ϫⲉ ⲙⲛ̄ ⲡⲉⲕⲡⲛⲉⲩⲙⲁ ϩⲱⲱⲕ. ⲁⲩⲱ ⲉϥϣⲁⲛⲟⲩⲱ ⲉϥϫⲱ ⲙ̄ⲡⲁⲓ ⲙⲁⲣⲉϥϫⲱ ⲟⲛ ⲉⲡⲗⲁⲟⲥ ⲛ̄ϩⲉⲛϣⲁϫⲉ ⲛ̄ⲥⲟⲗⲥⲗ. ⲉϥϣⲁⲛⲟⲩⲱ ⲇⲉ ⲉϥϯⲥⲃⲱ ⲙⲁⲣⲉ ⲡⲇⲓⲁⲕⲟⲛⲟⲥ ⲁⲗⲉ ⲉϩⲣⲁⲓ ⲉϫⲛ̄ ⲟⲩⲙⲁ ⲉⲩϫⲟⲥⲉ ⲛ̄ϥⲕⲩⲣⲓⲥⲍⲉ ϫⲉ ⲙ̄ⲡⲉⲣⲧⲣⲉ ⲟⲩⲁ ⲛ̄ⲛⲁⲡⲓⲥⲧⲟⲥ ϭⲱ ⲙ̄ⲡⲉⲓⲙⲁ. ⲁⲩⲱ ⲛ̄ⲧⲉⲓϩⲉ ⲉⲣϣⲁⲛ ⲡⲉⲡⲓⲥⲕⲟⲡⲟⲥ ϫⲉⲕ ⲛ̄ⲉⲩⲭⲟⲟⲩⲉ ⲧⲏⲣⲟⲩ ⲉⲃⲟⲗ ⲉⲧⲉϣϣⲉ ⲉⲧⲣⲉϥⲁⲁⲩ ⲉⲓⲧⲉ ϩⲁ ⲡⲉⲧϣⲱⲡⲉ ⲙⲛ̄ ⲡⲕⲉⲥⲉⲉⲡⲉ, ⲙⲁⲣⲉ ⲡⲇⲓⲁⲕⲟⲛⲟⲥ ϫⲟⲟⲥ ⲛⲁⲩ ⲧⲏⲣⲟⲩ ϫⲉ ⲁⲥⲡⲁⲍⲉ ⲛ̄ⲛⲉⲧⲛ̄ⲉⲣⲏⲩ ϩⲛ̄ ⲟⲩⲡⲓ ⲉⲥⲟⲩⲁⲁⲃ. ⲁⲩⲱ ⲙⲁⲣⲉ ⲡⲉⲕⲗⲏⲣⲓⲕⲟⲥ ⲁⲥⲡⲁⲍⲉ ⲙ̄ⲡⲉⲡⲓⲥⲕⲟⲡⲟⲥ ⲁⲩⲱ ⲛ̄ⲧⲉ ⲛ̄ⲗⲁⲉⲓⲕⲟⲥ ⲛ̄ϩⲟⲟⲩⲧ ⲁⲥⲡⲁⲍⲉ ⲛ̄ⲛⲉⲩⲉⲣⲏⲩ, ⲛ̄ⲧⲉ ⲛⲉϩⲓⲟⲙⲉ ⲟⲛ ⲁⲥⲡⲁⲍⲉ ⲛ̄ⲛⲉϩⲓⲟⲙⲉ.......................................

....

ⲙⲁⲣⲉ ⲛ̄ϩⲩⲡⲟⲇⲓⲁⲕⲟⲛⲟⲥ ⲇⲉ ⲉⲓⲛⲉ ⲛ̄ⲟⲩⲙⲟⲟⲩ ⲛ̄ⲧⲉ ⲛ̄ⲟⲩⲏⲏⲃ ⲉⲓⲁ ⲛⲉⲩϭⲓϫ ⲉⲡⲙⲁⲉⲓⲛ ⲛ̄ⲟⲩⲧⲃⲃⲟ ⲛ̄ⲛⲉⲩⲯⲩⲭⲏ, ⲉⲩϥⲓ ⲙ̄ⲙⲟⲟⲩ ⲉϩⲣⲁⲓ ϣⲁ ⲡⲛⲟⲩⲧⲉ ⲡⲡⲁⲛⲧⲟⲕⲣⲁⲧⲱⲣ. ⲁⲩⲱ ⲙⲁⲣⲉ ⲕⲉⲇⲓⲁⲕⲟⲛⲟⲥ ⲱϣ ⲉⲃⲟⲗ ϫⲉ

ⲙ̄ⲡⲉⲣⲧⲣⲉ ⲗⲁⲁⲩ ⲛ̄ⲕⲁⲧⲏⲭⲟⲩⲙⲉⲛⲟⲥ ϭⲱ ⲙ̄ⲡⲉⲓⲙⲁ.

ⲙ̄ⲡⲉⲣⲧⲣⲉ ⲟⲩⲟⲛ ϩⲛ̄ ⲛⲉⲧⲥⲱⲧⲙ̄ ⲉⲡϣⲁϫⲉ ⲙ̄ⲙⲁⲧⲉ ⲉⲙⲉⲩⲕⲟⲓⲛⲱⲛⲉⲓ ⲇⲉ ⲉⲙⲙⲩⲥⲧⲏⲣⲓⲟⲛ ⲉⲧⲟⲩⲁⲁⲃ ⲁϩⲉⲣⲁⲧⲟⲩ ⲙ̄ⲡⲉⲓⲙⲁ.

ⲙ̄ⲡⲉⲣⲧⲣⲉ ⲟⲩⲟⲛ ϩⲛ̄ ⲛ̄ⲁⲡⲓⲥⲧⲟⲥ ϭⲱ.

ⲙⲡⲉⲣⲧⲣⲉ ⲟⲩⲟⲛ ϩⲛ̄ ⲛ̄ϩⲁⲓⲣⲉⲧⲓⲕⲟⲥ ⲁϩⲉⲣⲁⲧϥ ⲙ̄ⲡⲉⲓⲙⲁ ⲛ̄ⲙ̄ⲙⲁⲛ ⲙ̄ⲡⲟⲟⲩ.

ⲙ̄ⲙⲁⲁⲩ ⲁⲙⲁϩⲧⲉ ⲛ̄ⲛⲉⲧⲉⲛϣⲏⲣⲉ.

ⲙ̄ⲡⲉⲣⲧⲣⲉ ⲟⲩⲁ ⲕⲁ ⲁⲣⲓⲕⲉ ϩⲙ̄ ⲡⲉϥϩⲏⲧ ⲉϩⲟⲩⲛ ⲉⲟⲩⲁ.

ⲙ̄ⲡⲉⲣⲧⲣⲉ ⲟⲩⲁ ⲁϩⲉⲣⲁⲧϥ ⲙ̄ⲡⲉⲓⲙⲁ ϩⲛ ⲟⲩϩⲩⲡⲟⲕⲣⲓⲛⲉ ⲏ ϩⲛ̄ ⲟⲩϩⲩⲡⲟⲕⲣⲏⲥⲓⲥ.

ϣⲱⲡⲉ ⲛ̄ⲧⲉⲧⲛ̄ⲥⲟⲩⲧⲱⲛ ⲧⲏⲣⲧⲛ̄ ⲉϩⲟⲩⲛ ⲉⲡϫⲟⲉⲓⲥ ⲡⲛⲟⲩⲧⲉ.

ⲙⲁⲣⲉⲛⲁϩⲉⲣⲁⲧⲛ̄ ϩⲛ̄ ⲟⲩϩⲟⲧⲉ ⲛ̄ⲧⲉ ⲡⲛⲟⲩⲧⲉ ⲙⲛ̄ ⲟⲩⲥⲧⲱⲧ.

Translation. HORNER, *Statutes of the Apostles*, pp. 342—344.

And when they have saluted him with the salutation which is in the Lord, let them read in the holy Gospels. And when they have finished reading the Gospel, let the bishop who has been ordained salute all the church, saying: "The grace of our Lord Jesus the Christ, and the love of God the Father, and the fellowship of the Holy Spirit (be) with you all." And let all of them answer: "With thy spirit also." And when he has finished saying this, let him also speak to the people with words of exhortation: then having finished his instruction, let the deacon mount upon a high place and proclaim: "Let no unbeliever remain in this place." And thus when the bishop has finished all the prayers which it is right for him to make, whether for the sick and also the rest, let the deacon say to them all: "Salute one another with a holy kiss."

And let the clergy salute the bishop, and let the laymen salute one another, and let the women also salute the women.............. ....[1].

Then let a subdeacon bring water, and let the priests wash their hands, for a sign of purity of their souls, lifted up to God the Almighty. And let another deacon cry out:

"Let no catechumen remain in this place.

Let not any of those who only hear the word, but who do not communicate of the holy Mysteries, stand in this place.

Let not any of the unbelievers remain.

Let not any of the heretics stand in this place with us to-day.

Mothers hold your children.

Let no one have a quarrel in his heart with another.

Let none stand in this place playing the hypocrite or with hypocrisy.

Be all of you sincere toward the Lord God.

Let us stand in fear of God[2] and trembling."

[1] The words omitted deal with the positions of the congregation.

[2] The Bohairic version omits 'of God.'

§ 65. ⲡⲣⲟⲥⲫⲉⲣⲓⲛ.

ⲡⲁⲓ ⲇⲉ ⲉⲩϣⲁⲛϣⲱⲡⲉ ⲙⲁⲣⲉ ⲛ̄ⲇⲓⲁⲕⲟⲛⲟⲥ ⲉⲓⲛⲉ ⲛ̄ⲛ̄ⲇⲱⲣⲟⲛ ⲉϩⲟⲩⲛ ⲙ̄ⲡⲉⲡⲓⲥⲕⲟⲡⲟⲥ ⲉⲡⲉⲑⲩⲥⲓⲁⲥⲧⲏⲣⲓⲟⲛ ⲉⲧⲟⲩⲁⲁⲃ ⲁⲩⲱ ϣⲁⲣⲉ ⲛⲉⲡⲣⲉⲥⲃⲩⲧⲉⲣⲟⲥ ⲁϩⲉⲣⲁⲧⲟⲩ ⲛ̄ⲥⲁ ⲟⲩⲛⲁⲙ ⲁⲩⲱ ⲛ̄ⲥⲁ ϩⲃⲟⲩⲣ ⲙ̄ⲡⲉⲡⲓⲥⲕⲟⲡⲟⲥ ϩⲛ̄ ⲟⲩⲉⲥⲩⲭⲓⲁ ⲙ̄ⲡⲉⲥⲙⲟⲧ ⲛ̄ϩⲉⲛⲙⲁⲑⲏⲧⲏⲥ ⲉⲩⲁϩⲉⲣⲁⲧⲟⲩ ⲉⲡⲉⲩⲥⲁϩ. ⲙⲁⲣⲉ ⲕⲉⲥⲛⲁⲩ ⲛ̄ⲇⲓⲁⲕⲟⲛⲟⲥ ⲁϩⲉⲣⲁⲧⲟⲩ ⲛ̄ⲥⲁ ⲡⲉⲓⲥⲁ ⲙⲛ̄ ⲡⲁⲓ ⲙ̄ⲡⲉⲑⲩⲥⲓⲁⲥⲧⲏⲣⲓⲟⲛ ⲉⲣⲉ ϩⲉⲛⲥⲁⲧⲱ ⲛ̄ⲧⲟⲟⲧⲟⲩ ⲉⲩϣⲟⲟⲙⲉ ⲉⲁⲩⲧⲁⲙⲓⲟⲟⲩ ⲉⲃⲟⲗϩⲛ̄ ϩⲉⲛⲛ̄ⲕⲁ ⲉⲩϣⲟⲟⲙⲉ ⲏ ϩⲉⲛⲙⲏϩⲉ ⲛ̄ⲧⲁⲱⲥ ⲏ ⲛ̄ⲧⲟϥ ϩⲉⲛⲫⲁⲕⲓⲁⲣⲓⲟⲛ ⲉⲩϣⲟⲟⲙⲉ ⲛ̄ⲥⲉⲑⲗⲟ ⲉⲃⲟⲗ ⲛ̄ⲛ̄ⲕⲟⲩⲓ ⲛ̄ⲥⲱⲛⲧ ⲉⲧϩⲏⲗ ⲉⲧⲙ̄ⲧⲣⲉⲩ ⲃⲱⲕ ⲉϩⲣⲁⲓ ⲉⲡⲡⲟⲧⲏⲣⲓⲟⲛ.

ⲁⲩⲱ ⲛ̄ⲧⲉⲓϩⲉ ⲙⲁⲣⲉ ⲡⲁⲣⲭⲓⲉⲣⲉⲩⲥ ⲥⲟⲡⲥⲛ̄ ⲉϩⲣⲁⲓ ⲉϫⲛ̄ ⲧⲉⲡⲣⲟⲥⲫⲟⲣⲁ ⲉⲧⲣⲉ ⲡⲉⲡⲛⲉⲩⲙⲁ ⲉⲧⲟⲩⲁⲁⲃ ⲉⲓ ⲉϩⲣⲁⲓ ⲉϫⲱⲥ, ⲡⲟⲉⲓⲕ ⲙⲉⲛ ⲛ̄ϥⲁⲁϥ ⲛ̄ⲥⲱⲙⲁ ⲙ̄ⲡⲉⲭⲣⲓⲥⲧⲟⲥ, ⲡⲡⲟⲧⲏⲣⲓⲟⲛ ⲇⲉ ⲛ̄ⲥⲛⲟϥ ⲙ̄ⲡⲉⲭⲣⲓⲥⲧⲟⲥ.

ⲁⲩⲱ ⲉϥϣⲁⲛϫⲱⲕ ⲉⲃⲟⲗ ⲛ̄ⲛⲉⲡⲣⲟⲥⲉⲩⲭⲏ ⲉⲧⲉϣϣⲉ ⲉⲣⲟϥ ⲉⲧⲣⲉϥϫⲟⲟⲩ, ⲙⲁⲣⲉ ⲡⲉⲡⲓⲥⲕⲟⲡⲟⲥ ϫⲓ ⲛ̄ϣⲟⲣⲡ, ⲙⲛ̄ⲛ̄ⲥⲱϥ ⲛⲉⲡⲣⲉⲥⲃⲩⲧⲉⲣⲟⲥ, ⲙⲛ̄ⲛ̄ⲥⲱⲟⲩ ⲛ̄ⲇⲓⲁⲕⲟⲛⲟⲥ, ⲁⲩⲱ ⲛ̄ⲧⲉⲓϩⲉ ⲛ̄ⲕⲉⲕⲗⲏⲣⲓⲕⲟⲥ ⲧⲏⲣⲟⲩ ⲕⲁⲧⲁ ⲧⲁⲝⲓⲥ, ⲙⲛ̄ⲛ̄ⲥⲱⲟⲩ ⲛ̄ⲧⲉ ⲡⲗⲁⲟⲥ ⲧⲏⲣϥ ϫⲓ. ⲉⲣⲉ ⲡⲉⲡⲓⲥⲕⲟⲡⲟⲥ ⲇⲉ ϯ ⲙⲁⲣⲉϥϫⲟⲟⲥ ϫⲉ ⲡⲁⲓ ⲡⲉ ⲡⲥⲱⲙⲁ ⲙ̄ⲡⲉⲭⲣⲓⲥⲧⲟⲥ: ⲛ̄ⲧⲉ ⲡⲉⲧϫⲓ ϩⲱⲱϥ ⲟⲩⲱϣⲃ ϫⲉ ϩⲁⲙⲏⲛ. ϩⲟⲙⲟⲓⲱⲥ ⲇⲉ ⲟⲛ ⲡⲇⲓⲁⲕⲟⲛⲟⲥ ⲉⲧϯ ⲙ̄ⲡⲡⲟⲧⲏⲣⲓⲟⲛ ⲙⲁⲣⲉϥϫⲟⲟⲥ ϫⲉ ⲡⲁⲓ ⲡⲉ ⲡⲥⲛⲟϥ ⲙ̄ⲡⲉⲭⲣⲓⲥⲧⲟⲥ ⲡⲁⲓ ⲡⲉ ⲡⲡⲟⲧⲏⲣⲓⲟⲛ ⲙ̄ⲡⲱⲛϩ: ⲛ̄ⲧⲉ ⲡⲉⲧϫⲓ ϩⲱⲱϥ ⲟⲛ ϫⲟⲟⲥ ϫⲉ ϩⲁⲙⲏⲛ. ⲁⲩⲱ ⲙⲁⲣⲟⲩⲯⲁⲗⲗⲉⲓ ⲉⲩϯ ϣⲁⲛⲧⲟⲩⲱ ⲉⲩⲥⲩⲛⲁⲅⲉ ⲧⲏⲣⲟⲩ. ϩⲟⲧⲁⲛ ⲇⲉ ⲉⲩϣⲁⲛϫⲓ ⲧⲏⲣⲟⲩ ⲁⲩⲱ ⲛ̄ⲧⲉ ⲛ̄ⲕⲉϩⲓⲟⲙⲉ ⲧⲏⲣⲟⲩ ϫⲓ ⲁⲩⲱ ϩⲙ̄ ⲡⲧⲣⲉ ⲡⲉⲯⲁⲗⲧⲏⲥ ⲗⲟ ⲉϥⲯⲁⲗⲗⲉⲓ, ⲙⲁⲣⲉ ⲡⲇⲓⲁⲕⲟⲛⲟⲥ ϫⲓ ϣⲕⲁⲕ ⲉⲃⲟⲗ ⲉⲩϫⲱ ⲙ̄ⲙⲟⲥ ϫⲉ.

ⲁⲛϫⲓ ⲧⲏⲣⲛ̄ ⲉⲃⲟⲗϩⲙ̄ ⲡⲥⲱⲙⲁ ⲙⲛ̄ ⲡⲉⲥⲛⲟϥ ⲉⲧⲧⲁⲉⲓⲩ ⲙ̄ⲡⲉⲭⲣⲓⲥⲧⲟⲥ ⲙⲁⲣⲉⲛⲉⲩⲭⲁⲣⲓⲥⲧⲟⲩ ⲛⲁϥ ϫⲉ ⲁϥⲁⲁⲛ ⲛ̄ⲉⲙⲡϣⲁ ⲙ̄ⲙⲉⲧⲉⲭⲉ ⲉⲛⲉϥⲙⲩⲥⲧⲏⲣⲓⲟⲛ ⲉⲧⲟⲩⲁⲁⲃ ⲁⲩⲱ ⲛ̄ⲁⲧⲙⲟⲩ ⲉⲧⲏⲡ ⲉⲙⲡⲏⲩⲉ. ⲁⲩⲱ ⲙⲛ̄ⲛ̄ⲥⲱⲥ ⲙⲁⲣⲉ ⲡⲉⲡⲓⲥⲕⲟⲡⲟⲥ ϣⲗⲏⲗ, ⲉϥϣⲉⲡϩⲙⲟⲧ ⲉϫⲙ̄ ⲡⲟⲩⲱⲙ ⲙ̄ⲡⲥⲱⲙⲁ ⲙⲛ̄ ⲙ̄ⲡⲉⲥⲛⲟϥ ⲙ̄ⲡⲉⲭⲣⲓⲥⲧⲟⲥ. ⲉϥϣⲁⲛⲟⲩⲱ ⲇⲉ ⲉϥϣⲗⲏⲗ ⲙⲁⲣⲉ ⲡⲇⲓⲁⲕⲟⲛⲟⲥ ϫⲟⲟⲥ ϫⲉ ⲕⲉⲗϫ ⲧⲉⲧⲛ̄ⲡⲁⲛⲉ ⲉⲡⲉⲥⲏⲧ ⲙ̄ⲡϫⲟⲉⲓⲥ ⲛ̄ϥⲥⲙⲟⲩ ⲉⲣⲱⲧⲛ̄. ⲁⲩⲱ ⲉⲩϣⲁⲛϫⲓⲥⲙⲟⲩ ⲙⲁⲣⲉ ⲡⲇⲓⲁⲕⲟⲛⲟⲥ ϫⲟⲟⲥ ⲛⲁⲩ ϫⲉ ⲃⲱⲕ ϩⲛ̄ ⲟⲩⲉⲓⲣⲏⲛⲏ.

§ 65. To offer. (Prospherin.)

Further, when these things have been done, let the deacons bring the gifts to the bishop at the holy altar. And let the presbyters stand on the right hand and on the left of the bishop in silence, in the form of disciples standing by their master. Let two other deacons stand on either side of the altar, with thin fans in their hands made of something thin, or feathers of peacocks, or again thin stoles, that they may cause to fly away the little flying creatures, so that they may not go into the cup.

And then let the Chief Priest supplicate over the Oblation, that the Holy Spirit may come upon it, and make the bread indeed Body of the Christ, and the cup Blood of the Christ. And when he has finished the prayers which it is right for him to say, let the bishop receive first, after him the presbyters, after them the deacons, and thus all the clergy according to order. And after them let all the people receive. And when the bishop gives, let him say: "This is the Body of the Christ," and let him who receives also answer: "Hamen." Then likewise also the deacon who gives the cup, let him say: "This is the Blood of the Christ; this is the cup of life." And let him also who receives answer: "Hamen."

And let them sing while they are giving, until all have finished communicating. Further, when all shall have received, and when all the women also have received, and when the singer has left off singing, let the deacon call out, saying: "We have all received the Body and the precious Blood of the Christ; let us give thanks to Him because He has made us worthy to partake of His Mysteries, holy and immortal, belonging to the heavens."

And afterwards let the bishop pray, giving thanks for the eating of the Body, and the drinking of the Blood of the Christ.

Further, when he has finished praying, let the deacon say: "Bend your head down to the Lord that He may bless you." And when they have received the blessing, let the deacon say to them: "Go in peace."

Sarapion's Liturgy. G. Wobbermin, *Altchristl. liturgische Stücke*, pp. 4—7.

εὐχὴ προσφόρου Σαραπίωνος ἐπισκόπου.

ἄξιον καὶ δίκαιόν ἐστιν σὲ τὸν ἀγένητον πατέρα τοῦ μονογενοῦς Ἰησοῦ Χριστοῦ αἰνεῖν ὑμνεῖν δοξολογεῖν· αἰνοῦμεν σὲ, ἀγένητε θεὲ, ἀνεξιχνίαστε, ἀνέκφραστε, ἀκατανόητε πάσῃ γενητῇ ὑποστάσει· αἰνοῦμεν σὲ τὸν γιγνωσκόμενον ὑπὸ τοῦ υἱοῦ τοῦ μονογενοῦς, τὸν δι' αὐτοῦ λαληθέντα καὶ ἑρμηνευθέντα καὶ γνωσθέντα τῇ γενητῇ φύσει· αἰνοῦμεν σὲ τὸν γιγνώσκοντα τὸν υἱὸν καὶ ἀποκαλύπτοντα τοῖς ἁγίοις τὰς περὶ αὐτοῦ δόξας· τὸν γιγνωσκόμενον ὑπὸ τοῦ γεγεννημένου σου λόγου καὶ ὁρώμενον καὶ διερμηνευόμενον τοῖς ἁγίοις· αἰνοῦμεν σὲ, πάτερ ἀόρατε, χορηγὲ τῆς ἀθανασίας· σὺ εἶ ἡ πηγὴ τῆς ζωῆς, ἡ πηγὴ τοῦ φωτὸς, ἡ πηγὴ πάσης χάριτος καὶ πάσης ἀληθείας, φιλάνθρωπε καὶ φιλόπτωχε, ὁ πᾶσιν καταλλασσόμενος καὶ πάντας πρὸς ἑαυτὸν διὰ τῆς ἐπιδημίας τοῦ ἀγαπητοῦ σου υἱοῦ ἕλκων. δεόμεθα ποίησον ἡμᾶς ζῶντας ἀνθρώπους· δὸς ἡμῖν πνεῦμα φωτὸς, ἵνα γνῶμεν σὲ τὸν ἀληθινὸν καὶ ὃν ἀπέστειλας Ἰησοῦν Χριστόν· δὸς ἡμῖν Πνεῦμα ἅγιον, ἵνα δυνηθῶμεν ἐξειπεῖν καὶ διηγήσασθαι τὰ ἄρρητά σου μυστήρια. λαλησάτω ἐν ἡμῖν ὁ Κύριος Ἰησοῦς καὶ ἅγιον Πνεῦμα καὶ ὑμνησάτω σὲ δι' ἡμῶν· σὺ γὰρ ὁ ὑπεράνω πάσης ἀρχῆς καὶ ἐξουσίας καὶ δυνάμεως καὶ κυριότητος καὶ παντὸς ὀνόματος ὀνομαζομένου οὐ μόνον ἐν αἰῶνι τούτῳ ἀλλὰ καὶ ἐν τῷ μέλλοντι· σοὶ παραστήκουσι χίλιαι χιλιάδες καὶ μύριαι μυριάδες ἀγγέλων ἀρχαγγέλων θρόνων κυριοτήτων ἀρχῶν ἐξουσιῶν· σοὶ παραστήκουσι τὰ δύο τιμιώτατα σεραφεὶμ ἑξαπτέρυγα, δυσὶν μὲν πτέρυξιν καλύπτοντα τὸ πρόσωπον, δυσὶ δὲ τοὺς πόδας, δυσὶ δὲ πετόμενα καὶ ἁγιάζοντα, μεθ' ὧν δέξαι καὶ τὸν ἡμέτερον ἁγιασμὸν λεγόντων· Ἅγιος ἅγιος ἅγιος Κύριος σαβαώθ, πλήρης ὁ οὐρανὸς καὶ ἡ γῆ τῆς δόξης σου· πλήρης ἐστὶν ὁ οὐρανὸς, πλήρης ἐστὶν καὶ ἡ γῆ τῆς μεγαλοπρεποῦς σου δόξης· Κύριε τῶν δυνάμεων, πλήρωσον καὶ τὴν θυσίαν ταύτην τῆς σῆς δυνάμεως καὶ τῆς σῆς μεταλήψεως· σοὶ γὰρ προσηνέγκαμεν ταύτην τὴν ζῶσαν θυσίαν τὴν προσφορὰν τὴν ἀναίμακτον· σοὶ προσηνέγκαμεν τὸν ἄρτον τοῦτον, τὸ ὁμοίωμα τοῦ σώματος τοῦ μονογενοῦς. ὁ ἄρτος οὗτος τοῦ ἁγίου σώματός ἐστιν ὁμοίωμα, ὅτι ὁ Κύριος Ἰησοῦς Χριστὸς ἐν ᾗ νυκτὶ παρεδίδοτο ἔλαβεν ἄρτον καὶ ἔκλασεν καὶ ἐδίδου τοῖς μαθηταῖς αὐτοῦ λέγων· Λάβετε καὶ φάγετε, τοῦτό ἐστιν τὸ σῶμά μου τὸ ὑπὲρ ὑμῶν κλώμενον εἰς ἄφεσιν ἁμαρτιῶν· διὰ τοῦτο καὶ ἡμεῖς τὸ ὁμοίωμα τοῦ θανάτου ποιοῦντες τὸν ἄρτον προσηνέγκαμεν καὶ παρακαλοῦμεν διὰ τῆς θυσίας ταύτης· καταλλάγηθι πᾶσιν ἡμῖν καὶ ἱλάσθητι, Θεὲ τῆς ἀληθείας· καὶ ὥσπερ ὁ ἄρτος οὗτος ἐσκορπισμένος ἦν ἐπάνω τῶν ὀρέων καὶ συναχθεὶς ἐγένετο εἰς ἕν, οὕτω καὶ τὴν ἁγίαν σου ἐκκλησίαν σύναξον ἐκ παντὸς ἔθνους καὶ πάσης χώρας καὶ πάσης πόλεως καὶ κώμης καὶ οἴκου, καὶ ποίησον μίαν ζῶσαν καθολικὴν ἐκκλησίαν· προσηνέγκαμεν δὲ καὶ τὸ ποτήριον τὸ ὁμοίωμα τοῦ αἵματος, ὅτι ὁ Κύριος Ἰησοῦς Χριστὸς λαβὼν ποτήριον μετὰ τὸ δειπνῆσαι ἔλεγε τοῖς ἑαυτοῦ μαθηταῖς· Λάβετε, πίετε, τοῦτό ἐστιν ἡ καινὴ διαθήκη, ὅ ἐστιν τὸ αἷμά μου τὸ ὑπὲρ ὑμῶν ἐκχυνόμενον εἰς ἄφεσιν ἁμαρτημάτων. διὰ τοῦτο προσηνέγκαμεν καὶ ἡμεῖς τὸ ποτήριον ὁμοίωμα αἵματος προσάγοντες.

ἐπιδημησάτω, Θεὲ τῆς ἀληθείας, ὁ ἅγιός σου Λόγος ἐπὶ τὸν ἄρτον τοῦτον ἵνα γένηται ὁ ἄρτος σῶμα τοῦ Λόγου καὶ ἐπὶ τὸ ποτήριον τοῦτο ἵνα γένηται τὸ ποτήριον αἷμα τῆς ἀληθείας. καὶ ποίησον πάντας τοὺς κοινωνοῦντας φάρμακον ζωῆς λαβεῖν εἰς θεραπείαν παντὸς νοσήματος καὶ εἰς ἐνδυνάμωσιν πάσης προκοπῆς καὶ ἀρετῆς, μὴ εἰς κατάκρισιν, Θεὲ τῆς ἀληθείας, μηδὲ εἰς ἔλεγχον καὶ ὄνειδος· σὲ γὰρ τὸν ἀγένητον ἐπεκαλεσάμεθα διὰ τοῦ μονογενοῦς ἐν ἁγίῳ Πνεύματι· ἐλεηθήτω ὁ λαὸς οὗτος, προκοπῆς ἀξιωθήτω, ἀποσταλήτωσαν ἄγγελοι συμπαρόντες τῷ λαῷ εἰς κατάργησιν τοῦ πονηροῦ καὶ εἰς βεβαίωσιν τῆς ἐκκλησίας.

παρακαλοῦμεν δὲ καὶ ὑπὲρ πάντων τῶν κεκοιμημένων, ὧν ἐστιν καὶ ἡ ἀνάμνησις (μετὰ τὴν ὑποβολὴν τῶν ὀνομάτων). ἁγίασον τὰς ψυχὰς ταύτας· σὺ γὰρ πάσας γινώσκεις. ἁγίασον πάσας τὰς ἐν Κυρίῳ κοιμηθείσας. καὶ συγκαταρίθμησον πάσαις ταῖς ἁγίαις σου δυνάμεσιν καὶ δὸς αὐτοῖς τόπον καὶ μονὴν ἐν τῇ βασιλείᾳ σου· δέξαι δὲ καὶ τὴν εὐχαριστίαν τοῦ λαοῦ καὶ εὐλόγησον τοὺς προσενεγκόντας τὰ πρόσφορα καὶ τὰς εὐχαριστίας, καὶ χάρισαι ὑγείαν καὶ ὁλοκληρίαν καὶ εὐθυμίαν καὶ πᾶσαν προκοπὴν ψυχῆς καὶ σώματος ὅλῳ τῷ λαῷ τούτῳ διὰ τοῦ μονογενοῦς σου Ἰησοῦ Χριστοῦ ἐν ἁγίῳ Πνεύματι· ὥσπερ ἦν καὶ ἐστὶν καὶ ἔσται εἰς γενεὰς γενεῶν καὶ εἰς τοὺς σύμπαντας αἰῶνας τῶν αἰώνων. ἀμήν.

μετὰ τὴν εὐχὴν ἡ κλάσις καὶ ἐν τῇ κλάσει εὐχή.

καταξίωσον ἡμᾶς τῆς κοινωνίας καὶ ταύτης, Θεὲ τῆς ἀληθείας, καὶ ποίησον σώματα ἡμῶν χωρῆσαι ἁγνείαν καὶ τὰς ψυχὰς φρόνησιν καὶ γνῶσιν. καὶ σόφισον ἡμᾶς, Θεὲ τῶν οἰκτιρμῶν, διὰ τῆς μεταλήψεως τοῦ σώματος καὶ τοῦ αἵματος, ὅτι διὰ τοῦ μονογενοῦς σοὶ ἡ δόξα καὶ τὸ κράτος ἐν ἁγίῳ Πνεύματι, νῦν καὶ εἰς τοὺς σύμπαντας αἰῶνας τῶν αἰώνων. ἀμήν.

μετὰ τὸ διδόναι τὴν κλάσιν τοῖς κληρικοῖς χειροθεσία λαοῦ.

ἐκτείνω τὴν χεῖρα ἐπὶ τὸν λαὸν τοῦτον καὶ δέομαι ἐκταθῆναι τὴν τῆς ἀληθείας χεῖρα, καὶ δοθῆναι εὐλογίαν τῷ λαῷ τούτῳ διὰ τὴν σὴν φιλανθρωπίαν, Θεὲ τῶν οἰκτιρμῶν, καὶ τὰ μυστήρια τὰ παρόντα· χεὶρ εὐλαβείας καὶ δυνάμεως καὶ σωφρονισμοῦ καὶ καθαρότητος καὶ πάσης ὁσιότητος εὐλογησάτω τὸν λαὸν τοῦτον καὶ διατηρησάτω εἰς προκοπὴν καὶ βελτίωσιν διὰ τοῦ μονογενοῦς σου Ἰησοῦ Χριστοῦ ἐν ἁγίῳ Πνεύματι καὶ νῦν καὶ εἰς σύμπαντας αἰῶνας τῶν αἰώνων. ἀμήν.

μετὰ τὴν διάδοσιν τοῦ λαοῦ εὐχή.

εὐχαριστοῦμέν σοι, δέσποτα, ὅτι ἐσφαλμένους ἐκάλεσας καὶ ἡμαρτηκότας προσεποιήσω καὶ ὑπερτέθεισαι τὴν καθ' ἡμῶν ἀπειλὴν φιλανθρωπίᾳ τῇ σῇ συγχωρήσας καὶ τῇ μετανοίᾳ ἀπαλείψας καὶ τῇ πρὸς σὲ γνώσει ἀποβαλών. εὐχαριστοῦμέν σοι ὅτι δέδωκας ἡμῖν κοινωνίαν σώματος καὶ αἵματος· εὐλόγησον ἡμᾶς, εὐλόγησον τὸν λαὸν τοῦτον, ποίησον ἡμᾶς μέρος ἔχειν μετὰ τοῦ σώματος καὶ τοῦ αἵματος, διὰ τοῦ μονογενοῦς σου Υἱοῦ, δι' οὗ σοὶ ἡ δόξα καὶ τὸ κράτος ἐν ἁγίῳ Πνεύματι καὶ νῦν καὶ ἀεὶ καὶ εἰς τοὺς σύμπαντας αἰῶνας τῶν αἰώνων. ἀμήν.

St Cyril of Jerusalem. Catechesis Mystagogica v. [Ed. J. Rupp.]

c. 3. ὁ διάκονος·
ἀλλήλους ἀπολάβετε, καὶ ἀλλήλους ἀσπαζώμεθα.

c. 4. ὁ ἱερεύς·
ἄνω τὰς καρδίας.
ἀποκρίνεσθε·
ἔχομεν πρὸς τὸν Κύριον.

c. 5. ὁ ἱερεύς·
εὐχαριστήσωμεν τῷ Κυρίῳ.
λέγετε·
ἄξιον καὶ δίκαιον.

c. 6. μετὰ ταῦτα μνημονεύομεν οὐρανοῦ καὶ γῆς καὶ θαλάσσης, ἡλίου καὶ σελήνης, ἄστρων καὶ πάσης τῆς κτίσεως λογικῆς τε καὶ ἀλόγου, ὁρατῆς τε καὶ ἀοράτου, ἀγγέλων ἀρχαγγέλων δυνάμεων κυριοτήτων ἀρχῶν ἐξουσιῶν θρόνων, τῶν χερουβὶμ τῶν πολυπροσώπων, δυνάμει λέγοντες τὸ τοῦ Δαβὶδ, μεγαλύνατε τὸν Κύριον σὺν ἐμοί. μνημονεύομεν καὶ τῶν σεραφὶμ, ἃ ἐν Πνεύματι ἁγίῳ ἐθεάσατο Ἡσαίας παρεστηκότα κύκλῳ τοῦ θρόνου τοῦ Θεοῦ, καὶ ταῖς μὲν δυσὶ πτέρυξι κατακαλύπτοντα τὸ πρόσωπον, ταῖς δὲ δυσὶ τοὺς πόδας, καὶ ταῖς δυσὶ πετόμενα, καὶ λέγοντα Ἅγιος ἅγιος, ἅγιος, Κύριος σαβαώθ.

c. 7. εἶτα...παρακαλοῦμεν τὸν φιλάνθρωπον Θεὸν τὸ ἅγιον Πνεῦμα ἐξαποστεῖλαι ἐπὶ τὰ προκείμενα, ἵνα ποιήσῃ τὸν μὲν ἄρτον σῶμα Χριστοῦ, τὸν δὲ οἶνον αἷμα Χριστοῦ.

c. 8. εἶτα μετὰ τὸ ἀπαρτισθῆναι τὴν πνευματικὴν θυσίαν...παρακαλοῦμεν τὸν Θεὸν ὑπὲρ κοινῆς τῶν ἐκκλησιῶν εἰρήνης, ὑπὲρ τῆς τοῦ κόσμου εὐσταθείας, ὑπὲρ βασιλέων, ὑπὲρ στρατιωτῶν καὶ συμμάχων, ὑπὲρ τῶν ἐν ἀσθενείαις, ὑπὲρ τῶν καταπονουμένων, καὶ ἁπαξαπλῶς ὑπὲρ πάντων βοηθείας δεομένων δεόμεθα πάντες ἡμεῖς καὶ ταύτην προσφέρομεν τὴν θυσίαν.

c. 9. εἶτα μνημονεύομεν καὶ τῶν προκεκοιμημένων, πρῶτον πατριαρχῶν, προφητῶν, ἀποστόλων, μαρτύρων, ὅπως ὁ Θεὸς ταῖς εὐχαῖς αὐτῶν καὶ πρεσβείαις προσδέξηται ἡμῶν τὴν δέησιν.

εἶτα καὶ ὑπὲρ τῶν προκεκοιμημένων ἁγίων πατέρων καὶ ἐπισκόπων καὶ πάντων ἁπλῶς τῶν ἐν ἡμῖν προκεκοιμημένων, μεγίστην ὄνησιν πιστεύοντες ἔσεσθαι ταῖς ψυχαῖς ὑπὲρ ὧν ἡ δέησις ἀναφέρεται τῆς ἁγίας καὶ φρικωδεστάτης προκειμένης θυσίας.

c. 11. εἶτα μετὰ ταῦτα τὴν εὐχὴν λέγομεν ἐκείνην ἣν ὁ σωτὴρ παρέδωκε τοῖς οἰκείοις αὐτοῦ μαθηταῖς.

c. 19. μετὰ ταῦτα ὁ ἱερεὺς λέγει·

τὰ ἅγια τοῖς ἁγίοις.

εἶτα ὑμεῖς λέγετε·

εἷς ἅγιος, εἷς Κύριος, Ἰησοῦς Χριστός.

c. 20. μετὰ ταῦτα ἀκούετε τοῦ ψάλλοντος μετὰ μέλους θείου προτρεπομένου ὑμᾶς εἰς κοινωνίαν τῶν ἁγίων μυστηρίων καὶ λέγοντος· γεύσασθε καὶ ἴδετε ὅτι χρηστὸς ὁ Κύριος.

c. 21. ...δέχου τὸ σῶμα τοῦ Χριστοῦ ἐπιλέγων τὸ ἀμήν.

c. 22. ...προσέρχου καὶ τῷ ποτηρίῳ...λέγων τὸ ἀμήν.

...εἶτα ἀναμείνας τὴν εὐχὴν εὐχαριστεῖ τῷ θεῷ τῷ καταξιώσαντί σε τῶν τηλικούτων μυστηρίων.

INDEX

For EU product safety concerns, contact us at Calle de José Abascal, 56–1°,
28003 Madrid, Spain or eugpsr@cambridge.org.

www.ingramcontent.com/pod-product-compliance
Ingram Content Group UK Ltd.
Pitfield, Milton Keynes, MK11 3LW, UK
UKHW012331130625
459647UK00009B/218

* 9 7 8 1 1 0 7 4 1 6 0 5 5 *